Billy Barcroft R.N.A.S.
A Story Of The Great War

by

Percy F. Westerman

Double9
BOOKS

Billy Barcroft R.N.A.S.
A Story Of The Great War
by Percy F. Westerman

ISBN: 978-93-59329-87-1

Published by

DOUBLE 9 BOOKS

2/13-B, Ansari Road
Daryaganj, New Delhi – 110002
info@double9books.com
www.double9books.com
Tel. 011-40042856

ABOUT THE AUTHOR

Joseph Hocking was a Cornish novelist and United Methodist Free Church clergyman who died on March 4, 1937. Hocking was born in St Stephen-in-Brannel, Cornwall, to tin mine owner James Hocking and his wife Elizabeth (Kitto) Hocking. He was ordained as a Methodist clergyman in 1884. He wrote his first novel, Harry Penhale - The Trial of his Faith, while in London in 1887, while working in various places of England over the next few years. He saw fiction as a powerful tool for communicating his Christian message to the public, and he balanced his writing with his church obligations until ill health compelled him to leave from the ministry in 1909. His final pastoral responsibility was the huge and significant United Free Church in Woodford, Essex, which he was influential in having renovated by the renowned arts and crafts architect Charles Harrison Townsend. Following his recuperation, he became a greatly sought-after preacher throughout the United Kingdom, and he traveled extensively in the Middle East. He continued to write and was the author of approximately 100 novels during his career. Although he is now completely forgotten, he was enormously popular in his day.

CONTENTS

PREFACE

THE GREAT WAR OF 1914 opened the floodgates of hatred between the nations which took part and this stirring story, written when feelings were at their highest, conveys a true impression of the attitude adopted towards our enemies. No epithet was considered too strong for a German and whilst the narrative thus conveys the real atmosphere and conditions under which the tragic event was fought out it should be borne in mind that the animosities engendered by war are now happily a thing of the past, Therefore, the reader, whilst enjoying to the full this thrilling tale, will do well to remember that old enmities have passed away and that we are now reconciled to the Central Powers who were opposed to us.

CHAPTER I
"YOUR BIRD!"

Two Bells of the First Dog Watch somewhere in the North Sea.

To be a little more definite it was bordering that part of the North Sea that merges into the narrow Straits of Dover and almost within range of the German shore batteries of Zeebrugge.

It was mid-October. The equinoctial gales had not yet arrived to convert the placid surface of the sea into a regular turmoil of short, broken waves. Hardly a ripple ruffled the long gentle undulations. Not a cloud obscured the sky. The slanting rays of the sun played uninterruptedly upon the sloping deck of H.M. Seaplane Carrier "Hippodrome" as she forged slowly ahead, surrounded by an escort of long, lean destroyers.

Her day's work was apparently over. The operations against the Zeebrugge defences—operations of almost a daily occurrence—had been carried out according to orders. The observation "kite" balloon had been hauled down and stowed in the "Hippodrome's" after-well; her brood of seaplanes had, save one, returned from their task of "spotting" for the guns of the monitors, and everything had been made snug for the run back to her base. She awaited only the reappearance of the stray "duckling" to increase speed for home waters.

"Billy's getting properly strafed, I fancy," remarked Flight-Lieutenant John Fuller as the distant growl of innumerable "antis" reverberated in the still air. "Wonder what the deuce he's doing? When we swung about over Position 445 he was heading almost due east."

"Billy won't suffer from cold feet," rejoined his companion—"a regular glutton for work. Give him a chance for a stunt (bombing raid) and he's all there. For a mere youngster, I say, he's——"

Further remarks concerning the rashness of Billy—otherwise Flight-sub-lieutenant Barcroft—were postponed by the appearance of yet another member of the "Hippodrome's" flying-officers.

"Young Barcroft's just tick-tocked through," he announced. "He's on his way back. Cool cheek, by Jove! Keeping the crowd of us waiting while he's joy-riding somewhere in the direction of Berlin. Wonder how far he went?"

From where they stood, just abaft the starboard funnel-casing, the officers scanned the horizon. The "Hippodrome," like most of her sisters, had at one time been a liner, but the building up of a launching-platform for seaplanes had resulted in considerable alterations to her external and internal appearance. Amongst other things she now had two funnels abreast and far apart in place of her original foremost one, in order to give full scope to the inclined plane that extended from her bows to within a few feet of the navigation bridge—a piece of new construction perched at least 150 feet further aft than the old bridge and chart-room of pre-war days.

The clank of a steam winch and the swinging overhead of a long steel derrick announced the fact that preparations were being made to welcome home the "stray bird." Although a seaplane could be launched with ease from the sloping platform, on her return she would have to alight in the water and "taxi" alongside her parent ship. Hence the necessity for a long and powerful derrick to swing the seaplane, with its broad expanse of wings, clear of the ship's side and deposit it carefully upon deck.

"Here he comes!" exclaimed Fuller, indicating a faint object in the eastern sky.

Rapidly it resolved itself into a large biplane with triple floats in place of the three landing wheels that form a necessary adjunct to army aeroplanes. Then the polished wood propeller, glinting in the oblique rays of the sun, could be discerned as it slowed down preparatory to the seaplane commencing a thousand feet glide.

With a succession of splashes the biplane took the water, "bringing up" with admirable judgment at a distance of less than fifty yards from the starboard quarter of the parent ship.

The seaplane carried a crew of two. The pilot pushing up a pair of goggles revealed a fresh-looking, clean-cut face that gave one the impression of a public school boy. Billy Barcroft was still in his teens. He had just another month to enter into his twentieth year. In height he was a fraction under five feet ten inches; weight—an important consideration from an airman's point of view—was "ten seven." Supple and active, he carried not an ounce of superfluous flesh. Standing up and lightly grasping a stay, he swayed naturally to the slight lift of the seaplane—the personification of that product of the Twentieth Century, the airman.

His companion, who had just completed the "winding in" of the trailing aerial, raised his head above the coaming surrounding the observer's seat.

In appearance he resembled Barcroft so strongly-that the pair might have been taken for twin-brothers. But no relationship, save the ties of friendship and duty, existed betwixt Billy Barcroft and his observer, Bobby Kirkwood. The latter was an Assistant Paymaster, who, deserting the ship's office for the freedom of the air, had already mastered the intricacies of "wireless" and other qualifications necessary for the responsible duties of observer.

"You've been a jolly long time, you belated bird!" shouted Fuller in mock reproof. "What's the stunt?"

"Couldn't help it," replied Barcroft with a broad grin. "If you were in my place and saw a crowd of Hun Staff officers pushing along in motor-cars wouldn't your idea of courtesy lead you to pay them a little attention? Kirkwood gave 'em a couple of plums and a whole drum. Result—a slight increase in the Hun death-rate."

Barcroft had, in fact, gone well inland over the German batteries, on a sort of informal joy-ride. From a height of 5,000 feet the observer had spotted what appeared to be a motor convoy bowling along the road between Zeebrugge and Bruges. With a daring bordering on recklessness the pilot had vol-planed down to within two hundred feet, greatly to the consternation of the grey-cloaked German Staff officers, who, leaving the shelter of their steelroofed cars, scurried with loss of dignity for the safety that was denied most of them. For with admirable precision Kirkwood had dropped two bombs fairly into the line of cars, following up the attack by firing a whole drum of ammunition from the Lewis gun into the fleeing Huns.

Deftly the flexible steel wire from the outswung derrick engaged the lifting hooks of the seaplane. The machine was just clear of the water when the order came "Avast heaving." Simultaneously a bugle blared. It was the call for Flying Officers.

Leaping into the stern sheets of a boat in attendance, Barcroft and Kirkwood were taken to the side of the "Hippodrome," where they gained the deck of the ship. Already Fuller and the rest of the airmen had gone aft. Something was literally in the air.

The signal commander held up a leaf torn from a signal pad.

"A wireless has just come through," he announced in clear deliberate tones. "A hostile plane has made a raid over parts of Kent. She is now on her way back, apparently heading for Ostend. Machines from Eastchurch have started in pursuit, but the Hun has a useful lead. Now, gentlemen, a nod is as good as a wink to a blind horse: we are between the raider and his base."

The assembly dispersed like magic, the airmen hurriedly donning leather jackets and flying helmets and giving peremptory orders to the mechanics in attendance. In less than five minutes the first of the stowed seaplanes was ready to glide down the inclined platform to take to flight.

Yet, from a starting point of view Barcroft had a decided advantage. His seaplane was practically ready. There was enough petrol for a lengthy flight, and a good reserve of ammunition for the Lewis gun. Bombs there were none, nor were any likely to be required for the task in hand. The chances of a hit on a small and rapidly-moving target were very remote. It was by machine-gun fire that the attack upon the returning raider was to be made.

With the motor throbbing noisily and with clouds of oil-smelling smoke pouring from her exhaust, Barcroft's seaplane taxied away from the towering side of her ungainly parent. Then, so gracefully that it was impossible to determine the exact moment when the aircraft ceased to be waterborne, the seaplane rose swiftly and steadily in the air.

Climbing in steep spirals the machine quickly rose to a height of 5,000 feet. It was enough for all practical purposes, allowing a margin of superior altitude to that of the expected Boche.

"Good enough!" shouted the flight-sub through the speaking tube. "Aerials paid out? All ready?"

"All serene," replied Kirkwood, affixing a whole drum of ammunition to the upper side of the breech mechanism of the deadly machine gun. "By Jove, we've all been pretty slick this time. The fifth bird has just got away."

Barcroft leant over the side of the fuselage. Seven hundred feet below and speeding away to the nor'-west were a couple of the "Hippodrome's" seaplanes. Two more, at a lower altitude but still climbing, were heading in a south-easterly direction. Thus, when the formation was complete, Barcroft's machine would be in the centre of a far-flung line thrown out to form a barrier betwixt the solitary raider and his base.

The British airmen were at an atmospheric disadvantage. Straight in their face came the rays of the setting sun, while the calm sea beneath them was one blaze of reflected light. Against that blinding glare it was almost impossible to distinguish the mere black dot in the vast aerial expanse that represented the returning hostile aviator; while on the other hand the Hun, with the sun at his back, would be able to discern with comparative ease the glint of the seaplane's wings.

The characteristic tick of the wireless brought. Kirkwood to attention. With the receiver clamped to his ear he took down the message and passed it on to his companion.

"Our pigeon!" soliloquised Barcroft grimly. The information was to the effect that the "Hippodrome" had first sighted the approaching Hun machine by means of telescopes. The hostile craft had previously spotted two of the intercepting seaplanes, and her pilot, taking advantage of the light, decided to make a vol-plane to within a few hundred feet above the level of the sea. By so doing he was sacrificing his advantage of altitude, but there was a chance of slipping unobserved under the British aircraft. Once through the far-flung cordon he hoped to rely upon superior speed and climbing powers to elude pursuit.

By this time Barcroft had "picked up" his opponent. At first sight it seemed as if the Hun were executing a nose dive. Keenly on the alert the flight-sub depressed the ailerons with a quick yet decided movement. There was no trace of jerkiness in the pilot's actions. All were performed with that smooth dexterity and rapidity that comprised the essential qualifications of a successful airman.

At an aggregate speed of nearly two hundred miles an hour the rival aeroplanes converged. It seemed as if each pilot were bent upon ramming his opponent and sending the colliding craft to a common destruction.

Barcroft, his hands resting lightly on the "joy-stick," was keenly alert to every forthcoming move of his adversary. Already the Hun observer was letting off rounds from his machine-gun in the vain hope that some of the hail of bullets would disable the British seaplane. On his part Kirkwood "stood by," ready at the first favourable opportunity to let the Hun have a taste of the Lewis gun—and the opportunity was not yet.

Suddenly the German monoplane straightened out, then, lifting, attempted to pass above the seaplane. Quick as a flash Barcroft grasped the situation. Round swung the British machine, though not before a dozen holes had been ripped in her wings, as, banking steeply, she presented a vast spread of canvas to the hostile machine-gun.

Through the turning movement of his opponent the Hun had gained nearly three hundred yards. The observer, swinging his gun aft, was busily engaged in fitting a new belt of ammunition.

It was now Kirkwood's chance. The hostile monoplane was still within easy range, although momentarily her superior speed was taking her further and further away from her pursuer. She had broken through the cordon. Ahead was a straight, unimpeded run for home.

The Lewis gun began to splutter. Half—three-quarters of the drum of ammunition was expended without tangible result. The Hun observer, too, had got his machine-gun in working order and was pumping out nickel at the rate of five hundred rounds a minute.

It was a duel to the death. At that dizzy height no human being could fall and reach the surface of the sea alive. No cover, no sheltering trenches protected the four combatants. In the blue vault of heaven they were compelled to kill or be killed, or even deal out complete and horrifying destruction to each other.

"Got him, by Jove!" shouted Kirkwood, as the Hun at the machine-gun threw up his arms and toppled inertly across the barrel of the weapon. For perhaps ten seconds he hung thus, till the monoplane, rocking through an air-pocket, tilted violently. For a brief instant the body trembled in the balance, then slipping sideways the dead Boche toppled over the edge of the fuselage and fell like a stone through space.

"Keep it up, you're on it!" yelled Barcroft, never for a moment taking his eyes off the fugitive monoplane.

His observer heard the shout but the words were unintelligible in the deafening rush of air Nevertheless he maintained a steady fire at the enemy machine.

To give the Hun pilot his due he made no attempt to throw up the sponge. He might have made a nose-dive, trusting to flatten out' and gain the surface of the water. The machine would have sunk like a stone, but there was a faint chance of the pilot being able to unbuckle the strap that held him to the seat and make an attempt to save himself by swimming.

The Hun did unfasten the leather strap, but for a different purpose. The monoplane, being of a self-steering type, could be relied upon to continue her flight more or less in a straight line, without a controlling touch on the rudderbar.

With a stealthy, cat-like movement the German made his way to the observer's seat, and gripping the firing mechanism of the machine gun prepared to return the dangerous greetings from his pursuer.

Less than fifteen miles off—twelve minutes flight—lay the flat outlines of the Belgian coast. Unless Fritz could be brought down rapidly the raider would win through.

Suddenly the monoplane tilted and settled down to a dizzy nose-dive. Whether a vital part had been hit or whether the uncontrollable drop was due to faulty construction neither Barcroft nor his companion knew. For the moment the flight-sub imagined that it was a daring ruse on the part of the Hun pilot, until he realised that the latter was in the observer's seat when the catastrophe occurred.

Down plunged the vanquished monoplane, spirally, erratically. The pilot was clinging desperately to the machine-gun. Even as the 'plane dashed through space the weapon, under the pressure of the Hun's hand, was aimlessly spitting out bullets.

Again the wireless ticked off a message. It was from another seaplane that, although far away in the original cordon, had swung round and joined in the pursuit. Kirkwood's eyes twinkled as he deciphered the dots and dashes: "Congrats: your bird!"

CHAPTER II
A PRICE ON HIS HEAD

FLIGHT SUB-LIEUTENANT BARCROFT scanned the expanse of water beneath him. The "Hippodrome" was now a mere speck far away to the west'ard. Four distinct trails of smoke betokened the fact that British destroyers were pelting to the scene of the seaplane's victory.

On all other points of the compass the surface of the sea was deserted.

"Wind up!" exclaimed Barcroft, using the speaking-tube for the first time since the opening of the duel. "I'm going to have a look at our bag."

The A.P. began to reel in the trailing length of wireless aerial, while the pilot, shutting off the motor, began a spiral volplane towards the surface of the water. His "opposite number"—the seaplane that had tendered her congratulations—was also gliding down towards the spot where the Hun aeroplane had struck the surface. Barcroft recognised her pilot as Lieutenant John Fuller.

The white patch of foam that had been created by the terrific impact of the wrecked machine had already vanished, but a series of everdiverging concentric circles of iridescent oil marked the spot. The monoplane had sunk like a stone.

"No use going any lower," announced the Flight-sub, as he prepared to restart the engine.

"Hold hard!" exclaimed the observer. "There's something floating. I believe, by smoke! it's the Boche pilot."

"That alters the case, then," decided Barcroft. "We'll investigate still further."

The Hun showed no signs of life. Kept up by his inflated jacket he floated on his back, his legs and arms trailing listlessly and his wide open eyes staring vacantly into the element through which a few minutes previously he had been flying for his life.

The British seaplane alighted within a stone's throw of the corpse. Gravely both pilot and observer saluted the vanquished. Whether he deserved the honour or not the victors did not pause to consider. He might have been the cause of the deaths of a score or more inoffensive civilians— women and children perhaps; but death wipes out old scores. Barcroft and his companion merely recognised the dead airman as an opponent worthy of their steel, and as such he was entitled to the homage that one brave man pays to another. Of his past record they knew nothing. Their tribute was the spontaneous acknowledgment of a well-contested fight.

Slowly the seaplane taxied until one of the floats was within a foot or so of the Hun airman's corpse. Agilely Kirkwood swung himself over the side of the fuselage and swarmed down one of the supporting struts to the broad float.

"Ugh!" he soliloquised. "The fellow's grinning at me."

Securing the body the A.P. deftly opened the leather jacket. From the inner breast pocket he withdrew a bulky pocket-book, a map and an envelope, sealed and addressed and enclosed in oiled silk. Further search produced a gunmetal watch. On the lid was inscribed in High German characters: "War substitute in lieu of gold watch patriotically surrendered by Unter-leutnant E. von Bülow und Helferich." A purse completed the list of articles found on the body.

"Buck up!" exclaimed Barcroft. "It will be dark in another twenty minutes."

Thus abjured Kirkwood opened the valve of the dead airman's inflated jacket. Slowly the corpse sank beneath the surface to find a temporary resting-place on the bed of the North Sea. Night had fallen by the time the seaplanes had returned to their parent ship and had been safely housed. The "Hippodrome," steaming with screened lights and escorted by the vigilant destroyers, resumed her belated run for home waters.

Barcroft and Kirkwood, in the large and well-lighted wardroom, were examining the "effects" of their victim, while a crowd of flying-officers stood round to watch the proceedings.

The A.P. had separated the Hun's personal belongings and was making them up into a parcel, to be sealed and delivered to the dead aviator's relatives when opportunity occurred. It was a point of etiquette faithfully carried out by the airmen of both sides whenever circumstances made it possible.

Barcroft was studiously scanning the documents that were not of a personal nature. The map was a German production, and comprised a large scale area of Kent. Probably it was based upon the British Ordnance Survey, supplemented by details gathered by the swarm of Hun spies who more or less openly infested the length and breadth of the British Isles, prior to the memorable month of August 1914. Yet there was clear evidence of the map being brought up to date, recently-erected munition factories and other places of military importance being faithfully recorded. The margin was embellished with photographic reproductions of views of conspicuous landmarks taken from a considerable altitude.

"Jolly rummy how these Boche birds get hold of these views," commented Fuller. "I swear they didn't take them unless they've been running daylight trips in noiseless and practically invisible 'planes. It's their strafed organisation that is so wonderful. Knock holes in that and it's all up with Hunland. Hullo, Billy, what's the excitement?"

Barcroft, holding up a paper he had taken from the pocket-book, was studying it with the deepest interest, while his face was dimpled with lines of suppressed laughter.

"By Jove!" he exclaimed. "Won't the governor be bucked? Listen to this, you fellows. I'll have to go slow, as some of the tongue-splitting words take a bit of translating:

"'It is my Royal and Imperial command that steps be taken to secure the person of the Englishman Peter Barcroft, residing at Rivers dale House, near Alderdene, in the county of Kent, the said Peter Barcroft having published or caused to be published books that—that—(can't quite make out what's Schriftsteller? Ah! I have it) of which he is the author, the same books treating Us with libellous contempt. To the good German who succeeds in producing the said Peter Barcroft alive on German soil will be paid the reward of twenty thousand marks. In the event of the said Peter Barcroft being slain by the act of one of my subjects the reward will be ten thousand marks.—Wilhelm, I.R.'"

"So that's what Unter-leutnant E. von Bülow und Helferich was on the stunt for," remarked Fuller. "Yes, by smoke! there's a red circle drawn round the village of Alderdene. Billy, my festive, your pater will have to look out for himself."

"Perhaps the Hun has already wiped Riversdale House out of existence," said Barcroft with a hearty laugh.

His brother officers looked at him in astonishment. His levity, at the possibility of his parent's annihilation by a few hundred pounds of high explosive, seemed altogether out of place.

"Steady, old man," exclaimed Tarleton, the senior "flight-luff."

"Can't help it," continued Barcroft, vainly endeavouring to suppress his mirth. "Fancy a Boche going all that way on a fruitless errand, even supposing he did drop a plum within half a mile of the house. The governor vacated the show last quarter-day, and it's still empty. There isn't another house within a couple of miles of it, and it belongs to a regular pig of a lawyer-josser who's at loggerheads with everybody. Let's hope, if the house is pulverised, that it isn't insured against hostile aircraft. I'm not vindictive, but it would serve the bounder right."

"Where's your governor now?" enquired Fuller.

"Eh? Entering for the Kaiser's Stakes, old man? Well, here's a clue. He's moved to Tarleigh, a little show somewhere in Lancashire. About six or seven miles from Barborough, I believe, and the same distance from anywhere else. At any rate, I'm off there directly I get my leave. By Jove, won't the old man feel honoured!—a price set on his head by Irresponsible Bill. He'll feel as proud as Punch. By the bye—don't all speak at once—who's pinched my matches?"

CHAPTER III
CONCERNING PETER BARCROFT

"AND Billy arrives by the ten-fifty. No, I don't think I'll wait here for three hours and then stand a chance of missing him. I'll get back home and give him a fitting welcome to the new house."

Thus meditated Peter Barcroft as he paced up and down the crowded up-platform of Barborough Station. He had studied with varying emotions a poster depicting a flabby, pigeon-toed child with one hand over that part of the human form known to infants as a "tummy" and supposed to be ejaculating, "I feel so jolly here." Even that mild excitement paled, and Mr. Barcroft pined for the congenial warmth of his study. The platform was cold and draughty, offering no inducements to linger for the arrival of the sure-to-be belated "ten-fifty."

Peter Barcroft was a thick-set man of fortyfive. In height he was a good two inches shorter than his airman son. He was clean shaven. Had he removed his Norfolk cap it might have been noticed that his iron-grey hair showed thin on his temples and was conspicuously absent on the top of his head. His forehead was high, and in conjunction with two vertical wrinkles extending upwards from the inner ends of his eyebrows, gave the appearance of a deep thinker. Otherwise there was little about him to give one the idea that he was engaged in literary pursuits. According to popular notions he ought to be wearing shabby clothes of eccentric, out-of-date cut; he should affect a weird type of soft collar and a flowing tie; his hair ought to be long and wavy. But Peter Barcroft had none of these qualifications. To judge him by appearances he was just an ordinary middle-aged man of powerful physique and retaining many of the qualities of a bygone athletic age.

He had been living only a fortnight in Lancashire. Why he migrated from Kent was a mystery to the friends he had left behind. Perhaps he did not know himself, unless it was surrender to a sudden, almost eccentric desire for pastures new.

Up to a certain point he possessed the artistic temperament. He worked only when it suited him, and generally seized every plausible excuse to "knock off." Yet, when he did settle to his task he wrote at a tremendous rate, and so vilely that often he was quite unable to decipher his own caligraphy. In financial matters he was as careless as a man could possibly be. Rarely he knew the state of his current account. Trivial matters in everyday life would send him into a towering rage, while the loss of a couple of hundred pounds hardly troubled him in the least degree. He would ransack the house to find a favourite pipe which he had mislaid, or waste half a day searching in vain for a certain pen which he felt sure he had left in such-and-such a place. On the other hand, when a valuable and almost new overcoat was stolen from the hall he just shrugged his shoulders and soon forgot all about it.

During the fortnight he had been the tenant of Ladybird Fold, Peter Barcroft had either "sacked" or had been "sacked" by three housemaids and two cooks, to the consternation and despair of his wife. The servant problem, probably more acute in the manufacturing district of Lancashire than anywhere else in the kingdom, was in this case rendered even more difficult by Peter's display of irritation at the manifold but trivial delinquencies of his staff of menials.

Mrs. Barcroft had gone on a visit to a relative in Cheshire on the strength of a vague report that there was a girl who might be willing to take the vacant place of housemaid at Ladybird Fold-His wife's absence for two days had given Peter the excuse to "knock off." It was one of his avowed peculiarities that he could not write a stroke unless his wife were with him in the study. So Mr. Barcroft had gone for a jaunt in his light car.

After the splendidly-surfaced gravelled or tarmac roads of Kent the greasy granite setts and bumpy slag roads of the north came as an unpleasant surprise to the easy-going Peter. A couple of punctures in addition to a slight collision with a "lurry"—a type of vehicle hitherto known to him as a lorry—did not improve his peace of mind, while what ought to have been the climax to a day of mishaps was the sudden failure of the magneto at a desolate spot on the western slope of the Pennine Hills.

But unruffled Peter pushed the car on to the side of the road and tramped stolidly into the nearest village—a good three miles. Here, in an interview with the decrepit motor-engineer (Barcroft guessed rightly that he was too *passé* even for munition making), he learnt that at least a month must elapse before the magneto could be re-wired. He received the intelligence with equanimity, for in his pocket was a telegram to the effect that Billy was coming home that night. Nothing else mattered.

"Which is the Tarleigh train?" enquired Mr. Barcroft of a porter.

"Next one in on this side," replied the man gruffly.

Half a minute later the train rumbled into the station. Mr. Barcroft, realising that up to the present he had not mastered the intricate system of train-service of the Lancashire and Yorkshire Railway, and having had many previous experiences of being misinformed by surly servants of the various railway companies, addressed himself to a passenger who was about to enter a carriage.

"Tarleigh? Yes, you're quite right. At any rate, I'm for Blackberry Cross."

"Thank you," replied Peter.

"Motorist?" enquired the other laconically. "Yes; had a breakdown."

The ice was broken. The studied, almost taciturn reserve of the typical level-headed Lancashire man was not proof against the claims of motoring. Before the train glided out of the station the two passengers were deep in the subject of cars and their peculiarities.

"Dash it all! we seem a long time getting to Two Elms," remarked the stranger.

He drew aside the blind and peered into the darkness. At that moment the train rumbled under a broad bridge.

"Sorry!" he exclaimed. "We're already half way between Blackberry Cross and Tarleigh. We must have taken the wrong train: it's a non-stop to Windyhill."

"Don't mention it," rejoined Peter affably. "I'm quite enjoying your society. An hour or so won't make very much difference provided I can get home before eleven. I hope you won't be inconvenienced?"

The stranger laughed.

"I'm secretary of the Tarleigh and Blackberry Cross Golf Club," he explained. "Entwistle—Philip Entwistle—is my name. By profession I am what is commonly known as a vet. It's our Annual General Meeting, and I'm due there at eight."

"'Fraid it will have to stop at the due," said Mr. Barcroft grimly. "It's 7.30 already."

"You'll be all right," continued Entwistle. "There's a train back from Windyhill at 10.5, You're a stranger to the district?"

"Fairly so," admitted Peter. "I've take Ladybird Fold for three years."

"Your name doesn't happen to be Norton—Andrew Norton?"

"No," was the reply. "Barcroft's my name. I know Norton. He's a newcomer. Only been here a week, I believe; and in that time he's frozen on to me. Kind of companionship in a strange land, so to speak. He seems a very decent sort; in fact, I rather like him. He's my nearest neighbour and he lives at least half a mile from Ladybird Fold."

"What is he?" asked Entwistle. "Independent?"

"So I should imagine. He has plenty of time on his hands, and spends a good part of it with me, except when I have to choke him off. He'll be sitting in my study when I get home, for a dead cert. Already he's made it a practice of looking me up at ten o'clock of an evening, after I've knocked off. You see," he added apologetically. "I have to work."

"At what?" enquired his companion, the Lancashire thirst for knowledge ever in the foreground.

"I am a professional liar," announced Peter with mock gravity.

"A what? Oh, I suppose you mean that you're a lawyer?"

"Heaven forbid!" protested Mr. Barcroft piously. "You misunderstand me. I am a novelist. Modesty forbids me to give you my *nom de Plume*. At present, however, I am engaged upon a book of a technical character dealing with the conduct of the war. Perhaps some of my theories will be a bit startling when pushed on to the British Public, but they'll be vindicated."

"Hang it all!" exclaimed Entwistle. "I have heard of you already."

"Have you really?" enquired Peter. Professional vanity—although he was not afflicted with "swollen head"—made him perhaps justifiably keen on hearing outside opinions of his literary efforts.

"Yes," continued his companion. "It was the Vicar of Tarleigh. He was in Wheatcroft's place—down the bottom of Blackberry Hill and while he was talking to the old man a car came along driven by you. In it were two sheep dogs barking like fury. I think I am right in the description?"

Peter nodded appreciatively.

"Says the vicar, 'And what might that terrific disturbance mean?' 'Eh, parson,' replied Old Wheatcroft, ''tis but that there novel-writing chap as lives in Ladybird Fold.' So you see they've got you posted up all right. But here we are," he continued, as the train came to a standstill. "It's a jolly draughty station to hang about."

"It is," admitted Barcroft. "But fortunately there's very little wind. A proper Zeppelin night."

"Suppose so," admitted Entwistle. "You see, we don't worry very much about those gentry. Now, in Yorkshire, for instance, it would be otherwise, but we are on the right side of the Pennines. I don't for one moment think that a Zep. will ever get so far as this."

Peter shrugged his shoulders. On that matter, he preferred to maintain silence.

Up and down the bleak platform the two men paced until Entwistle, glancing at his watch in the feeble glimmer of a shaded lamp, exclaimed — "Twenty-five to eleven. Bless my soul, the time has gone quickly. That confounded train is late."

Before Barcroft could offer any remark the platform lights were turned off. Simultaneously, the electric signal lamps ceased to give forth their red and green warning.

"What's up?" demanded Entwistle. "Failure of the gas works and the Company's electric light station?"

"Hanged if I know," declared Peter. "It strikes me very forcibly that we'll have to walk those seven miles. I suppose it means twelve for you? A taxi, or even a humble four-wheeler is an impossibility in this forsaken hole."

A man, stumbling across the rails in the darkness, clambered upon the platform within a yard of the two would-be passengers.

"Sorry, sir," he muttered apologetically.

"What's all this about?" enquired Entwistle. "Why have the lights gone out? Are there no more trains to-night?"

"No, sir, no more trains yet awhile," replied the porter, for such he was. "They've just got a warning through. Them swine of Zeps. is somewheres about."

CHAPTER IV
WHEN THE ZEPPELIN WAS OUT

"WE'LL have to foot it, man," declared Entwistle decidedly. "Unless we can get a car to pick us up on the road. Zeppelins, by smoke! Whoever would have thought it? I didn't; not this side of the Pennines."

"So I believe you said," replied Peter Barcroft, as the two men swung down the inclined approach to the station and gained the setts of the dingy street. "Still, they may be miles away. These official warnings are the pattern of eccentricity. You know the road?"

"Yes fortunately Dash it all! I don't mind the excitement. It's my wife I'm thinking about, if they should come to Barborough. Ever seen a Zep., Barcroft?"

"Several," replied Peter. "They are fairly common objects down in Kent. Get quite accustomed to them. Latterly I have slept soundly, in spite of the noise of the engines. Of course they didn't drop any bombs in that particular district. In point of fact they eventually dumped their dangerous cargo into some fields a few miles from anywhere. Our lighting restrictions are far more stringent than they are up here. Barborough is a blaze of light compared, say, with Tangtable or Cobley, the nearest large towns to Alderdene, where I used to live."

"You used to sleep through it," repeated Mr. Entwistle. "That reminds me. I noticed that when we were walking up and down the platform just now you invariably got round to my left as we turned. Are you deaf in one ear?"

"Yes," replied Peter. "Stone deaf in my left. A really valuable asset when one has to be in the presence of bores, or enduring curtain lectures and the like."

"Then we may congratulate ourselves," was his companion's response. "I, too, am deaf, only in my right ear. When I was at school at Scarborough a brute of a master hiked me up by my ears. Result, deafness in one of them. Yes, I agree, it's very convenient at times."

By now they had breasted the steep rise out of Windyhill and had gained the bleak summit of the lofty ridge. In ordinary circumstances would be seen the twinkling lights from scores of factories—"works" as these are termed locally—in the five distinct valleys that radiate from this particular spur. All was now in utter darkness, save for a feeble glimmer from an isolated signal-box at the entrance to a deep cutting.

"That chap's looking for trouble," declared Barcroft, indicating the dim patch of luminosity. "They would spot that for a distance of ten miles. I say, isn't the atmosphere clear for this part of the country, and in autumn, too. It's the first absolutely fine night I have seen since I've lived here—ideal for Zeps., too. No wind to speak of and pitch dark. Listen."

The two men stopped abruptly. Above the faint rumble of the evening breeze could be distinguished a subdued and distinct hum.

"That's the brute," declared Peter. "It's a Zep, sure enough."

"Certain?" asked Entwistle anxiously.

"Rather—and it's coming this way."

In silence the two pedestrians waited. Nearer and nearer came the now increasing buzzing of the engines of the immense gas-bag. Vainly they attempted to detect the elongated airship. With heads thrown back they strove to pierce the black vault above. The "thing" was there, but it was invisible from where they stood. Only by the sinister sounds did they know of its presence. Then with the same rapidity as the unseen had approached the whirr grew fainter and fainter until it was heard no longer.

"Phew!" ejaculated Entwistle, mopping his forehead. "I'm not of a funky nature, but, by Jove! I'm glad that beastly thing's gone. It gives a fellow a peculiar sensation somewhere in the region of the stomach. What's the time?"

"About eleven, I should imagine," replied Barcroft. "I won't strike a match. Well, I suppose the Zep. has missed Barborough by this time—unless she's slowed down and circling over the town," he added in an undertone.

They were descending into one of the numerous valleys that lay betwixt them and Tarleigh. The effluvium of a neighbouring bleaching works was wafted to their nostrils.

"Rufford's Works," explained Entwistle. "Lucky that Zep didn't drop a bomb. There are hundreds of gallons of benzine stored there.... Yes, I fancy it's all right as far as Barborough is concerned. Wish a car would overtake us. Notwithstanding the fine night I don't feel particularly keen for a long tramp."

"Let me give you a shakedown at Ladybird Fold," suggested Peter. "You can telephone through to Barborough and let your wife know where you are."

"No, no, my dear fellow," protested Entwistle. "It's imposing on your good nature. Besides, you mentioned that your son was coming home on leave."

"Yes," said Mr. Barcroft. "Wonder if he's arrived yet, or is held up at some out-of-the-way railway station or in a tunnel. That won't make any difference. If it did I shouldn't have mentioned the matter. I can be as confoundedly blunt as you Lancashire people when I want."

"So I believe," rejoined Entwistle tersely. "Well, I'll accept your offer with pleasure. Now for the next hill. It's a regular brute, even for this part of the world. When a fellow is past forty he's not so good at this sort of work as he was. One has to admit the fact however much one tries to stifle the discovery. I used to pride myself on being a runner, and it came as a nasty shock when my fifteen-year-old son beat me in a 440 sprint—not by so very much, though," he added in defence of his bygone prowess.

"The third milestone," announced Peter pointing to a weatherbeaten slab just visible in the gloom.

"Yes, and the highest part of the road," added Entwistle. "It is about——".

He stopped abruptly. Away to the southward a vivid flash illuminated the sky, followed by three more in quick succession. Summer lightning would pale into insignificance compared with the intensity of those momentary sheets of lurid light.

"Good heavens—Barborough!" ejaculated the vet.

Barcroft made no remark. Failing his inability to read the face of his watch he placed the fingers of his right hand on his left wrist and carefully counted the pulse beats.

"Forty-five!" he announced calmly as the first of four loud detonations rent the air.

Crash—crash—crash—crash. It was as if he had been inside a tin bath and some one was belabouring it with a wooden mallet. Even allowing for the distance of the source of the sound the din was terrible.

A minute later came two more flashes, almost simultaneously, with forty-eight beats before the reports. Then one solitary flash followed by an even greater interval ere the detonation was heard.

"The brutes!" muttered Entwistle.

Again Peter made no audible comment. He was making a rapid mental calculation. Seventy pulsations to a minute: sound travels at roughly 365 yards to a second. Yes, that placed the scene of the raid at a distance of nine miles, and judging by the direction it was that populous town that had been the target for the missiles of the Zeppelin.

"She's gone, at any rate," he said.

"Yes, but goodness only knows what damage she's done in that minute and a half," added Entwistle. "What's more we're between her and that cursed Germany. Come on, man, let's hasten."

It was half-past twelve as the two pedestrians made their way through the village of Scatterbeck. Almost the whole of the population was astir, discussing in the shrill rapid Lancashire dialect the totally unexpected visit of the aerial raider. Thrice enquiries on the part of Barcroft and his companion brought the disconcerting information that no vehicle of any description was available. There was nothing for it but to continue their long tramp.

At length the summit of Tarleigh Hill was surmounted. Here they encountered a belated wayfarer—a watchman from the neighbouring works.

"Eh, maäster," he replied to an anxious question. "I'm thinkin' 'tes Barborough right enow. Seed 'em drop mysen, an' agen ower Percombe way. Eh, but there'll be a rush to t' recruitin' office after this. Lancashire's done main well in sojerin', but this'll cap everythin'. This night's work'll cost that there Kayser summat when the Barborough lads in t' trenches get to know o' it."

"That fellow's right," commented Mr. Barcroft after the watchman had taken a by-road. "These Zeps, do very little military damage. They don't intimidate or terrify the people, except, perhaps, those in the actual district raided. The German bombs are like the dragon's teeth of mythology; sown, they spring up as British soldiers, eager to avenge themselves upon the Kaiser's troops. If I had my way I'd run cheap excursions to the raided areas from Bristol, Exeter and other towns as yet not troubled with the Zeps. to let the people see the damage done to British homes. That would stir their imaginations and let 'em think strongly. Instead, all details of raids are kept, or are endeavoured to be kept, a profound secret by our wiseacres in authority. The report of the damage done is minimised—not that I would suggest making the news public as far as buildings of military importance are concerned—and the result is that the phlegmatic Briton who is not directly affected by the raid merely reads the bald newspaper account, mentally consigns the Government to perdition and forgets all about it."

"According to that American lecturer, Curtin, they do things better in France," added Entwistle. "The French allow full descriptions of the Zeppelin raids in their country to be published, and the result is discouraging to the Huns. At the time we were referring to these raids taking place in the 'eastern counties,' when the Germans knew exactly where they had been. I shouldn't wonder if this night's affair is described as taking place on the East Coast or the South Midlands instead of within sight of the Irish Sea."

"And yet nothing did more to depress the Germans than the humorous and true accounts of the Zep, raids that were eventually allowed to appear in the British newspapers."

"Except when we do bag half a dozen of them at one swoop," added the vet. "Mark my words, we'll get our own back with interest."

"What's the matter?" asked Peter, noticing that his companion had reduced his pace and was limping slightly.

"Galled heel, worse luck," replied the vet. Even in the darkness Barcroft could discern his face twitching. "But it's nothing. I'll stick it."

"Look here," declared Barcroft authoritatively. There were times when the easy-going Peter could make himself obeyed. "It's all jolly rot your carrying on. You'll be lame in another mile. You must stick to the original programme, and stop at my place. What's happened at Barborough has happened, and your presence there to-night won't mend matters. Besides, there's the telephone."

Entwistle capitulated. In fact he was in great pain. The injury to his foot was more than he cared to admit. Not only was his heel badly chafed, but he had twisted his ankle on a loose stone.

"All right," he replied. "But suppose I can't get through on the 'phone?"

"You will," said Barcroft confidently. "Now: hang on to my arm. It's only a couple of hundred yards up the hill."

The last two hundred yards was a pilgrimage of pain. The approach was along a narrow lane paved with irregular slabs and enshrouded: with trees that threw the path into even greater gloom than the high road. The blackness was so intense that it appeared to have weight—to press upon their eyeballs like a tightly adjusted bandage. Away to the left came the gurgle of a mountain stream as it flowed swiftly through a deep cutting in the rocks.

"Here we are," said Peter at last.

"Yes," agreed Entwistle. "I know the place."

They were now clear of the trees. Looming mistily against the dark sky was a long, rambling, two-storeyed building surrounded by a roughly built stone wall. The latticed windows were heavily curtained. Not a light nor a sound came from the isolated dwelling.

"So Billy hasn't turned up yet," remarked Barcroft senior as he fumbled for his key. "Why, by Jove, the door's wide open!"

CHAPTER V
AT LADYBIRD FOLD

"COME in," he continued, assisting his companion over the threshold. "I won't switch a light on in the hall until I close the door. Jolly queer about it being open. There'll be a court of enquiry in the morning."

A violent scratching upon the study door attracted his attention.

"That's Ponto and Nan—my sheep-dogs," he explained. "Wonder why they are locked in? They ought to be in the kennels. They're quiet enough: they won't bite."

Entwistle smiled grimly. Peter's idea of quiet seemed rather peculiar, for the animals were barking furiously and redoubling their attacks upon the door.

"The paintwork?" echoed Barcroft in answer to his companion's enquiry, as he proceeded to hang up his cap and coat. "Oh, that won't matter. You see, there's a curtain on the inside and that hides the marks."

He opened the door of the study, to be greeted with a blaze of dazzling light and a couple of shaggy-haired dogs, who hurled themselves upon him in an ecstasy of delight.

"Down, down, both of you! Kennel up," ordered their master.

The dogs obeyed, Ponto retiring to the limited space between the pedestals of the roll-top desk while Nan bounded into the large arm-chair by the fire.

"That's better," said Barcroft composedly, glancing at the desk to see if any letter had arrived. "Now take it easy for a bit. There's the telephone. I'll scout round and see what's going. Whisky? Good! Excuse me a minute while I look for some stuff for your foot."

Philip Entwistle settled himself in the only vacant arm-chair and took stock of his immediate surroundings. The study was a fairly large room, measuring, roughly, thirty feet by twenty. On the side facing south were three broad casement windows, now heavily curtained with a light-proof fabric. The door was on the eastern side, opening into a spacious hall. The remaining walls were blank except for the old-fashioned fireplace. Oak panelling and massive beams of the same material—wood that had been in position for close on three hundred years—gave an old-time appearance to the room. The furniture was hardly in keeping with the place. Presumably it was for utility. The large pedestal, roll-top desk occupied a proportionate position against the west wall. Almost every available bit of wall-space was taken up with book-cases groaning under the weight of volumes of all sizes and ages, from the leatherbound tomes of the late Stuart period to the modern "sevenpenny." Not a picture was in evidence. Instead, above the book-shelves the walls were adorned with pieces of medieval armour and weapons ranging from the Elizabethan musketoon and pike to the latest type of magazine rifle. Above the fireplace was a seven-feet-scale model of a super- Dreadnought that, in its sombre garb of battleship grey, contrasted strongly with the black and yellow striped hull and dun-coloured canvas of an eighteenth century frigate that adorned another part of the room.

The study, like the rest of the house, was lighted by electricity—a discovery that Peter Barcroft had made with huge satisfaction. It was, indeed, a rare chance to hit upon an isolated dwelling, in a commanding, lofty situation, well-built and supplied with water, gas and electricity. The secret lay in the fact that at one time it had been the residence of the manager of the nearest bleaching works. Had it been daylight one would have noticed a line of hefty posts supporting a cable-system that ran up hill and down dale almost as far as the eye could reach. At certain intervals the supports bore a large board on which was painted in bold letters: "Dangerous—10,000 volts"—a warning to the youth of the district who might feel tempted to fly kites over the wires or even to climb the poles out of sheer exuberance of juvenile spirits.

It was from this cable by means of a "transformer" that Ladybird Fold derived its supply of electric current, and, as it happened, the works had not received any warning that night of the raid—a circumstance that contributed greatly to the comfort of Peter Barcroft's den.

From his chair Entwistle glanced at his host's desk and shuddered. The cover had been left rolled back, disclosing a veritable chaos of papers, reference books, writing materials, pipes and two large tobacco-jars. The pigeon-holes were crammed to bursting-point with a medley of papers, particularly the one labelled "Letters to be answered." From another gaped the crumpled ends of what were evidently a number of cheques that awaited a favourable opportunity on the part of the busy author (he put in an occasional two hours a day, be it remembered) to be paid into the Barborough Bank. A thick layer of dust covered the desk, although everything else in the room was fairly clear if the patches of tobacco ash on the carpet square were not taken into account. It was part of Peter's creed to knock out his pipes on the heel of his boot and deposit their remains on the floor, convenient ash-trays notwithstanding. For one thing it kept the moth away.

The dust, too, upon the desk was the result of studied design. The "help" from the village—a temporary importation pending Mrs. Barcroft's return and provided she was successful in her distracting quest—had been strictly enjoined, browbeaten and threatened with divers pains and penalties, not to disturb Peter's papers. With luck he could find what he wanted in five minutes; without, in an hour. That is, if the desk had been left severely alone. Otherwise, should the timorous female dare to "side-up"—a Lancashire expression that puzzled Barcroft tremendously at first—the quest would be almost hopeless.

Had Philip Entwistle been more inquisitive and observant he might have noticed that on the top of the pile of literary debris were two objects that showed no signs of a coating of dust. One was a bound volume entitled *The Theories of Modern Naval Warfare*—a work of Peter's that had been responsible for a price being set upon the head of that as yet unconscious-of-the-fact worthy. The other was a batch of manuscript comprising his nearly completed book *The Great Reckoning—and After*.

The reappearance of his host with a tray bearing a tantalus, syphon and a couple of glasses, cut short Entwistle's casual survey.

"How goes it now?" asked Barcroft. "Telephoned?"

"You certainly said, 'There's the telephone,'" replied his guest, "but failed to explain to my satisfaction where 'there' is. Consequently that solemn and protracted rite has not yet been performed."

"Sorry," said Peter with a laugh. "My mistake entirely. I ought to have mentioned that that convenient but much maligned instrument is in the hall. There's a great-coat hanging over it: my device to deaden the nerve-racking sound of the bell."

Entwistle shuffled across the room. In spite of the fact that he was now wearing a pair of his host's capacious slippers the injured foot occasioned him more pain than while he was on his way to the house.

He left the door ajar. Barcroft could hear him thumping the as yet unresponsive machine. Quite five minutes passed before his guest could "get on."

"Number four four five, Barborough ... what—engaged ... no reply? Well, try again."

More violent manipulation of the telephone accompanied by a flow of forcible language resulted in the desired object being attained.

"That you, Vi?... Yes,.. yes,.. no, I wasn't injured ... what's that? Church Street knocked out of existence.... Not nervous? That's good. I'm speaking from Ladybird Fold, Tarleigh. Tell Jarvis to run the car over for me in the morning. Yes, about ten. Good-night."

Returning to his study he found Peter at his desk.

"Needn't have worried so much about my wife," he announced. "She's quite plucky over it. She even chipped me at having missed the excitement."

Barcroft did not reply. He was regarding his desk with a distinctly preoccupied air.

"Dash the L.L.P." he exclaimed, addressing the room in general rather than his guest. "I'll swear she's been meddling with my papers. And she left that door open. I'll let her know who rules this show."

"Who's L.L.P.?" enquired Entwistle.

His host laughed.

"Merely the help," he replied. "Carter's her name. I call her Little Liver Pill—she reminds me of one. L.L.P, for short, you know."

"Might be your friend Andrew Norton," suggested the other.

"By Jove, yes! I hadn't thought of that," was the reply. "All the same, I don't think he would touch my desk. It's just likely that in a preoccupied moment (although as a rule he isn't given that way) he may have gone home and left the lights switched on and the door open. Hulloa, this looks queer! I wonder if Norton got into a funk over the Zep.?"

Barcroft pointed to a pipe lying on the mantelpiece. It was freshly filled and the tobacco was slightly charred, indicating that the owner had been interrupted in the act of lighting up.

"His pipe," he continued. "And he seems a fairly methodical fellow, not likely to leave anything behind. Hope he's all right. If it wasn't for the fact that I've had a long tramp and it's close on one thirty I'd run across to his place."

"What sort of a man is he?" enquired Entwistle.

"Decent—quite. Nothing of the bore about him, or I would have choked him off very quickly," replied Barcroft grimly. "Quite informal, and different from the ordinary type of caller when a fellow comes into a fresh district. You know the sort—stiff-necked blighters of both sexes who pay formal calls for the sole purpose of finding out who you are, what you are and what you've got. In my case, I suppose, they expect to find a sort of untamed curiosity: that's how they regard literary men, I believe. But my time is too precious to waste in that way, so I let them know it pretty quickly. Ah, there are the trains running again," he added as a dull rumble was borne to their ears. "Zep. show's over for to-night. Keen on bed?"

"Not very," replied Entwistle. "Are you?"

"I'm going to wait up for Billy," said the fond parent. "Wonder what the young bounder is doing now?"

As he spoke came the sounds of quick, firm footsteps up the cobbled path. Before Peter could get across the room the door was thrown open and Flight-Sub-lieutenant Barcroft, his face blackened with smoke and dust and his great-coat bearing signs of rough usage, burst into the room.

"Cheer-o, pater!" he exclaimed. "Sorry I'm late. Some night, eh, what?"

CHAPTER VI
KIDNAPPED

IT will now be necessary to set back the hands of the clock to the hour of ten on the evening of the Zeppelin's visit to Barborough.

At that hour Mr. Andrew Norton was knocking on the door of Ladybird Fold, and vainly endeavouring to restrain the boisterous attentions of Ponto and Nan.

"Good evening, Mrs. Carter," he said as the door was opened revealing the domestic stopgap with her head covered by a shawl—the recognised head-dress of the working-class women of industrial Lancashire. "Any one at home?"

"Only mysen, master," was the reply. "An' in another minute you would be findin' me gone. Mr. Barcroft he's out, but he'll not be long, I'm thinkin'. An' young Mr. Barcroft—'im as is in the Navy—is expected home to-night. But come in, you're kindly welcome."

"And at what time is young Mr. Barcroft expected?" he asked in a tone that implied mild curiosity, as he stepped over the threshold.

"I'm not for sayin' for certain. Master had a telegram. You'll not be wantin' anythin', sir?"

Norton shook his head. Accompanied by the two dogs he entered the study and switched on the lights. As he did so he heard the door slam and Mrs. Carter's retreating footsteps on the hard path.

He knew how to make himself at home during his friend's absence. He was one of those men who have the happy knack of forming quick friendships, and the somewhat easy-going Peter was a good subject in that respect.

Andrew Norton was a man of forty-five, although he looked considerably younger. He was of medium height, full-featured and inclined to stoutness. A keen motorist, he had attracted Barcroft's attention on the very first day of his taking possession of "The Croft," when he was endeavouring to take a large car up the difficult lane beyond Ladybird Fold. Since there was plenty of accommodation in the outbuilding utilised as a garage at Barcroft's house

Peter's suggestion that it would be easier for the newcomer to The Croft to keep his car there and thus save a steep and loose ascent was accepted with profuse gratitude.

From that moment the friendship ripened. Almost every evening after the literary man's strenuous labours were completed for the day Andrew Norton would drop in for a smoke and a yarn.

"Rotten nuisance!" mused the hostless guest as he settled himself in an easy chair. "If only I knew what time he was returning. The uncertainty will probably make a regular mess of present arrangements."

It might have been idle curiosity that prompted him to cross over to the desk and examine Peter's uncompleted work; sheer anxiety that led him to the open window to listen intently for the sound of his absent friend's footsteps.

Through the uncurtained window three shafts of brilliant light were flung upon the closely-cropped lawn, the limit of the rays being defined by a thick hedge dividing the lawn from the rose-garden.

"No signs yet," he muttered, as he glanced at the clock for the twentieth time. "Friend Barcroft's regrettable absence is spoiling my evening. I'll get back to The Croft."

He drew the curtains with deliberate care, so that no stray ray of light should escape. Lighting restrictions were lax in that part of Lancashire, as the twinkling glimmers from the houses in the valley testified; for in the district where he had previously lived for two years there were drastic observances on that score, and now the habit of conforming to the requirements of the authorities was not lightly to be dropped.

"I'll give him five minutes more," he soliloquised as he drew a pipe from his pocket and charged it with great deliberation. This he proceeded to light, making use of a paper spill. Here he showed a marked contrast to the easygoing methods of the occupier of Ladybird Fold. In spite of their high price, Peter invariably used matches—and plenty of them. Usually the hearth was littered with the burnt-out stumps, for Barcroft always had a pipe in his mouth when he was writing. It might go out twenty times before the tobacco was expended, but every time a fresh match was struck and flung away to augment the already numerous accumulation in the fireplace.

Just then the two dogs sat up and barked. Norton started nervously. He was only just beginning to get used to the sturdy, shaggy animals.

"Quiet!" he shouted.

A peremptory knock sounded on the door. The still burning spill fell from the man's fingers. He made his way into the hall, shutting the study door upon the dogs. Vainly he groped for the switch operating the front door light.

"Who's there?" he demanded.

"Telegram for Mr. Barcroft," replied a deep voice.

Had Norton paused to consider the likelihood of a telegram being delivered at a very late hour in a remote country district he might have saved himself from a great deal of personal inconvenience. But he did not.

He threw open the door. His eyes, still dazzled by the quick transition from the brilliant light within to the intense darkness without, stared vacantly into the night, while his right hand groped furtively for the expected orange coloured envelope.

As he did so a pair of powerful hands grasped his ankles. His involuntary exclamation of mingled astonishment and indignation was stifled by a thick cloth twisted over his mouth and round his head, while simultaneously his arms were pinioned to his sides.

Unable to move a limb, much less to struggle, he found himself lifted from the ground and borne away as helpless as an infant.

"Fools!" he spluttered. "Fools! You'll be sorry for this."

Whether his captors heard his muffled protests or not they paid no heed save to give the cloth that encircled his head an extra twist. The pressure upon his nose was painful. He had difficulty in breathing, so, realising that his stifled exclamations were futile, he wisely held his peace from a vocal point of view, although inwardly he was raging furiously.

He could hear the boots of his captors clattering on the cobbles until the crisp-sounding footfalls told him that the men had gained the cinder path on the east side of the house. Then, with considerable effort on the part of his bearers, he was lifted up a flight of four stone steps, beyond which, he knew, was an extensive grassfield that rose gradually for the next half mile.

Grunting and obviously short of breath the men trudged stolidly onwards for perhaps nearly two hundred yards. Once Norton thought fit to make a sudden effort and wriggle from his captors' grasp, but the attempt ended disastrously to himself. Brutally they bumped him upon the ground. The shock to the spinal system was excruciating, but it had the desired effect. The prisoner's spirit of resistance was broken; even the stern mandate, "Quiet, or you are a dead man," was unnecessary.

The scarf or cloth that enveloped his head had slipped during the struggle. He could now see. Either his kidnappers had not noticed the fact or else they regarded it as of no consequence.

He could discern the faces and upper portions of the bodies of the two men. They were tall burly fellows dressed in black oilskins. In spite of their powerful physique they were breathing stertorously; they reeked of petrol.

Another fifty yards and they came to a halt. Norton turned his head and saw what appeared at first sight to be the dark grey body of a motorcar. It was quivering under the application of some unseen influence, yet there was no purr of internal mechanism to justify the belief that it possessed self-contained machinery.

"Lash that schweinhund's ankles, Pfeil," ordered one of the fellows in German. "That is right; now do you enter first and I'll heave the English fool up so that you can get him inside."

"Now is the dangerous time," commented his companion as he scrambled through a narrow aperture.

"It is ever a dangerous time with us," rejoined the other gloomily.

"Ah, yes; but now? Supposing the wire is insufficient to take the strain?"

"It will bear thrice our total weight," replied the first speaker, "frail though it looks. No fear of that breaking. It is that highly-charged electric cable that worries me. We must have landed nearer to it than we should have done, yet it looks further away on the map."

The fellow completed his difficult task of lifting Norton into the interior of the covered-in car—the observation room of a Zeppelin floating motionless five hundred feet or so overhead.

The commander of the giant aircraft had successfully carried out a daring manoeuvre with the ultimate object of taking prisoner the man on whom his imperial master the "All-Highest" had set a price for his capture. Taking advantage of an almost imperceptible breeze and knowing his position to an almost dead certainty by means of exact cross-bearings afforded by three reservoirs, conspicuous even in the darkness, he had caused to be lowered the aluminium observation car.

In flight this contrivance is slung close under the after part of the Zeppelin, but when necessary it can be lowered by means of a fine but enormously strong flexible steel wire to a maximum distance of two thousand feet beneath the giant envelope. Thus it is possible for a Zeppelin to remain hidden in a bank of clouds and lower the observation car to within a few hundred feet of the ground. Its comparatively small size and inconspicuous colour would render it invisible even at that short distance, and give the observer an uninterrupted view of the country. By means of a telephone he could then communicate with the commander of the airship and indicate the objects singled out for attack.

On this occasion the aluminium box was lowered till it touched the ground. The two men purposely told off for the work in hand had anchored the car, thereby keeping the Zeppelin stationary also. In the event of a surprise the airship's crew would unhesitatingly sever the wire and leave the car and their two comrades to their fate.

And now most of this particular enterprise had been carried out. The supposed object of their attentions lay gagged and bound within the aluminium cage. All that remained to be done was to break out the grapnel and signal to the men in the Zeppelin to wind in the steel cable.

"All ready?" enquired Pfeil through the telephone. "Good! When I give the signal will you forge ahead to the north-east? Why? Because we are much too close to the high tension cable which Herr Leutnant knows of."

He leant through an aperture in the side of the cradle and listened intently. At the first sound of the airship's propellers he jerked a tripping-line smartly. The fluke of the grapnel folded as he did so, and the car, no longer held captive, slid jerkily over the grass.

"Up!" telephoned the German.

The next instant Norton felt himself being lifted through the air as the car ascended swiftly at a rate of five feet a second. In less than two minutes the cradle's supplementary movement ceased. It was hauled hard up against the immense bulk of the Zeppelin and secured with additional lashings.

The wind was now shrieking through the lattice work of the airship, as gathering speed she flew through the still air at a rate of nearly fifty miles an hour, or a little more than half her maximum speed.

It was cold—horribly cold. Lightly clad and coming from a warm room the prisoner felt the change acutely. He shivered in spite of his efforts to the contrary.

Gripped by the ankles he found himself being dragged like a sack of flour from the detachable car to the V-shaped gangway connecting two of the fixed gondolas. The lashings securing his lower limbs were cast off, and, thrust forward by the powerful Pfeil, he was made to walk along the narrow corridor.

"Here is the Englishman, Herr Leutnant," announced the German addressing a short, corpulent officer who stood by the bomb-dropping apparatus in the centre of the gondola.

"Good!" was the appreciative reply. Ober-leutnant Julius von Loringhoven squirmed in anticipation of winning more than a half of the promised guerdon. A share—a considerable share unfortunately—was owing to a certain individual who, acting as an agent of the German Government, had given valuable aid in snaring the proscribed Englishman. His assistance was necessary, of course, but that meant a sensible reduction of the sum of paper money with which von Loringhoven hoped to restore the fortunes of his impoverished house.

"Good!" he repeated. "Remove that covering and let me look at the pig."

Pfeil obeyed smartly. With a savage jerk he exposed the face of his captive.

"Utter idiot!" shouted Andrew Norton in German. "Imbecile! You've blundered and spoilt everything."

CHAPTER VII
THE RAID

OBER-LEUTNANT JULIUS VON LORINGHOVEN recoiled a couple of paces in sheer amazement. The compartment in which he stood was strictly limited in point of size, or he might have stepped back even more, so great was his consternation. For some seconds he stood with his shoulders against the aluminium bulkhead, his small eyes protruding to their utmost capacity.

"Von Eitelwurmer!" he gurgled at last. "What does this mean?"

"It means," retorted Andrew Norton furiously, "that your men have wrecked everything. It is their duty to wreck everything English, I admit, but they have overreached themselves."

"I am sorry," said the ober-leutnant humbly, though the apology needed an effort. "The culprits will be duly punished."

"And serve them right," interrupted the kidnapped man. "But that will not mend matters. Our plans are completely upset; Barcroft will take warning; there will be no plausible excuse for my sudden departure—Ach, it is intolerable. Is it possible to set me down?"

Von Loringhoven shook his head.

"Impossible," he replied. "You must return with us to the Fatherland. Meanwhile I must take steps to justify the presence of this war-machine over the hated country."

Siegfried von Eitelwurmer was one of the German super-spies—a class far and above the host of ordinary spies that, in spite of the utmost vigilance on the part of the British government, still continue their activities although in a restricted form. To all outward appearance he was English born and bred. His mannerisms were entirely so. Even in his most excitable moods, for Teutonic stolidity was almost a stranger to him, he would never betray by word or gesture the fact that he was of Hunnish birth and sympathies. When he spoke in English his inflexion was as pure as a typical Midlander; his knowledge of British habits and customs was profound. In short, he was one of the most dangerous type of German agents that ever set foot on British soil.

It will be unnecessary to detail his past activities, which almost invariably he carried out successfully and without giving rise to suspicion, even at times when the espionage mania was at its height, and Britons were being arrested and detained on suspicion for various slight acts of indiscretion that they had committed in pure ignorance. A man might in all good faith take photographs of a place of national interest; an artist might make a sketch in the grounds of his own house—and be promptly haled before the magistrates and fined. The "powers-that-be" seem to be blind to the fact that a trained spy would not attempt to use a conspicuous camera. An instrument of the vest-pocket type would serve his purpose equally well and with little chance of detection.

It was the Kaiser's manifesto relating to the capture of the "dangerous" Peter Barcroft that turned the course of von Eitelwurmer's activities in the direction of Ladybird Fold—not wholly for the sake of the pecuniary reward, but with the idea of gaining additional kudos at the hands of his Imperial master.

The spy had little difficulty in tracing Barcroft's movements from the time he vacated Riversdale House in the village of Alderdene. The information that his quarry had removed to Tarleigh in Lancashire he had communicated to Berlin, but owing to a delay the news was not in time to prevent the Hun airman, von Bülow und Helferich, making his ill-fated flight to the south-eastern part of England.

Von Eitelwurmer's method of communicating with Berlin was simplicity itself, and as such ran less chance of detection than if he had resorted to elaborate and intricate means.

He would obtain catalogues from manufacturers living in the same town in which he had taken up his temporary abode. On the pages he would write with invisible ink—or even milk or lemon, both of which when dried naturally show no trace of their presence—his reports, taking the additional precaution of using a cipher which he could retain mentally and thus do away with the risk of incriminating documents.

The next step was to get possession of a printed wrapper bearing the name and address of the firm in question. The catalogue, enclosed in the wrapper, was then sent to a pseudo Englishman living in Holland, who, almost needless to say, was a German agent.

These reports were then sent in duplicate, one preceding the other in the space of three days. Fortunately or otherwise—according to the standpoint taken by interested parties—the first secret dispatch related to the movements of Peter Barcroft was lost in a Dutch mail-boat that a German submarine had sent to the bottom. The second resulted in Ober-leutnant von Loringhoven being dispatched on a Zeppelin raid with the primary intention of kidnapping the proscribed Englishman.

Julius von Loringhoven was an officer of the Imperial German Navy. In his youth he had served before the mast on board several British coasters with the idea of gaining intimate local knowledge of the harbours of the land that in due course would be an integral part of the vast and unassailable German Empire; for, like thousands of Germans he held the firm belief that the Emperor Wilhelm II was the rightful heir to the British throne by virtue of his descent through the eldest child of the late Queen Victoria.

It was on one of these coasting trips that von Loringhoven then a stripling of seventeen—was within an ace of losing his life. Ordered aloft on a winter's night to furl the topsail of the schooner "Pride o' Salcombe," he was benumbed with the piercing cold as he lay along the lee yard-arm. A burly British seaman saved him just as he was on the point of relaxing his hold. Gathering him in his arms the man brought him down on deck, little knowing what manner of young reptile he was nursing in his bosom. If von Loringhoven had had any spark of gratitude it had been smothered by the passion of "frightfulness" as expressed by dropping powerful explosives upon the defenceless civil population of the country to one of whose sons he owed his life.

A brief training at Friedrichshaven was followed by an exacting period at Borkum which qualified von Loringhoven for a series of flights across the North Sea to the East Coast of England. As yet he was merely a tyro, gaining practical experience under a veteran Zeppelin commander. But at last the day came when he was given sole charge of one of the Kaiser's giant gas-bags.

"Go and raid the counties of Yorkshire and Lincolnshire," were his superior officer's instructions. "That's a fairly safe game. You'll find little more than dummy guns against you. Acquit yourself well and you will be given an opportunity to take part in the forthcoming gigantic raid upon London."

This was before the time when, as the Huns knew to their cost, the "swarm of hornets" promised by a former First Lord of the Admiralty proved their existence.

And now, after twelve months of active Zeppelin service von Loringhoven was over Lancashire. One part of his mission foiled he had yet to exhibit Teutonic frightfulness to the dwellers of the large manufacturing town of Barborough.

The second in command of the Zeppelin was an unter-leutnant of the name of Klick. It was one of his triumphs to announce that he had been arrested in England as a spy. That was in those distant pre-war times. He had been "spotted" by a sentry while in the act of sketching a fortification in the neighbourhood of an important naval station, arrested and charged at a police-court. Committed to the County Assizes he was politely told by the judge that espionage was dishonourable. Klick smiled inwardly. To him spying was part of an important German military training—an organised procedure. Nevertheless he was agreeably surprised when he was allowed to go with the admonition, "Don't do it again."

Fortunately for Great Britain such misplaced leniency is a thing of the past. On Unter-leutnant Klick it was entirely thrown away. His typically German mind read the clemency as a sign of weakness. He came from a country where the only strength is "force majeur."

"Well, Herr von Eitelwurmer," exclaimed the ober-leutnant after he had recovered from his surprise. "If you wish to see how our in comparable Zeppelins set to work you had better station yourself at this observation scuttle. I will lend you a fur coat."

"Pity you hadn't lent me one long before," growled the spy, as one of the crew helped him into the warm garment. "Yours is a cold business, von Loringhoven."

"Not when we get to work," corrected the other with a grim laugh. "Excitement stirs our blood to boiling point."

A telephone bell tinkled softly. The commander took up the receiver.

"Ach!" he replied. "That is good."

The message was from Unter-leutnant Klick, announcing that the airship was immediately over the large town of Barborough. Von Loringhoven glanced at the altitude indicator. It registered 2,000 metres—too great for practical purposes where no danger was to be anticipated from anti-aircraft guns. The speed of the Zeppelin was now less than ten miles an hour, just sufficient to keep her stationary over her objective.

The commander gave an order. A man on duty in the gondola thrust down a lever, Instantly the gas in several of the ballonets was withdrawn and forced under great pressure into a strong metal tank. This answered to the old-fashioned method of releasing gas from a balloon by means of an escape valve, but with a vast difference. The hydrogen was not wasted; it was merely stored for further service.

Down dropped the airship to less than a thousand feet. Von Eitelwurmer, leaning over the sill of the large scuttle, peered downwards. By means of a pair of powerful night-glasses he could locate his position with great accuracy. He recognised most of the conspicuous land marks of Barborough, in spite of their unfamiliar appearance when viewed from a height. There was the town-hall—a pile of smoke blackened stonework. The railway station with its web of steel lines radiating in four different directions; the huge factories, working day and night at high pressure; the main thoroughfares, rendered even more pronounced by the blue flashes of the electric tram-cars. The Zeppelin had the town at its mercy.

Ober-leutnant von Loringhoven was also examining the scene beneath him. He had no occasion to consult the spy. He knew quite as much as von Eitelwurmer of the topography of the district; thanks to the accurate air-maps supplied by the German government.

"Now, watch!" he exclaimed, at the same time holding up four fingers as a sign to the airman at the firing apparatus to release the missiles of destruction.

Von Eitelwurmer held his breath. He clearly heard the four metallic clicks as the man released the bombs at quick intervals. Seven seconds after the first had left the dropping apparatus a lurid flash threw the underside of the enormous envelope into an expanse of reflected light. A roar like the concentration of half a dozen thunder peals tore the air, followed by the rumbling of falling masonry. The other explosions took place in rapid succession, causing the Zeppelin to sway and rock in the violently disturbed atmosphere.

The place where the bombs had burst was hidden in a thick pall of smoke and dust. Tongues of red and yellow flames flickered through the vapour.

"Two more," ordered von Loringhoven.

By this time the Zeppelin, forging ahead, was nearly a quarter of a mile from the scene of her first attempt. The objective was a purely conjectural one, for the missiles burst in a street in one of the poorer quarters of the town.

"Two more!"

The two bombs were released, but only one exploded. The other failed to detonate, but the raid was over. In a little over a minute and a half death had been poured upon the unprepared town.

"I can claim the big munitions factory," remarked the ober-leutnant as he telephoned to the navigating gondola for full speed. "Those first four had it to a nicety. The others—well, they did some damage."

The spy smiled.

"Yes; it all helps," he said. "Frightfulness always scores,"

"Realising, as we do, that every English baby is a potential enemy to Germany," added von Loringhoven. "Not necessarily in a military sense, but in the forthcoming commercial war."

Von Eitelwurmer glanced at his companion,

"The forthcoming commercial war," he repeated. "Our Emperor will see to it that there will be no British Empire to threaten our mercantile supremacy."

The commander of the Zeppelin shrugged his shoulders.

"I trust you are right," he rejoined, "but you do not realise the big task in front of us. These Englishmen are only just beginning to bestir themselves. We hoped to have beaten them long ago. Time is no longer on our side, and——"

Then, realising that his digression was bordering upon dangerous lines, he broke off.

"And now, von Eitelwurmer, we are homeward bound. In four hours I hope to shake hands with you on German soil."

The spy merely grunted. He was thinking regretfully of his lost chance in the share of the twenty thousand marks.

CHAPTER VIII
'MIDST THE SCENE OF RED RUIN

FIVE minutes before the fall of the first bomb, Flight-Sub-lieutenant Barcroft alighted from a tram-car in the market square of Barborough.

The stopping of the railway service had upset his calculations, for instead of the train running into Barborough Station it had come to a stand still at Wolderton, a little town five miles from his destination.

"Can't go no further yet awhile, sir," replied a porter in answer to the flight-sub's enquiry. "They say as 'ow Zeps is about, though I fancy they won't come to Lancashire, sir. Don't hold wi' these silly scares mysen."

"Where are we?" asked Barcroft, striving vainly to read the name of the unlighted station. "Wolderton, sir; if you're for Barborough you can get a car just outside. They are runnin', Zep, or no Zep."

The young officer alighted, made his way out of the station and boarded the first northbound car, which in due course deposited him at Barborough—a stranger in a strange land.

"For Tarleigh, sir?" rejoined a policeman to his question. "Matter o' four or six miles. No, sir, you'll not be findin' a taxi to-night, I fancy. Just you go along yon road, take first on your right then straight on till you come to Chumley Old Road. There you'll find a car that'll take you as far as Black Pit Brow, and it'll be forty minutes sharp walking to Tarleigh."

Somewhat bewildered Barcroft set out to follow the constable's directions. He found himself slipping on the rough and greasy setts, jostling people in the darkened streets, and barking his shins against obtrusive door steps. The road was a mean and narrow one—a short cut to a main thoroughfare. A dank unwholesome smell permeated the misty air. It struck the young officer as being worse than the atmosphere of the lower deck of a battleship battened down during a three-days' gale.

Suddenly the darkness was rent by a terrific flash. The light was so dazzling that Barcroft was under the impression that it came from the centre of the street. Stunned by the deafening crash he felt himself lurching against a wall, amidst a shower of broken glass.

Another explosion followed and then two more. The flight-sub felt the wall of the house rock with the concussions. He was quite prepared to see the building collapse under the impact of the displaced air. Fragments of slates and tiles, mingled with shattered woodwork, hurtled overhead. Glass tinkled upon the setts. The rumble of falling masonry was added to the uproar, while flames shot up from a mound of debris that a brief instant earlier had been the homes of three English families, and threw a fitful glare upon the scene of destruction.

"Factory explosion, I suppose," thought Barcroft. "Can't be a Zep., or I should have heard her engines."

He put his hand to his cheek. It was warm and moist. Blood was welling from a deep gash. He hardly noticed it. His attention was attracted by the shouts and screams of the terrified inhabitants of the neighbourhood — those whose houses having escaped annihilation but were within the danger zone, had fled pell-mell into the streets.

Other crashes followed, but at a greater distance.

"Then it is a Zep., by Jove!" declared the young officer. For the first time he realised his helplessness. He was virtually one of the thousands of civilians unable to raise a hand in self-defence against the cowardly night-raider. A Tommy in a trench with only a rifle — an almost useless weapon against an aircraft of any description — has the satisfaction that he is armed. He is willing to take his chance. But here the townsfolk were utterly at a loss to defend themselves, and it was sorry consolation to be told by the authorities that the inhabitants of raided districts are only sharing the dangers to which the troops in the trenches are exposed.

"If only I were up aloft with young Kirkwood," thought Barcroft. "We'd make the beggars skip out of that gas-bag. Perhaps some day—"

A woman, with her shawl wrapped tightly round her head, came hurrying in the opposite direction to which the stream of terrified people forced its way.

"Eh!" she exclaimed. "An' I left t'owld mon's supper on t' stove. I'll be fair angry if 'tis spoilt."

It was genuine anxiety. Even in the midst of the scene of destruction her thoughts dwelt upon the little cares of everyday domesticity.

With the sailor's typical eagerness to render aid Barcroft hurried down the street. Already the ebb-tide of fugitives was thinning and giving place to the flood-tide of willing helpers. Here and there men staggered and groaned, bleeding from serious wounds caused by the flying fragments of the deadly missiles. Here and there came others supporting or carrying victims unable to help themselves—stalwart men, frail women and puny children reduced in the fraction of a second to mangled wrecks.

Pungent, asphyxiating fumes drifted slowly down the narrow thoroughfare, while the glare of the burning buildings threw an eerie light upon the surroundings.

In the street not one panel of glass remained intact. Cast-iron stack-pipes were riddled with holes cut as cleanly as with a drill. Brick walls were perforated like paper; stone-steps—the "scouring" of which is a solemn rite with Lancashire folk—were chipped and splintered like glass. Doors were burst open as if with a sledge-hammer. And this was fifty yards or more from the scene of the actual explosion.

Where the first bomb had fallen nothing remained of the house except a mound of smoking rubbish. The two adjoining buildings were cut away from top to bottom almost as evenly as if severed by a saw. In one the roof was exposed on the underside. The slates were still in position but riddled like a sieve. So violent was the force with which the flying fragments were projected upwards that the fragile slates were perforated before they had time to crack or be dislodged from the rafters.

In the house on the other adjoining side the parting wall had vanished, leaving the remaining walls and flooring practically intact. A fire was still burning in the kitchen grate, and on it an iron pot was simmering. In front of the fire were three pairs of "clogs" of varying sizes—the footgear of a family that was no longer in existence.

It was the same story. The raid from a military point of view was of no consequence. The munitions factory, in spite of von Loringhoven's assurances, had been missed—missed handsomely.

The flight-sub did not linger at this particular spot. Human aid was unavailing as far as those ruined houses were concerned, but on the other side of the street groans and cries of pain told him that here at least there was work to be done.

Through an open doorway Barcroft dashed. The woodwork of the door was in splinters. Part of the floor had vanished. The place was full of smoke, while gas from a severed pipe was burning furiously.

Grasping a large fragment of paving-stone the flight-sub battered the pipe.

"Iron, worse luck," he exclaimed. "Wonder where the meter is?"

He discovered it just above the door. In the absence of a key to turn off the inflammable gas he knocked the lead pipe flat. The flame began to die down until it gave a fairly safe illumination.

Up the rickety stairs the young officer made his way. With smarting eyes and irritating throat he groped through the stifling smoke, guided by the cries of the injured victims. The room was feebly lighted by a nightlight set in a basin of water. The light flickered in the breeze that swept in through the glazeless window, while its intensity was even more diminished by the eddying smoke. Yet it was sufficient to enable Barcroft to take in his surroundings.

The ceiling had fallen. Plaster and broken glass littered the floor, and every object presented a flat, face-upward surface. On the walls were crude prints hanging at grotesque angles and ripped by flying fragments. Pieces of broken furniture were everywhere in evidence.

In one corner of the room was a bed. One leg had been torn off, causing it to touch the floor. On the bed was a grey-haired woman, groaning feebly and with her forehead dabbled in blood.

She opened her eyes as Barcroft approached, then raising one hand pointed to the side of the bed. There was a cradle that had hitherto escaped his notice, and in it was a baby of but a few months old. Although the old woman could not speak she made it known that the rescuer should first save her grandchild.

Even in that scene of desolation Barcroft could not bring himself to lift the baby from its cot. Dimly he fancied that he might harm it. He hadn't the faintest notion how to hold an infant of tender years.

Lifting the cot bodily he bore it with its contents down the stairs and out into the night. By this time other rescuers were hard at work. Two of them seeing the flight-sub issuing from the house came up to him.

"D'ye want a hand, sir?" they asked.

The uniform imparted an air of authority, and instinctively the men realised the fact. True the naval rig was foreign to them. For all they knew Barcroft might be a sanitary inspector or a school-attendance officer, but his peaked cap and naval blue coat denoted an official of some sort, and, in cases of this description, the distinction carries weight.

"Yes, there's a woman injured in that house," replied the flight-sub, setting down his burden. One of the men bent over the cradle and drew back the covering. Then he hastily replaced it.

"Might have saved yourself the trouble, sir," he gulped. "Those baby-killing swine! If that cursed Zep, should happen to fall anywhere round about and any of the devils are left alive, I bet my last shilling the women-folk o' Barborough 'ud tear 'em limb from limb. An' serve 'em right. Lead on, sir."

Not until the last of the living victims of the outrage had been removed from this section of the bombed district did Barcroft and his willing helpers desist from their arduous labours. Nothing more could be done until daybreak. Police guarded the approaches to the devastated street, while firemen stood by, ready at the first sign to tackle a fresh outburst from the still smouldering ruins.

"Suppose I ought to try for an hotel," soliloquised the flight-sub. "I don't know. I'm in a horrible mess. Feel like a dustman or a scavenger. Perhaps I'd better carry on. The governor might be a bit anxious if I don't."

Receiving fresh directions Barcroft stepped out briskly. Taxis and even tramcars were now out of the question.

"Most confusing place I've struck for many a day," he muttered. "I feel completely out of my bearings. I'm supposed to be going north; it's my belief I'm making in a southerly direction."

Vainly he looked aloft to "verify his position by stellar observation." Not a star was visible. He was now clear of the town. The road ran steeply up a bleak hillside and was bounded by rough stone walls. Doubtless there were plenty of houses scattered about in the surrounding valleys, but these were not in evidence. Every light still burning had been carefully screened. It was a case of shutting the stable door after the horse had been stolen.

Presently he reached the junction of two fork roads, either of which might lead to Tarleigh. A tantalising sign-post afforded no information, for upon swarming up the post the flight-sub was unable to read the weather-beaten directions.

"What on earth possessed the pater to hang out in this benighted spot I cannot imagine!" exclaimed Barcroft disgustedly. "Suppose I must wait here in the hope that some one will be passing this way. It seems the safest chance."

CHAPTER IX
BETTY

"THAT'S more hopeful," ejaculated Flight sub-lieutenant Barcroft. "I hear footsteps."

For perhaps half a minute he listened intently. He was not mistaken in his surmise, but there was still the haunting doubt that the benighted wayfarer might be proceeding in a different direction. But no; the footsteps came nearer and nearer. It was not the firm tread of a man, nor the clatter of a pair of Lancashire clogs.

"A woman, by Jove!" muttered Billy. "I'll have to be jolly careful not to give her a fright. Rummy idea having to hail a craft of that sort at this time of the morning. Wonder what brings her out in this isolated spot?"

In his anxiety not to unduly alarm the approaching woman, the flight-sub began to walk in her direction. It was, he decided, a better course than to stand back until she passed.

"Excuse me," he said touching his cap, "but can you direct me to Tarleigh?"

"Yes, I am going part of the way," was the reply in a decidedly clear and pleasant voice, which spoke with perfect composure. "If you like I'll go with you as far as Two Elms. It is then a straight road."

"Thank you," said Barcroft, falling into step with his unknown benefactor. "You see, I'm quite a stranger here."

"Hang it all!" he mused. "That voice seems familiar. A trim little craft, too, I should imagine, although I can't see her face. Wonder who she is?"

"You are a naval officer, I see," remarked the girl.

"Yes," admitted Billy. "On leave and going to a home I've never seen. This raid affair made me late."

"And so it did me," added his companion. "By the bye, where was your home before?"

"At Alderdene in Kent," replied Barcroft, somewhat taken aback at the question. "Why do you ask?"

"I thought so," was the composed reply. "And your name is Barcroft—Billy Barcroft."

"By Jove!" exclaimed the young officer. "How on earth do you know that? I'm afraid I don't recognise you."

"You always had a bad memory for certain things, Mr. Barcroft," the girl laughingly reminded him. "I felt almost positive it was you directly you spoke. You see, the uniform and you have a most characteristic helped me, manner of speaking."

"Have I?" asked Billy, still mystified. "And you have a good memory, I presume?"

"Fairly reliable," admitted the girl.

"Then let us hope that your recollections of me are of a favourable character," continued the flight-sub. "Now, tell me; what is your name?"

"There is no immediate hurry for that," she protested. "Before I reveal my identity suppose I remind you of some of your girl friends at Alderdene—Ada Forrester, for instance."

Yes, Billy remembered Ada Forrester very well—a short, podgy kid, he reflected, who by no possible chance could have developed into the tall, graceful girl by his side.

"And Betty Deringhame," continued his inquisitor. "One of the noble army of flappers. Rather a shallow-headed kid and a bit of a tomboy, wasn't she?"

"A tomboy—yes," agreed the flight-sub, "but I cannot admit the other. We used to be good pals, but that was three years ago. I was in my Third Term at Dartmouth when her people left Alderdene."

"You taught her to signal in Morse, I think," pursued the girl. "You used to exchange messages until that little pig, Pat o'Hara, the vicar's son, learnt it too and told tales to her mother."

They walked in silence for some moments. Barcroft had almost forgotten his surroundings. His thoughts had taken him back to those far off, pre-war days in sunny Kent.

"Yes," he said at length in his deep manly voice. "It is absolutely great to be with Betty Deringhame again."

"So you've guessed at last," said Betty. "It's a strange world, isn't it?"

"And a mighty pleasant one, barring the Huns and others of that crowd," added Billy. "Now, tell me, what are you doing here?"

"Walking with an old acquaintance upon a long road that leads to Two Elms and Tarleigh."

"Obvious—we will not dispute the fact," rejoined the young officer. "To put the question in more exact terms: where are you living, and what brought you to this part of England?"

"I think I said I was living at Two Elms. To be more precise, at Mill View. That doesn't sound particularly cheerful, does it? We came here to live after we left Alderdene, shortly after war broke out. I am now employed in a munitions works."

"Munitions works! Whatever are you doing that for?" asked Billy surprised beyond measure. It seemed incredible that the slim, light-hearted girl of his boyhood days should be toiling in this manner.

"Because I had to do something," replied Betty simply. "We lost almost everything. Besides, it was an opportunity to do something practical for the war. People of all social grades do, you know."

"I'm sorry about your financial misfortune," said Barcroft sympathetically.

"And so am I—very," added the girl frankly. "But it is unnecessary to enter into details. This is my home."

They came to a standstill in front of a row of two-storeyed houses. Owing to the darkness it was impossible for the flight-sub to form an accurate idea of the pretensions of the place; but at any rate it was a pitiful contrast to "The Old Rectory," the Deringhames' house at Alderdene.

"The works were nearly hit by the bombs," continued Betty. "We had just started the night-shifts, but the girls were sent off after the raid was over. One of them was so frightened that I had to take her home. That's why I was late."

"Fortunately for me," declared Billy earnestly.

"Yes, a stranger would have some difficulty to find his way on a night like this," said Betty inconsequently. "You are on a straight road now, until you come to a railway arch. Just beyond you'll notice a line of overhead wires if you keep your eyes open. Just beyond is a path on the left. That will take you past Ladybird Fold."

"I'll call in the morning," said Barcroft.

"We—that is, mother and I, will be pleased to see you," replied the girl. "Goodnight—Billy."

For the rest of the distance the flight-sub trod literally on air until he reached the path that Betty had mentioned. Tripping over a slab of stone he came to earth in a double sense.

"Dash it all!" he exclaimed as he picked himself up. "Has the governor defended Lady bird Fold with entanglements and pitfalls? By Jove, this is a night!"

Groping his way Billy ascended the steeply sloping cinder path across the meadow. Another stile and a broad stretch of rugged ground had to be negotiated before he saw a dark mass looming up in front. By this time he was feeling particularly stiff, hungry and cold. The keen air of the hillside made him regret the absence of his airman's leather coat.

"Wonder if this is the show?" he mused as he surveyed the isolated and apparently deserted building.

He stopped and listened intently. Voices were heard within, behind the thickly-curtained window. He recognised one of the speakers.

"That's the governor, right enough," he exclaimed, all traces of annoyance vanishing at the pleasurable discovery.

The outer door was unlocked. Billy threw it open and burst into the well-lighted study.

"Cheer-o, pater!" he exclaimed. "Sorry I'm late. Some night, eh, what?"

CHAPTER X
THE SEAPLANE'S QUEST

"S' LONG, you festive blighters! Good luck!"

With this typically airman's farewell ringing in his ears Flight-lieutenant John Fuller, D.S.O., clambered lightly into the pilot's seat of Seaplane 445B.

Owing to Billy Barcroft's absence on leave a change round had been effected in the composition of the crews of the seaplane carrier "Hippodrome's" little nest of hornets, and as a result Fuller found himself in company with Bobby Kirkwood as his observer.

It was the night of the Barborough raid. The "Hippodrome," bound for the Firth of Forth, had picked up a wireless when some where off the Yorkshire coast, reporting the presence of four Zeppelins. Aeroplanes and seaplanes attached to the north-eastern bases had already ascended in the hope of cutting off the returning air-pirates, and in conjunction with these operations the "Hippodrome" was about to send out her airmen to grapple with the enemy in the darkness.

It was indeed a formidable and hazardous undertaking. The returning Zeppelins would certainly take advantage of the stiff westerly breeze. By keeping to a great altitude and shutting off their engines they drift, silent and unseen, over the East Coast, until it is deemed advisable to restart the motors. Even the disadvantage caused by the immense bulk of the vulnerable envelope would be discounted by its invisibility in the darkness of the night.

The Zeppelins could keep "afloat" by the buoyancy of their hydrogen-charged ballonets; the aeroplanes, being heavier than air, could not, except for a comparatively brief vol-plane, without the aid of their propellers, The roar of the latter would betray their presence to the watchers on the silent airship.

Altogether the seaplane's task savoured of a wild goose chase, only by a pure fluke might one of the aeroplanes "spot" one of the returning raiders, but on the remote chance of being able to do so the "Hippodrome's" aerial flotilla set out on its hazardous flight.

For three-quarters of an hour No 445B flew to and fro parallel to the coast. It was bitterly cold. At a minimum height of five thousand feet was a vast bank of clouds that drifted steadily eastwards.

Occasionally Kirkwood took down a wireless report from the parent ship and handed it to the pilot. Hardly a word was spoken. The voice tube was resorted to only once in that forty-five minutes.

"I'm going further out," announced Fuller. "We'll clear that patch of clouds."

With her motors purring rhythmically and the pistons throbbing in perfect tune the seaplane swung round and settled in an easterly direction, the while climbing steadily. Behind her was the tail end of a nimbus; above, through a vast rift the stars twinkled in the cold sky; beneath, thousands of feet down, was the sea, its vicious, steep waves invisible in the kindly darkness.

Suddenly, from the enshrouding masses of cloud, a dark, symmetrically elongated shape shot rapidly into the starlight. It was a Zeppelin in full flight. Columns of smoke were issuing from her exhausts, but the throb of the seaplane's motors drowned the drone of her powerful engines.

"Good!" ejaculated Fuller, actuating the rudder bar with his feet and elevating the ailerons. "That's our bird. If they don't spot us before they gain that bank of clouds, she's ours."

Eagerly yet methodically Kirkwood brought the Lewis gun ready for action. It was to be the last resource in attack, to be used only if the seaplane failed to gain the aerial "weathergage"—a superior altitude to that of her bulky antagonist.

For the present the odds were level as regards speed. The seaplane's greater rate of flight was counterbalanced by the fact that she had to climb in order to get above her intended prey and drop a bomb upon the immense and fragile bulk of the Zeppelin's envelope.

And Fuller was achieving his object. Already Seaplane 445B was passing diagonally upwards through the raider's smoking trail, the oil tinged vapour from her exhaust pipes. Every moment tended to bring the protruding stern portion of the Zep, betwixt her crew and the steadily climbing aeroplane, thus diminishing the risk of detection.

Fuller was about to check the upward climb and overhaul his antagonist when the Zeppelin appeared almost to stand on end. The whole of her upper surface was exposed to the British airmen's view. Then, almost simultaneously the seaplane seemed to be following.

It was a form of optical delusion. She was still climbing steadily. The Zeppelin had spotted her small and dangerous foe. Dropping a quantity of ballast *en bloc* the airship shot vertically upward to a terrific height. It was this motion that had given Fuller the impression that the seaplane was dropping.

"She's twigged us!" he shouted through the voice tube. "Let her have it."

The A.P. promptly began to let loose a whole drum of ammunition. The Zeppelin was instantly enveloped in a cloud of smoke. Into the pall of vapour the Lewis gun pumped its nickel missiles, yet no crippled flaming fabric crashed helplessly to the surface of the sea.

The smoke was a "blind." Fuller realised that. Screening herself by the dense vapour the Zeppelin had ascended almost vertically until safe from observation in the dense clouds overhead.

"Missed her, by Jove!" ejaculated the flight-lieutenant.

"More than she did us," replied Kirkwood coolly, in spite of his keen disappointment, for a small-calibre bullet had ripped the ear-pad of his airman's helmet. Whether his ear was hit he knew not. The intense cold had numbed all sense of feeling. The shot was evidently from a Maxim and one of many, but in the darkness it was impossible to see whether the seaplane had sustained any damage. Judging by her behaviour Kirkwood thought not.

Yet Fuller was loath to discontinue the chase. On and on he flew, further and further away from the "Hippodrome" and the shores of Britain, vainly hoping to pick up his quarry when the Zeppelin again emerged from the cloud banks.

"I'll swear she's shut off power and is floating somewhere in that cloud," he soliloquised. "Well, I'll have a shot at it, even if we charge smack into the brute."

With this desperate yet praiseworthy resolution the flight-lieutenant swung his frail command about and began to climb steadily towards the mass of dark clouds. Ten minutes later the seaplane entered the lower edge of the nimbus. It was like tearing through a dense fog. All sense of direction was lost. Whether the machine was climbing, banking or descending was a matter of conjecture, since the darkness and the moisture made it impossible to consult the aeronautical instrument. Ahead was nothing but an opaque curtain of mist. On either side the tips of the planes merged into invisibility. Only astern were there any light-sparks from the hot exhaust throwing a faint, ruddy glare upon the wisps of trailing vapour that followed, circling and writhing, in the wake of the swiftly-moving machine.

"If the Huns are anywhere in this stuff they'll get in a rare funk even if we don't run across them," thought Fuller, Unmindful of the danger of his own seeking he mentally pictured the panic-stricken condition of the raider, as hearing the roar of the seaplane's motors and unable to locate its position, they were in momentary peril of being rammed by an object tearing at ninety miles an hour through an optically impenetrable darkness.

Kirkwood, too, realised the risk. With nerves a-tingle he awaited developments. Faith in Fuller's prowess gave him confidence. With one hand resting lightly on the lever operating the bomb-dropping gear he waited, ready at the first signal to release the missiles of annihilation.

Suddenly the muffled roar of the exhaust gave place to a series of rapid explosions. Instinctively Kirkwood likened it to a boy rasping a stick along a row of iron palings. At the same time a succession of spurts of flame streaked overhead. The seaplane had only just scraped the underside of her antagonist. The upper planes had missed the Zeppelin's 'midship gondola by inches, and the flashes he had seen were from the airship's machine-gun as the Huns blazed furiously and erratically at their unseen but unpleasantly audible foe.

Up spun 445B, until she seemed to stand almost on her tail. Then tilting until she was in imminent danger of side-slipping, she sought to make good her discovery. Vainly Fuller circled and circled, striving to pierce the vault of inky blackness. The Zeppelin was no longer there. Whether she had thrown out some more ballast or had trusted to her motors to bear her away from the unseen terror he knew not.

He was not a man to admit defeat readily.

"I'll make 'em have cold feet in any case," he decided, as he removed his mist-dimmed goggles and peered into the luminous compass bowl. "Due east till we get out of this cloud, and then I'll wait for the brute."

Unfortunately, as far as he was concerned, Fuller's decision could not be carried out, for from no apparent cause the motors raced at unprecedented speed for a brief instant and then stopped.

The contrast from the noise of the engine to the stillness of the upper regions was the feature that impressed him most. The seaplane, at a height of ten thousand feet, and in the midst of a dense cloud, was beginning to fall. Vainly the pilot strove to avoid the nerve-racking "tail-spin." His sense of direction gone he could only jiggle the joy-stick in the hope that the terrific headlong, erratic downward rush might be checked.

Kirkwood, secured by the broad leather safety strap, also realised the danger. He was conscious of being whirled round and round with his body in a horizontal position. He could feel the rush of air as the seaplane dropped, otherwise silently, towards the sea. Unless the machine could be got under control their fate was sealed. The frail floats would be pulverised and splintered with the terrific impact, and the wreckage, weighted down by the heavy motor, would sink like a stone.

For sixty seconds—it seemed like sixty hours—the uncontrollable plunge continued, then like a flash the tail-spinning machine emerged from the under side of the cloud into the comparatively clear atmosphere. With an almost superhuman effort Fuller readjusted the sorely tried ailerons. The resistance on the planes was tremendous, but the fabric and the tension wires were British made, with a sickening jerk the seaplane described a complete loop. In the nick of time the resourceful pilot caught her on the "swing" and flattened out.

Once the motion was sufficiently retarded he commenced a vol-plane. It was, perhaps, prolonging the agony, since there could be little hope of rescue on a dark night, even if the waves did not overwhelm the frail craft.

"Stand by!" shouted Fuller. "Look down—on your right."

The A.P., well nigh breathless through the pressure of the belt upon his ribs, leant over the side of the chassis. Two thousand feet below, with her drawn-out shape glittering dully in the starlight, was another Zeppelin. The first, silhouetted against the faint light, had presented a black shape; this one showed up clearly in her aluminium garb against the darkness. She was proceeding rapidly at a height of about three thousand feet, and now less than a thousand beneath the vol-planing British craft.

"Our luck's in!" exclaimed the flight-lieutenant, his thoughts only for the immediate present. It would be sufficient to consider the end of that terrific vol-plane when the moment arrived. For the present it was not even a secondary matter—it did not enter into the intrepid airman's calculation.

"Stand by!" roared Fuller again. "For Heaven's sake don't miss."

Down swept the noiseless biplane upon its unsuspecting prey. According to Fuller's plans he would approach the Zeppelin in the same vertical plane but at an acute angle—both aircraft proceeding in the same direction. This would give the bombs a better target than if the seaplane was cutting across the path of the airship.

So swift was the descent that the Zeppelin appeared to be rising in the air to meet her opponent. Her huge, long-drawn-out mass grew bigger and bigger until it seemed as if a miss would be an impossibility.

"Now!" shouted the flight-lieutenant.

With a swift, decided movement Kirkwood thrust over the releasing-gear lever. There was no resistance. Unaccountably the flexible wire operating the release catch had been detached. Without a moment's hesitation the A.P. unbuckled his belt and, bending, groped on the floor of the fuselage for the business-end of the wire. Just then the Zep, opened fire with her machine-gun.

Fuller, leaning over the side waited in eager expectation of the anticipated explosion, quite prepared to find the seaplane capsized under the blast of the terrific detonation. But there was none, and already the vol-planing machine was beyond and on a level with the Zeppelin. Without the aid of the motor it was impossible to return to the attack.

Savagely Fuller swung round with the intention of demanding the reason of his observer's blunder. To his surprise the A.P., was not to be seen.

"Plugged!" ejaculated the pilot. "Well, here goes; another two minutes will decide."

The Zeppelin was now out of his mind. His whole attention was devoted to the impending impact with the surface of the water. Every thing depended upon his skill and judgment, with a fair element of luck thrown in. In the darkness it was impossible to gauge with any degree of certainty the height of the descending machine above the sea. If the pilot "flattened out" too soon the seaplane would fall like a stone; if, on the other hand the vol-plane were maintained the fraction of a minute too long the impact would either result in the shattering of the floats or in the machine describing a somersault—possibly both.

With a double plash the flat-bottomed floats smacked the waves. The "landing" was successfully accomplished, but the unpleasant fact remained that Fuller and Kirkwood were afloat in a frail cockleshell in a fairly "jumpy" sea and on a pitch-dark night. Without water and provisions and with no aid in sight and already sixty miles or more from land they were rapidly drifting out to sea nearer and nearer the hostile shores of Germany.

CHAPTER XI
THE TERRORS OF THE AIR

SIEGFRIED VON EITELWURMER, the German Secret Service Agent, sat and shivered in the after-gondola of the returning Zeppelin. He was not feeling at all happy. Apart from the physical discomfort—for in addition to the effect of the cold he was under the influence of air-sickness—his mind was harassed by wellfounded thoughts that something might happen to the gigantic but obviously frail gas-bag.

Like most Germans his faith in Count Zeppelin's cowardly and diabolical invention was unshaken—so long as he could remain on terra-firma. But whereas the stay-at-home Hun satisfied himself by reading of the colossal achievements of the German aerial fleet, von Eitelwurmer knew by actual observation that the raids failed to justify one-tenth, nay, one-thousandth part of the claims put forward by the authorities at Berlin.

In pre-war days he had seen experimental Zeppelins dashed to pieces in a vain attempt to regain the shed. He had seen others destroyed by fire. He remembered seeing a "leader" in a British newspaper in which it was solemnly declared that the sympathies of the civilised world will go out to the aged Count in the hour of his grief at the failure of his life's work.

And now, in addition to the ordinary risks of aviation the returning airship was liable at any moment to the attack of the "hornets" that were known to be on the look-out for the raiders. Here he was, carried off against his will, suspended like Mahomet's tomb 'twixt heaven and earth, and faced with the prospect of a swift journey to a place not included in the above category.

Ober-leutnant von Loringhoven left his passenger severely alone. For one thing the commander's attention was almost entirely taken up with the work of navigating his cumbersome craft back to the Fatherland; for another he mistrusted spies, even when they were Germans and notwithstanding the fact that he himself had indulged in that dangerous pastime. But there was this difference. Von Loringhoven was a naval officer while von Eitelwurmer was a civilian. He had heard of German spies renouncing their allegiance and acting for the country in which they were to be working on behalf of the authorities at Berlin.

The spy had been accommodated with a camp-stool. On either side of the narrow compartment was a window fitted with double plate-glass windows. The for'ard bulkhead was pierced by a door leading to the cat-walk or suspended bridge communicating with both the 'midships and for'ard gondolas. Aft was another bulkhead separating a portion of the compartment from that containing the motors actuating the two rearmost propellers. The floor was in a state of continual tremor under the pulsations of the engines and the rattle of the two endless chains that transmitted the power to the two outboard propellers.

The limited space was still further taken up by two machine-guns mounted on aluminium alloy pedestals and capable of being trained through a fairly broad arc. By these stood four of the crew, ready at the first alarm to lower the glass panes and bring the weapons into action. The men were taciturn and obviously nervous. When flying over the unprotected towns and dropping their murderous cargoes they could be boisterous enough, but now, knowing that they had to run the gauntlet, they were feeling particularly cowed. The fear of being paid back in their own coin—a possibility that alone makes the Hun howl—gripped them, and held them in a state of prolonged mental torture.

Presently at an order communicated by telephone from the foremost gondola, the machine-gunners lowered the sashes of the windows. The temperature, already -2 °C. fell rapidly to -10 °C. Warm air-currents from the motor-room drifted through gaps in the partition and condensing fell upon the floor in the form of globules of ice.

Up and up climbed the Zeppelin. She was approaching the East Coast.

Von Eitelwurmer, overcoming his torpor, went to the window. One of the men was about to motion him to his seat, when another touched him on the shoulder and pointed.

Far below the whole country was in darkness. The spy could not tell whether it was land or water. Away to the southward a group of searchlights swept the sky, the beams impinging upon a bank of clouds that floated at a height of nearly a mile. Still further away more electric rays swayed slowly to and fro. At intervals the searchlights of the nearmost station crossed those of the one more remote, while in turn these effected a luminous exchange with rays still further away. As far as the eye could see there appeared to be a continuous barrage of light through which the returning raider must pass before gaining her base.

At an order the motors were switched off. Almost absolute silence succeeded the noisy roar of the seven 240-horse-power engines. The airship, at the mercy of the winds, began to turn broadside on to the aerial drift, yet the while, by means of ballast thrown overboard and the release of more compressed hydrogen from the cylinders into the ballonets, was steadily climbing.

It was von Loringhoven's aim to ascend until the Zeppelin was above the clouds. Screened from those dangerous searchlights the airship would then drift over the coast-line until such times as it would be deemed safe to restart the motors.

With the altitude gauge hovering at 4,000 metres the raider found herself just above the natural screen. The belt of clouds was not more than three hundred feet in height—sufficient to hide her from the earth, yet transparent enough to allow the rays of the searchlight to penetrate the vapour.

To the spy the outlook resembled the view from a railway carriage when dense clouds of steam waft past the windows. So powerful were the rays of the searchlights that the stratum of the vapour was flooded with silvery luminosity, while—ominous sign—the beams no longer swayed to and fro as previously, but hung with sinister persistence upon the bank of clouds with which the airship hoped to screen herself from observation.

Even as von Eitelwurmer looked a huge dark shadow eclipsed the concentrated beams. It was moving slowly at a rate hardly exceeding that of the airship. For that reason the object could not be an aeroplane. Perhaps it was some deadly invention that the English had brought into action against the Zeppelins—a sort of aerial torpedo steered by wireless electric waves?

The machine-gunners saw it too. The last atom of courage literally oozed out of their boots, yet almost automatically they gripped the handle that would liberate shots at the rate of 500 a minute if to the voidless night.

It was fortunate for them that they did not open fire. The shadow was that of another Zeppelin that at less than a hundred feet below was slowly forging ahead in a southerly direction under the action of her throttled-down motors, and with her exhausts carefully muffled.

In five minutes the novel Zeppelin eclipse was over, although at no time was the actual airship to be seen. She had previously been fired upon by the anti-aircraft guns on the coast and was now cautiously smelling her way through the clouds in order to find an undefended gap in the defences.

Another half-hour passed in acute suspense, Three times the anxious crew heard the terrifying sound of an aerial propeller. Somewhere in the darkness the British hornets were up and searching for their lurking foe—so far without success unless the moral effect be taken into consideration.

Presently the Zeppelin drifted beyond the glare of the fixed searchlights, but not until another twenty minutes had passed did von Loringhoven give orders for the engines to be restarted. At that terrific altitude the noise was considerably diminished in volume. Instead of the explosions of the motors resembling a succession of rifle-shots the sounds were like those of a whip being cracked, yet as the airship descended steadily to a height of five thousand feet the noise resumed its normal and distracting violence.

The spy sat down again. His torpor was returning. The sudden change of altitude had resulted in a steady flow of blood from his nose, while his ear-drums throbbed until they seemed on the point of bursting. At that moment he felt that he would not have minded had the airship been blown to atoms.

But the next instant his lassitude vanished, as the loud pop-pop-pop of two of her machine-guns roused him from his stupor. The weapon on the starboard side was trained as far as possible abaft the beam and was pumping out nickel into the darkness.

Craning his neck over the shoulders of the men serving the belt-ammunition von Eitelwurmer saw a sight that caused his agonies of mind to return with redoubled violence.

Just visible against the loom of the starlit sky was a huge biplane that, climbing steeply, seemed to be steadily overhauling the airship. Serenely unmindful of the hail of bullets aimed at her the seaplane held on with the obvious intention of getting astride her prey.

Mingled with the detonations of the machine-guns were the clanging of telephone bells, the clank of machinery and the excited voices of the crew. Then with a jerk that threw the spy violently against the after bulkhead the Zeppelin leapt skywards. Simultaneously dense volumes of black smoke eddied in through the open windows.

Sprawling in the intense darkness upon the ice-encrusted floor of the gondola the spy vainly strove to shriek, but only a gurgled sound came from his lips. He had not the slightest doubt but that the airship was on fire and on the point of crashing to her doom.

Hearing the stifled cry, for again the motors were stopped, one of the crew gripped him roughly by the arm, and set him on his feet.

"Silence!" he hissed. "A noise like that may betray us."

A seemingly interminable interval followed. The Zeppelin, floating motionless in a dense and opaque bank of clouds, was endeavouring to evade her comparatively small but highly dangerous antagonist, the loud buzzing of whose engine could be distinguished with all too forcible certainty.

With every light switched off the crew of the unwieldy gas-bag waited in breathless suspense, knowing that at any moment a bomb might explode with annihilating result in the midst of the vast store of highly inflammable hydrogen above their heads.

For how long this state of almost unbearable suspense and nerve-racking tension lasted von Eitelwurmer had not the slightest idea. In Cimmerian darkness he sat, shivering with cold and fear, his eyes fixed upon the motionless form of one of the machine-gunners who, leaning out of one of the open apertures, was striving to locate the presence of the unseen but audible British seaplane.

Every time that the drone of the biplane's engine rose to a crescendo the spy's finger-nails cut into the palms of his benumbed hands. Vaguely he wondered what the end would be: whether the intense cold would give place to violent heat as the Zeppelin, a mass of flames, crashed headlong, or whether in the absence of an explosion the agony would be prolonged until the gondola, pinned down by the weight of the shattered framework of the gas-bag, would plunge beneath the waves and cause him to drown like a rat in a trap. He gave no thought to his companions. It was he that mattered. He was in peril. The rest—well, that was their affair. They had undertaken the raid and its attendant risk to themselves. It seemed hard that he—an involuntary passenger—should be faced with the immediate prospect of being burnt to a cinder in mid-air or stifled in the icy waters of the North Sea.

The whirr of the seaplane's propeller increased in volume, more than at any previous time during the Zeppelin's sojourn in the clouds.

Suddenly the machine-gunner uttered an exclamation and nudged his companion. A succession of blinding flashes and the rapid rattle of the automatic weapon dazzled the eyes and dulled the hearing of the demoralised spy. Yet, impelled by an unseen force, von Eitelwurmer raised himself and peered out of the scuttle.

The sight that met his eye was enough to appal a man of high moral and physical fibre, let alone the nerve-stricken spy; for, apparently heading straight for the Zeppelin and with her planes distinctly visible in the flashes of the machine-gun, was the avenging British seaplane. With a wild, unearthly shriek von Eitelwurmer threw up his arms and fell unconscious upon the floor of the gondola.

CHAPTER XII
THE RAIDER'S RETURN

SIEGFRIED VON EITELWURMER opened his eyes. His first thoughts were those of curious wonderment. It seemed remarkable, almost disappointing, that he found himself still alive.

More, he was still on board the airship, but his surroundings were different. The intense darkness had given place to light—not artificial luminosity of electric agency but the welcome light of day. His quarters had been changed. During his period of unconsciousness he had been taken along the narrow cat-walk (perhaps it was well for him that he had no recollection of that perilous passage along the V-shaped gangway) and had been placed in the centre gondola.

This move had been made at Ober-leutnant von Loringhoven's orders. During the nerve-racking journey over the sea-frontier of England the Hun commander had given scant thought to the comfort of his guest, but with immediate prospects of a safe return, he had recalled the advisability of giving the Kaiser's emissary those honours that his position albeit a despised civil one demanded.

"Are you feeling better now?" enquired von Loringhoven.

The spy sat up and passed a hand over his forehead.

"Where are we now?" he asked, ignoring the ober-leutnant's question.

"In sight of German soil," was the reply. "Yonder can be discerned our incomparable island fortress of Heligoland. No, we do not descend there, nor at Tondern or Borkum. Unfortunately that dare-devil of an Englishman has done us some damage, so we go on to the repairing sheds at Kyritz—they, fortunately, are beyond reach of hostile aircraft. At least, so I hope, but there is no telling what these English seaplanes will do next."

With von Loringhoven's reassurances bringing comfort to his tortured mind the spy's mercurial spirits rose. Yet not without a shudder he recalled his last conscious moment in the horrors of the pitch-black cramped interior of the after gondola.

"Himmel!" he exclaimed. "That was a nightmare. I little thought to be alive, and now I am tempted to shout 'Hoch! Hoch!' at the top of my voice."

"The bracing upper air," commented the ober-leutnant. "It is superb for raising one's spirits. Yes, it was an anxious time. I admit it. For the moment I thought that the cursed seaplane was going to hurl herself straight through the envelope. It is a thing that these mad Englishmen would do. I know them."

Von Eitelwurmer nodded in silent accord.

"But," continued the commander, "it was otherwise. Possibly our fire distracted the pilot, or he may have changed his mind at the last moment. Yet it was so close that I doubt whether there was anything to spare between the tip of one of his planes and the underside of the rear gondola. To me, looking aft, it seemed the narrowest shave possible. However, she missed us, and I immediately gave orders for the motors to be restarted. Heaven be praised, we never saw that seaplane again."

"And the damage?" enquired von Eitelwurmer.

"Not enough to prevent us continuing the voyage," replied von Loringhoven. "Two of the after ballonets are perforated too badly to be patched. A couple of my men succeeded in plugging the holes with the special preparation we use in such contingencies. You will observe that this floor inclines considerably in spite of the redistribution of ballast. We are down by the stern. Well, what is it?" he asked curtly as Unter-leutnant Klick entered the compartment.

"A wireless has just been received, sir," replied Klick, saluting his superior. "It appears that two of our airships have failed to return."

"*Donner wetter!* Two out of twelve!" exclaimed von Loringhoven furiously. "This is serious. But it might have been worse," he muttered in an undertone, as he glanced at the drooping end of the large envelope.

The spy went to one of the windows. The air was still sharp but mild in comparison to the piercing cold of the night. Already the sun was well above the horizon. Two thousand feet or less beneath the airship—for on approaching land the Zeppelin had descended considerably—could be discerned with remarkable clearness the green grass and red sandstone of the island of Heligoland with a strand of white sand adjoining one face of the cliffs. A short distance beyond was the flat, semi-artificial island of Sandinsel, with its batteries, concealed when viewed from the sea, standing conspicuously against the dunes.

Still further away were the flat, receding shores bordering the estuary of the Elbe, but vainly the spy looked for any signs of the vaunted High Seas Fleet. Even the well protected triangular expanse of water was desolate of shipping, save for a few small craft engaged either in laying additional mines or conveying stores to the island fortress.

At that height the varying depths of the sea could be noted owing to the changing colour of the water—not that that fact interested von Eitelwurmer in the slightest. He was a landsman out and out. He was content to leave the difficult task of wresting the trident from Britannia's grasp to others. The matter did not concern him. He specialised in the arts and intrigues of espionage.

Von Loringhoven was cast in a different mould. Although his present energies were centred upon the air service he was at heart a seaman. He, too, was examining the expanse of sea, but with the skill of a practised navigator.

"Look!" he exclaimed, pointing to a small, indistinct object from which emanated two ever-diverging lines of ruffled water. "Do you know what that is? Here, take these binoculars and look. Now, perhaps, you see what I mean?"

The spy brought the glasses to bear.

"A fish, I suppose," he remarked.

"A fish of sorts," added the ober-leutnant. "One's sense of proportion is deceived at this height. It is an unterseeboot. I do not fancy it is ours, otherwise why should she keep submerged when close to our territorial water?"

He lifted the receiver of the telephone.

"Wireless cabin. Report to the commandant of Heligoland that there is a submarine in the south channel. Ask if it is one of our unterseebooten."

In a few minutes came the reply.

"No German submarine operating sub merged off the fortress. Can you attack?"

"No, I cannot," declared von Loringhoven bluntly, directing his remarks to his companion. "She's a British submarine. Those fellows nose their way everywhere. She, evidently, is inside the outer minefield. And they want me, crippled as this airship is, to attack. It is unreasonable; besides, the wind is increasing in strength and we have yet to make a landing."

So, giving by wireless the bearings of the daring submarine, von Loringhoven "carried on" in the knowledge that the dangers of this flight were by no means over. Already the wind was blowing with a velocity of thirty miles an hour—a rate that would make landing a difficult matter—and, what is more, its strength was hourly increasing.

At ten in the morning the Zeppelin came in sight of the sheds at Kyritz, a town in the province of Brandenburg and roughly sixty miles north-west of Berlin. This was the base for airships that had sustained damage likely to take a considerable time to repair. The German authorities, profiting by the lessons of the British air raids on Friedrichshaven and other Zeppelin stations within range of aeroplanes operating either from the sea or from the hostile frontiers, had taken the precaution to remove the repair depots well inland. In such places as Borkum there were Zeppelins in commission ready for making flights to the British Isles, but at the first intimation of a raid upon the airship sheds the mammoth gas-bags would fly inland until the danger was past. In the case of a Zeppelin undergoing extensive repairs such a course would be impossible; hence the establishment of the base at Kyritz.

Turning head to wind the crippled Zeppelin descended slowly and cautiously towards a field surrounding the three large sheds. The sheds themselves were marvels of scientific ingenuity. For one thing they were easily collapsible. By means of mechanical appliances the roof could be parted lengthways and each section allowed to fold against the walls. The walls could then be lowered until the whole structure lay flat on the ground. The fabric, composed of steel sheeting on girders of the same material, was covered with stucco that strongly resembled the surrounding ground. Viewed from a height there would be great difficulty in distinguishing between the collapsible sheds and the adjoining land. The buildings, of course, could only be lowered when not tenanted by airships, but such was the deliberate thoroughness of the Huns that they had to provide for this contingency in the possible yet improbable event of a British aircraft raid.

Another feature of the sheds was the fact that each was built upon a gigantic turn-table, so as to enable the openings to turn away from the prevailing wind and thus facilitate landing operations; while by a system of disc signals the commander of the returning Zeppelin was informed of the direction and strength of the breeze.

Yet, in spite of these precautions, the landing operations were fraught with danger, especially in the present case.

As the crippled airship approached the shed, ropes were lowered from bow and stern. These were seized by swarms of trained air-mechanics, and as gently as possible the huge envelope was brought upon an even keel. All the while the propellers kept revolving in order to enable her to counteract the force of the head wind.

Then other ropes were lowered from the 'midship portion of the Zeppelin while simultaneously gas was exhausted from some of the ballonets to neutralise her buoyancy.

All that seemingly remained was to shut off the motors and drag the mammoth into its lair.

Suddenly a strong gust of wind, eddying past the shed, struck the bow of the Zeppelin. The men holding the bow ropes were thrown in a struggling heap of humanity upon the grass. In an instant the whole of the for'ard portion of the Zeppelin reared itself in the air. The aluminium longitudinal girders were not proof against the unequal strain, and with incredible rapidity the frail fabric buckled.

"Jump!" shouted von Loringhoven, his voice barely audible above the excited yells of the men and the rending of metal.

Setting the example the commander dropped from the cat-walk, followed by Unter-leutnant Klick and most of the crew. A few, imprisoned in the foremost gondola, were crushed under the ruins of the girders.

For a moment the spy hesitated to follow the example of his companions in peril. Taking his courage in his hands, he lowered himself over the latticed sides of the gangway. There he hung until half stupefied by the fumes of the escaping hydrogen; then, relaxing his hold he dropped, landing in a most undignified manner upon the equally ruffled von Loringhoven as he crawled from under the wreckage.

In five minutes nothing remained of the raider but a mass of gaunt and twisted girders from which fluttered the remains of the envelope in the grip of the now howling wind.

Two hours later, Siegfried von Eitelwurmer found himself in the presence of the Director of Aeronautical Intelligence in the official quarters of the Air Department—a pretentious building in the Wilhelmstrasse at Berlin.

With him were Ober-leutnant von Loringhoven and half a dozen commanders of the Zeppelin Squadron that had just carried out the raid over the British Isles. The task of reporting upon the raid was about to commence. Already the British communiqué had been received, and it was now considered advisable to issue a statement for the benefit of the German people.

The only person not present was Otto von Lohr, the commander of the air squadron, and until he put in an appearance the business could not be started.

A telephone bell rang. A uniformed secretary took up the receiver.

"Yes, Herr Schneider, he is here," he replied. "I will inform him of your request."

Replacing the instrument the secretary crossed the room and addressed the spy.

"Herr Kapitan-leutnant Schneider wishes to see you, Herr von Eitelwurmer," he announced obsequiously.

"Very good," replied the spy. "Inform me when the conference begins."

Kapitan-leutnant Schneider, the German Naval Censor-in-Chief, was a bald-headed, loose-lipped man of past middle age. He looked, and was, a typical Prussian, subserviently polite to his superiors and pointedly arrogant to those who were not. Von Eitelwurmer belonged to the former category, for although not of the military caste, he enjoyed the confidence of the Emperor. That in itself was sufficient to cause Kapitan-leutnant Schneider to squirm like an eel. It was his way of showing his pleasure at his visitor's presence.

"I wish to ask you, von Eitelwurmer," he remarked after the preliminary courtesies were exchanged, "concerning the effect of our reports—my work, you understand—upon the English people. You, living as an Englishman, ought to be in a position to inform me."

"My private opinion, or my official one?" enquired the spy bluntly.

The Censor shut one eye solemnly.

"Your private opinion," he said.

"The German communiqués seem to be a source of amusement to the English," began von Eitelwurmer in the same bold tone, for not being under the kapitan-leutnant's jurisdiction and having an old grievance against him he could afford to "rub it in." "In fact, the censorship in both countries is one of the chief weapons of their antagonists. In England bad news that we already know of is suppressed, and consequently all sorts of disquieting rumours get around. The same holds good in the Fatherland. It is like sitting upon the safety valve of a boiler: sooner or later——"

"Yes, yes," interrupted Schneider. "But as far as we Germans are concerned it matters little. If the people grow restive, if their hunger— and hunger amongst the lower classes is acute—goads them to attempted violence the danger ends there. Unlike the English we have organised the nation. Every man, woman and child realises his or her duty is to obey, otherwise we might see the business of Louvain enacted upon German soil."

"The English are of a different temperament," remarked the spy. "Reverses do not seem to damp their spirits. They have a firm faith that in spite of blunders everything will come out right for them at the finish. It is the fatalism based upon centuries of history. Why their government does not take them into its confidence puzzles me."

The Censor shrugged his shoulders.

"I do not believe in governments of that description," he said. "Give me our all powerful machinery—the War Council. No government yet won a war, but many a government has lost one. Now tell me——"

A discreet tap upon the door interrupted the official's words.

"Enter!" he bellowed.

A messenger crept stealthily into the room. By his manner it seemed evident that he expected to have a book hurled at his head. It was one of the kapitan-leutnant's usual *plaisanteries*, but on this occasion von Eitelwurmer acted as a moral shield.

The Censor took the proffered paper, read it and burst into a roar of laughter.

"Wait a moment, Herr von Eitelwurmer," he said when his mirth had subsided. "The conference won't start for some time. There's a fellow wanting an audience—an author, curse him! I'll let the press and their parasites depending upon it know that there is a censorship. This fellow wrote a book: *With von Scheer off Jutland* he called it. Since we must do something to justify our existence I smashed it. The fellow had no influence, so what matters? And now, I suppose, he's kicking. Send him in, you thick-headed numbskull; send him in."

The author of the banned book entered the room. He was of short stature, being barely five feet two in height, inclined to corpulence, and very white-faced. His heavy, bristling, up-turned moustache contrasted incongruously with his small beady eyes that peered through a large pair of spectacles of enormous magnifying powers.

For quite two minutes Kapitan-leutnant Schneider hurled a torrent of abuse at the head of his caller, punctuating every sentence with furious oaths. Yet, somewhat to the Censor's surprise, the little man showed no signs of quailing under the onslaught.

"Might I ask what there is in the book to which you take exception?" he asked.

"The whole of it," thundered the despot.

"Could not certain portions be revised?"

"No; I object to it in its entirety."

"Then, since the story is based upon Admiral von Scheer's report you object to the official dispatch?"

For a moment the Press Censor was taken aback. It never entered into his head that this meek and mild man could or would put a poser like this.

"No; I won't say that," replied Schneider. "But either you are a perverter of the truth or you know too much. The work has had the highest Admiralty consideration, and, as you ought to know, censorship has only one object in view, namely, the public interest. If you are ordered to say that black is white you must say it. You haven't, and you must abide by the consequences."

"One moment," interposed the still unruffled man. "Can you give me one solitary instance of what you object to in the book?"

The kapitan-leutnant puckered his shaggy eyebrows.

"No, I cannot," he replied, with considerable mildness. "I have forgotten all about it."

"And that is what you term the highest Admiralty consideration," added the author cuttingly. "Very good; I will not trouble you further at present, except to show you this: a commendation from no less a personage than Admiral von Tirpitz."

"Himmel!" gasped the astonished official. "Why did you not tell me this before?"

"Because I had not the chance," replied the caller gathering up his papers. "Good afternoon."

"You are perhaps sorry I waited?" remarked von Eitelwurmer, when the two were again alone.

Schneider frowned.

"If the fool had only made out that we had won a great victory all would have been well," he replied. "The Press and its satellites— —"

"The Conference has started, Herr von Eitelwurmer," announced the secretary. "I could not inform you before as the Kapitan-leutnant was engaged."

The spy returned to the council-room. Seated at a long table were the Zeppelin commanders. As each made his report the statement was taken down by an official shorthand writer, while the aviators were subjected to a stiff examination by the Director of Intelligence.

Some were most emphatic in their statements. They knew exactly where they had been; others were not so sure, but believed that they had been to such and such a town; others, somewhat indiscreetly but honestly, confessed that they had lost their bearings. All were agreed, however, that the Yorkshire towns of Brigborough and Broadbeck had been missed by the raiding aircraft.

"It seems pretty certain that the geography of the English authorities is at fault," commented the Director. "They report that our Zeppelins visited a North Midland county—that referred to your part of the business, von Loringhoven; I always thought that Lancashire was one of the six northern counties of England: let us hope that some day it will be one of a German dependency. However, we'll issue a report that our airships bombed Brigborough and Broadbeck. Then these English will think that you do not know where you have been, and that is exactly what we want them to think. Now, von Papen, draw up a suitable report for home consumption. In these strenuous times we must satisfy the public demands. It will keep the common people quiet for a time, and, if they *do* find out, there may then be something good to detract their attention."

The spy smiled grimly. He recalled a saying quoted by a German officer to his captor: "We Germans can never be gentlemen—you English will always be fools." The first part held good, but as for the second, his residence in Great Britain had taught him that behind the apathy of the British nation there was Something—a Something that, when aroused, would form more than a match for the cunning and brutality of his fellow countrymen. Reluctantly he had to admit that.

"Why do you smile?" asked the Director, fixing von Eitelwurmer with his eye.

"I was thinking," replied the spy. "Thinking of how I can get back to England. My good work there is not yet completed."

"Those twenty thousand marks, hein?" enquired the president, and the rest of the assembly laughed uproariously at the director's jest.

CHAPTER XIII
EXIT SEAPLANE No. 445B

"WHY did I leave my comfortable bunk and try my hand at fishing at night upon the wild North Sea?" enquired Lieutenant Fuller as he withdrew his benumbed hands from his airman's gauntlets and fumbled ineffectually for his electric torch. "Dash it all, man! What are you fiddling about with?"

"Only that releasing lever," replied Kirkwood from the depths of the fuselage. "That confounded Zep! If only the blessed thing hadn't jibbed I'd have strafed her, sure as fate."

"Chuck it!" ordered Fuller. "Let the beastly thing alone, or you may drop a plum. This child doesn't want to be hoist with his own petard. Well, thank goodness we're afloat. That's some consolation. Where the hooligan Harry is that confounded torch?"

"Take mine," said the A.P. passing for'ard the desired article. "Say, old man, we appear to be rolling more to starboard than to t'other side. Hope the float isn't leaking."

Fuller leant over the side. It was too dark to discern anything. Prudence forbade him to flash the torch upon the invisible support—a support so light and frail that the wonder of it all was that it hadn't given way under the force of the impact with the waves.

The crippled seaplane was tossing and rolling under the combined action of the short crested waves and the stiff breeze. It wanted about two hours to daylight. Meanwhile every minute saw the amphibious craft drifting further and further from shore.

There were no signs of the "Hippodrome." Possibly the seaplane carrier had resumed her voyage, in the supposition that the missing hornet had made one of the fishing harbours on the Yorkshire coast. The absence of any wireless call rather knocked that theory on the head. On the other hand the "Hippodrome" could not, without great risk of being submarined, since she was unaccompanied by destroyers or patrol-boats, steam seaward on an apparent wild-goose chase for her errant child.

"She's holding, I fancy," said Fuller referring to the suspected float. "Anyhow we've kept afloat so far and there's no reason why we shouldn't do so until I tackle this most refractory motor."

Making cautious use of the flash lamp the pilot minutely examined the complicated mechanism. It was not long before the mischief was discovered. Not only was the petrol-tank completely perforated by three shrapnel bullets, but the pipe leading from it to the carburetter had been cut clean through. That accounted for the engine running for some seconds before coming to a stop. Until the last of the petrol in the carburetter had been drawn into the cylinders firing was still taking place.

Further examination revealed the fact that, the motor was otherwise undamaged, although, judging by the holes in the fuselage and through the planes, it seemed wonderful that pilot and observer had escaped being hit.

"Can I bear a hand?" enquired Kirkwood.

"No, thanks," was the reply. "Close enough quarters as it is. We should only be tumbling over one another."

By the aid of a piece of flexible tubing lined with indiarubber the broken portions of the petrol pipe were temporarily reunited. The next step was to plug the holes in the tank. This task was performed by means of a metal instrument consisting of a metal rod of about a third of an inch in diameter and four inches in length. Two thirds of the length was threaded and fitted with a "butterfly" nut in front of which was a cylindrical plug of guttapercha faced with indiarubber. At the other extremity was a swivelled cross-bar of about an inch in length and so arranged that it could lie in a straight line with the rod.

This end Fuller inserted in one of the perforations in the side of the tank. Then, giving the rod half a turn, he allowed the swivel bar to fall into a position at right angles to the rod. It was then impossible to withdraw the latter owing to the cross-piece engaging on the inner side of the tank.

The flight-lieutenant's next move was to screw the pliable plug hard against the perforated metal by means of the "butterfly" nut, and by so doing hole No.1 was repaired—the first of six. While Fuller was engaged upon the work of making good defects Kirkwood, his mind still uneasy on the subject of the float, lowered himself over the side.

Gaining the upper side of the float he felt along it with his hand. As he did so a wave swept the frail buoyant structure.

"By Jove!" he exclaimed. "This is a treat. The water is quite warm."

Compared with the intense coldness of the upper air the sea, at this time of the year, was indeed tepid. The contrasted temperature acted like balm to his numbed hands. He revelled in the comfort.

While thus engaged the A.P. discerned a large object looming through the darkness—a cylinder nearly a yard in diameter. It was floating with very little of its bulk showing above the surface, and, owing to the comparatively rapid drift of the seaplane, it appeared to be moving steadily through the water and bearing straight down upon the float.

For a brief instant Kirkwood remained stock still in his recumbent position, unable to raise a finger or utter a cry. The object was a floating mine.

He could discern the horns with remarkable clearness, for the thing seemed surrounded by an aura of phosphorescent light. One blow from the underside of the float upon those delicately adjusted projections with which the mine simply bristled would result in utter annihilation.

Kirkwood's mind was steeled to the dangers of a ten or fifteen thousand feet fall through space; but this, to him, unusual danger literally took the wind out of his sails.

Then, like a flash, the reaction set in. The will to cope with sudden perils asserted itself. A plan, unpretentious in all its details, formulated in his active brain.

Throwing himself flat upon the float and grasping one of the supports with his left hand, the A.P. hung as far in front as he possibly could without losing his balance. His outstretched hand came in deliberate contact with the drifting horror. The smooth, slimy surface—for the mine had evidently been in the water for some time—offered no resistance, and he thrust until his fingers "brought up" against one of the horns.

How far short of the minimum pressure required to snap the brittle projection and allow the chemicals contained therein to ignite Kirkwood was never to know. He was just aware that either the seaplane or the mine was swinging clear—perhaps it was a mutual "get out of my way" affair.

Scraping the for'ard outer corner of the float by a bare six inches the infernal contrivance, fended off by the A.P.'s outstretched hand, glided past, until with a sigh of relief the observer watched it disappear in the darkness.

For quite a minute he hung on, his heart beating like a piston, his eyes peering through the blackness ahead. Floating mines, he knew, were generally in considerable numbers. The fact that one peril had been averted was no guarantee that all danger from these jettisoned cylinders of potential death was over.

"Where the Christopher Columbus are you, old bird?" exclaimed Fuller, who, pausing in his work, had missed the rest of the "crew." "What, down on that float? What's wrong now?"

"We nearly bumped into a mine," reported the A.P. "The beastly thing was within six inches of my nose."

"A miss is as good as a mile," remarked the pilot nonchalantly. "If the thing had gone up six inches or six feet wouldn't have made any difference. They wouldn't have found either of us, and there wouldn't be enough of the pair of us to make a satisfying meal for a solitary North Sea herring. Look here. Up with you and give me a hand at filling the tank. I want to test my handiwork."

By the time the repairs were completed to the satisfaction of all hands, grey dawn was breaking over the wild North Sea. As far as the eye could penetrate the haze that hung about in detached patches the expanse of water was unbroken. Not a sail of any description was in sight and the beetling cliffs of the Yorkshire coast had long since dipped beneath the horizon.

"Fill her right up now," continued the pilot, indicating the repaired tank. "It's lucky we had so many spare tins of stuff on board. We'll mop up most of the petrol during the plug home against the wind, I reckon."

Fuller, deep in final adjustments, and Kirkwood hard at work emptying the contents of the petrol-cans into the tank, were unaware of the new menace that threatened them, until a huge grey shape loomed up within fifty yards to windward of the seaplane.

The shape was a German submarine mine-layer, She was running awash, while on the short, narrow platform in the wake of her conning-tower stood a couple of officers and a half a dozen seamen.

"You vos surrender make!" shouted one of the Germans.

"I'll see you to blazes first!" retorted Fuller as he frantically manipulated the starting mechanism.

For once the accurately-timed engine failed to respond to the master-hand. A mutinous back-fire was the only result. Fuller tried again but ineffectually.

The Hun submarine then thought it time to butt in. This she did most neatly but none the less completely by running her nose into the resistless structure of the jibbing seaplane. Her rate of speed was but three or four knots, but that was enough. Amidst the rending of struts, the crashing of the shattered floats and the harp-like twang of severed tension-wires the luckless 445B turned absolutely over and disappeared beneath the waves, leaving pilot and observer struggling in the water.

"Dash it all!" soliloquised Fuller as he struck out for the submarine. "This is the second time the Huns have nabbed me. I'll bet there'll be a third. Just my rotten luck. Come on, old bird, half a dozen more strokes. They are going to heave us out of the ditch."

CHAPTER XIV
BUTTERFLY

"I SAY, pater."

"Eh?" ejaculated Peter Barcroft without looking up from his work, which happened to be revising a proof.

"I saw Betty Deringhame last night. I forgot to tell you," began Billy as a "preliminary canter" to the recital of his raid-night adventure.

"More fool you," grumbled his parent.

"I beg your pardon——" began the flight-sub, rather taken aback not by his sire's brusqueness, for Barcroft Senior when engaged in the non-creative work of proof-reading was like a bear with a sore head, but by the off-hand manner in which he had received the announcement of the girl's name.

"Look here!" exclaimed Peter, throwing down his pen and incidentally bespattering with ink the long, narrow sheet of printed matter. "Why on earth you want me to preach you a homily on the evils of betting——"

"Betting?" interrupted Billy. "I said nothing about betting. What I said was: 'I—saw—Betty—Deringhame—last—night.'"

Peter swung round in his revolving chair, and raised his eyebrows in mild surprise.

"Did you?" he asked. "My mistake, but why did you murmur that most interesting news into my deaf ear? What's she doing in this part?"

Billy duly reported the state of affairs.

"Jolly hard lines on the girl and her mother, too," was his parent's verdict. "Of course women of all classes are making munitions now, and all praise to them for doing it. I am not referring to that, but to the fact that Mrs. Deringhame has had a come-down in life. Did you ever hear how it occurred?"

"No," replied the young officer. "You see, I really didn't like to ask Betty, and she's too jolly brave to whine over her troubles."

"Sit down and fill your pipe," continued Barcroft Senior. "No matches? Hang it, there were three or four boxes on my desk this morning. Here, never mind, use a spill."

Billy laid a restraining hand upon his father's arm.

"Don't use your precious proofs, pater," he observed.

"Bless my soul! You were only just in time, my boy. Another second and that printed stuff would have been mingling in the form of smoke with the Lancashire atmosphere. Ah, yes; we were discussing the Deringhames. The same old tale, Billy: an inexperienced woman and a rascally lawyer. Not that all lawyers are rascals, you understand, but the profession contains a high percentage of rogues who, but for their knowledge of the law and of how far to go without overstepping the lawyer made laws of the land, would be doing time. This chap was a cute one. He persuaded Mrs. Deringhame to invest most of her capital in certain concerns of which he was a sort of sleeping partner. In five years he had literally done her out of a cool £ 6,000; and then, pretending to set matters right, he prevailed upon her to mortgage her house at Alderdene. Nominally he was her agent; in reality he was agent for the mortgagee, who was himself. You see the move?"

"Then, when war broke out, he drew in the mortgage, bringing an excuse that tightness of money necessitated the step. Mrs. Deringhame was unable at short notice to meet the demand. In vain she pleaded for time. Her last remnant of capital vanished into the rogue's clutches."

"The rotter!" ejaculated Billy indignantly. "And what is the bounder's name. Do you happen to know?"

"Yes," replied Mr. Barcroft. "Let me see—yes I have it: Antonius Grabb, of the firm of Grabb and Gott, of Ely Place."

"By Jupiter!" muttered Billy.

Mr. Barcroft raised his eyebrows enquiringly, but his son made no further audible comment. He had made the unpleasing discovery that the man who had wronged Betty and her mother was Bobby Kirkwood's uncle, and when, in the natural course of events the aforementioned uncle died, the A.P., should he be still surviving, would benefit considerably under the will of Antonius Grabb.

"By the bye," said Peter abruptly changing the subject. "Seen anything of Entwistle?"

"Met him coming from the bath-room half an hour ago; he was limping a good deal," replied Billy. "I don't suppose it will be long before he's down."

"I've a job for you, my boy," continued Peter. "They've just telephoned through to say that Entwistle's car won't be able to fetch him. My perambulating box of tricks and petrol is out of action somewhere in the hills. So I want you to drive our guest in the trap to Barborough. I'd go myself if it weren't for these confounded proofs. That idiot of a comp, will persist in printing 'stem' for 'stern.' The drive will do you good — blow some of last night's cobwebs away."

"Steady, pater," protested Billy with a hearty laugh. "I am no hand at driving horseflesh. Give me something in the motor line and I'm all there."

"You'll be all right with Butterfly," declared Barcroft Senior. "She's the steadiest-footed quadruped that ever stepped it out in shafts. A perfect gem, and the envy of the countryside."

He spoke with conviction, but the good character bestowed upon the animal was based simply upon hearsay. "Butterfly" was a new importation, having joined the establishment of Ladybird Fold only a week previously, and during that period she had either rusticated in the adjoining meadow or in her stable.

The flight-sub walked across the study to the open window. Without, hill and dale were bathed in the autumnal sunlight, and, having reviled the neighbourhood of Tarleigh in the darkness of the previous night, Billy felt compelled to render ample reparation to its charms as revealed by the light of day.

For miles there was a succession of hills and valleys, until the vista was terminated by the frowning Pennines. The country was well wooded, except for the grassy moorlands and bare yet picturesque outlines of the pikes and fells. Here and there were signs of human habitation in the form of well-built stone cottages, while in some of the steeper valleys could be discerned the chimneys and roofs of various mills and bleaching works. Nor did these lofty "stacks" disfigure the landscape. They seemed to harmonise with nature. The only blot in the vista was perhaps the line of electric cables with which the Zeppelin's observation car had so nearly collided with disastrous result on the previous night.

In the middle distance a haze of smoke through which a regular forest of factory chimneys could be dimly discerned marked the position of Barborough. Distance had lent not exactly enchantment but a discreet contrast to the rural outlook, and while taking in the panoramic effect with its attendant peacefulness Billy Barcroft could hardly realise that eight hours previously a cowardly night-raider had been hurling down her death-dealing missiles upon this portion of Britannia's sea-girt domain.

"Right-o, pater!" he exclaimed. "I'll risk it."

He spoke feelingly. The perils of his profession he regarded with equanimity. It was his choice, and he had no cause to regret it. But the idea of driving a quadruped of sorts along those steep roads and through the crowded streets of Barborough filled him with genuine apprehension.

"Hang it!" he soliloquised. "There's no cut-out on a gee-gee. I know how to stop an engine right enough, but a horse has a brain of its own and can be jolly erratic when it wants to. What on earth possessed the governor to go in for a quadruped when he has a rattling good car?"

Just at that moment the harmony of the morning was interrupted by the high-pitched voice of Mrs. Carter engaged in animated conversation with Mrs. Sarah Crumpet, the D.T.—otherwise Domestic Treasure—who "did" for Andrew Norton, Esquire.

Although the two ladies were at a side door that opened directly into the scullery their voices could be heard with astounding clearness.

"Eh! An' tha' found tha bed not slept upon?" she exclaimed. "Mr. Norton may ha' been called away a-purpose."

"Nay, that 'e wur not, Jane," declared Mrs. Crumpet. "I'm a-tellin' on ye, sitha'. Mr. Norton 'e meant to come back, for the whisky was on th' table."

"Methinks he looks to my employer for his nightcap," remarked Mrs. Carter with asperity.

"An' I was so overcome like," continued Sarah ignoring the insinuation, "that I simply 'ad to 'ave a drop-the first time I ever 'ad a chance up yonder."

"'As 'e paid thee thy brass?" enquired the sympathetic Mrs. Carter.

"Ay, that 'e did, thanks be. But it seems most strange-like, this business."

"I'll tell th' master," asserted Mrs. Carter as the other woman walked away. "An' sitha', if you're feelin' out o' sorts again, Mrs. Crumpet, now's your chance afore the bottle's locked up."

With this parting injunction the "help" of Ladybird Fold shut the door and made her way to the study.

"Yes, I know," said Mr. Barcroft when the Little Liver Pill had duly reported the absence of Mr. Norton. "He was here last night and left in a hurry before I returned; I'll stroll across in the course of the forenoon. Ah, good morning, Entwistle; how's that foot?"

"Better, thanks," replied his guest. "Gives me a bit of a twinge when I set it to ground. Well, what's the morning's news?"

"Papers not in yet, not that I expect any enlightenment on the subject of the raid in the Press report. There are all sorts of rumours flying about, as is to be expected. But it will be all right some day—when we tackle the business properly. These Zeps. will come once too often. It's a mystery to me that they haven't summed up the results and come to the conclusion that these haphazard raids aren't worth the candle."

"Unless it is to divert the attention of the German people from the Western Front," remarked Entwistle.

"Quite possible," agreed Peter. "Now to breakfast. I'm sorry your car couldn't come to fetch you—not that I want to lose you exactly, although I have a batch of proofs in hand," he added bluntly. "You understand? Billy will drive you into Barborough."

"And what do you think of the measures taken to combat the Zeppelin menace?" enquired Entwistle addressing himself to Billy. The flight-sub shook his head.

"I'm afraid I cannot venture an opinion," he replied. "Both branches of the Air Service are doing their level best—they cannot do more."

"You won't be able to draw Billy, Entwistle," added his parent with a laugh. "Even I cannot get him to talk shop."

"Pity some military men I know aren't like him," said the vet. "Nowadays it's either too much shop or too much official reticence. The middle path seems to have been lost sight of. But any more of the mystery of your friend Andrew Norton? I couldn't help hearing your housekeeper holding forth just now."

"Can't understand it," replied Barcroft Senior. "Why Norton should bolt out of my house and desert his own all night is a complete puzzle. I can only put forward the theory that the Zep. raid made him lose his mental balance—and he's a fellow with a steady head, I fancy. If he doesn't put in an appearance before lunch time I feel it is my duty to report the circumstances to that pillar of intelligence the Tarleigh police sergeant."

"And possibly get yourself arrested on suspicion," chuckled Entwistle. "Norton was last seen in this house, remember."

"It would be an experience that would afford practical knowledge as far as my work is concerned," decided Peter. "Nothing like real life to work into a plot, you know."

Breakfast over, Entwistle and the flight-sub went out into the garden for the time-honoured matutinal pipe until it was time for Peter's guest to take his departure.

"Warranted quiet in harness," quoted Billy as his parent cautiously retrieved the shaft. "My word, pater, there's not much room between the dock-gates. Think she'll take it?"

"Ought to," replied Barcroft Senior dubiously. "Now, have another shot. I wish the brute had a reverse gear."

By dint of mingled coaxing and physical force Butterfly was backed between the shafts. Then both men regarded the result of their triumph with chastened looks.

"Strikes me we've missed this sling arrangement on the starboard side," remarked Billy. "That leather thing ought to be round the shaft. She'll have to forge ahead a bit."

"Right-o!" assented his parent. "Gee-up. Oh, dash it all! That's my toe this time."

For Butterfly, in "forging ahead" had brought her hind hoof heavily upon Peter's foot, which happened to be encased in a carpet slipper.

At length the evolutions arrived at a state that found the donkey in the shafts. Father and son stood back to admire their handiwork and to puzzle out the way to adjust the seemingly chaotic tangle of harness.

"Why not ask Entwistle?" suggested the flight-sub. "He's a vet. He ought to know how this gear is rove."

Mr. Barcroft shook his head. He did not like to admit defeat.

"Can't ask him to hobble out here with that sprained ankle of his," he said. "Unfortunately I'm not used to the job."

"So I should imagine, pater," added Billy pointedly. "Well, we've got to get on with the business. I'll make sure that everything's lashed up securely. That's the main point. If it isn't right it can't be helped."

The task of harnessing completed Butterfly was led out of the stable, an operation that nearly resulted in Peter being pinned against the door-post by one of the wheels.

"She's perfectly docile now she's in the trap," he decided as the donkey walked demurely round to the front of the house. "That's right, Entwistle. Another hour will see you safely home. Good-bye, don't forget to look me up at any time. Up you get, Billy."

"Thanks, I'm not having any at present," decided the flight-sub. "I'll lead her down the narrow lane until we get to the high-road. Now, then, my hearty; easy ahead once more."

we get to the tram-lines or she'll try conclusions with a car. I tell you what: while you are in Barborough— —"

"If we ever get there," muttered Billy.

"You ought to get that brute shod. She may do better on the metallic roads."

Two hours later Butterfly and party were in the thickest part of the traffic. To the flight-sub it was a sort of nightmare. Tram after tram had to be stopped to enable the erratic animal to pass, while a crowd of urchins (practically all the unwashed of Barborough, Billy thought) tailed on to the "Dead March in Saul" procession and contributed rounds of applause as Barcroft steered the donkey through the traffic mostly by means of his shoulders directed against the animal's ribs.

"Come in," said Entwistle as the party finally drew up outside the vet's house. "Put your steed in the stable and stop and have lunch."

"Thanks all the same," said Billy. "I must be getting back, or it will be dark before I see Ladybird Fold again."

The two men said good-bye, and Barcroft, leading the animal, set off on the return journey.

"I'll leave the moke at a blacksmith's, and while the thing's being shod I may as well call and see Betty," he decided, and proceeded to put his plan into execution by enquiring of one of the attendant throng—he suffered their presence with equanimity by this time—where a shoesmith was to be found.

"Fine animal, sir," remarked the smith. "Best I've seen for a long time. Won't hurry, eh? Well, p'raps 'tes not being shod. How long will it take? Say half an hour."

Billy deliberated. It was not much use going to "Mill View" if he had to be back in thirty minutes. On the other hand he could easily put up the animal at Two Elms and save time on the return journey. Besides, curiosity prompted him to watch the forthcoming operation.

The smith was a powerfully-built fellow from his waist upwards. His chest was of enormous depth, his breast and arm muscles stood out like the gnarled trunk of a tree. But his lower limbs were so thin that they seemed incapable of supporting the bulky "upperworks."

Butterfly submitted graciously to the initial stages of the operation, but when it came to shoeing the off-side fore-foot she exhibited signs of obstinacy.

"I'll have to throw her, sir," declared the smith. "Stand aside a bit."

Bending he gripped the donkey's legs and applied his huge bulk to her ribs. Like a felled ox Butterfly fell.

"Keep 'er 'ead down, sir," cautioned the smith. "I won't be long."

At length the last shoe was nailed on and filed smooth. Billy had had about enough of it, for the pungent smell of the forge was far from pleasant. But not so Butterfly. Apparently smarting under the indignity she refused to rise.

The smith applied a leather strap, but unavailingly. He gripped her head and tried to lever it up. The donkey lashed out, narrowly missing Billy's shins.

"Dunno as 'ow I seed such a brute afore," said the smith, scratching his head. "Look 'ere, sir; do you 'old her tail and pull, and I'll tackle her 'ead. Now, up you come."

Butterfly did. With a series of frantic kicks she regained her feet, sent the astonished smith flying in one direction and Billy in another.

For some seconds the flight-sub was too dazed to take any active interest in the sequence of events, but when at length he picked him self up and ran to the smithy door, Butterfly's heels were just visible as at a good fifteen miles an hour she disappeared round the corner of the street.

CHAPTER XV
RECALLED BY WIRE

"SHE'S off home, sir," said the smith. "Don't you fash yousen about 'er. The cart? Run it in 'ere. 'Twill be all right."

Billy paid for the shoeing and walked slowly down the street.

"No good going to see Betty at lunchtime," he soliloquised. "Might just as well see about something to eat."

He made his way towards the cornmarket. Here the traffic was at its height. Nobody would have thought that twelve hours ago a Zeppelin had sought to terrorise these Lancashire folk with a display of "frightfulness," and that within two hundred yards a devastated street bore testimony to the Huns' feeble efforts.

"By Jove, if this had been Karlsruhe or Berlin, wouldn't the Kaiser be shedding floods of tears!" thought Billy. "Good old British public. 'Carry on, carry on—we'll come out top-dog all in good time'—that's the spirit."

A crowd outside the window of a news office attracted his attention. He crossed the road in order to read a broadsheet giving the latest war news. It was cheerful enough, in all conscience:

"Two Zeppelins Down. Official."

"Brief and to the point," exclaimed Billy. "Gives a fellow quite an appetite for lunch. Wonder if any of our crowd scored the winning hits?"

Ten minutes later, while awaiting lunch, Billy bought a paper still damp from the press.

"Honours even!" he exclaimed. "The R.F.C. bring down one gas-bag in Lincolnshire; our fellows bag another twenty miles off the Yorkshire coast. Hullo! Here's the fly on the ointment: one of our seaplanes missing."

He glanced casually at the rest of the news, which consisted mostly of ambiguous and contradictory Allied and enemy reports from the various fronts, a couple of columns of local news and a similar space devoted to racing and football. The whole of the front page was taken up with an advertisement of somebody's Autumn sale.

"Rot!" commented Billy forcibly, "They talk about paper shortage, cut down the paper by a third, and yet accept a whole page advertisement of this trash. The back page, I presume, is taken up with photographs of engaged nonentities that are not of the faintest possible interest to decimal ought-ought-one of the readers."

But the young officer was only partly right. In one column was an item of "Stop Press News" printed in blurred type:—

> "The Missing Airmen: Admiralty report that missing seaplane was piloted by Flight-lieutenant John Fuller, with Assist.-Paymaster Robert Kirkwood as observer."

For some moments Billy stared vacantly at the paper. He could hardly realise the truth of the bald statement. It seemed incredible. Never before, during the "Hippodrome's" commission, had a seaplane set out on a particular duty and failed to return. Fuller was a thoroughly capable man; Kirkwood—yes—there was nothing to complain about the way in which he carried out his duties. Had he, Billy, not been on leave the possibilities were that Kirkwood would have flown with him.

Barcroft was essentially of a sanguine nature. He had pictured several of his brother-officers coming a "crash," but never himself. It is the same sort of spirit that pervades the men in the trenches. Others might "go west" but not themselves. It is only on rare occasions that a fighting man has a presentiment that he will go under.

"I'm frightfully sick that I wasn't on board instead of being on leave," thought the flight-sub. "Just my rotten luck. Wonder what has happened to Fuller and Kirkwood? Missing. Perhaps; but I'll stake my all on Fuller. He'll turn up trumps right enough."

Nevertheless Barcroft spent a miserable afternoon. He felt too unsettled to carry out his original programme of calling at Mill View. The desertion of Butterfly he had practically forgotten. All he wanted to do was to go home and await news of his missing chums.

* * * *

Meanwhile Peter Barcroft, having completed his precious proofs to the accompaniment of a choice selection of literary profanity, set out to post the result of his labours.

It was a good mile to the nearest pillar-box, which was on the summit of the hill overlooking Blackberry Cross, and was cleared at the early hour of four p.m.

"Nice walk on a fine day," commented Peter, "but there'll be trou'ole when it blows, rains or snows. A bit of a change from having a pillar-box outside one's door, and where one can post at ten in the evening with the absolute certainty of the letter being delivered in Town the next morning. Wonder if I'll meet Billy on his way back?"

He whistled for the two dogs and, checking their impetuosity, walked briskly down the lane.

"Pity the car's crocked," he soliloquised. "Might have taken Billy round and shown him the country. By Jove, this air is fine! Makes a fellow glad to be alive. Hope Billy will have fine weather while he's here."

His plans for the entertainment of his sailor son were interrupted by his being nearly run down by a cyclist postman, who, turning sharply from the high road into the lane leading to Ladybird Fold, managed to miss the occupier of that delectable spot by a few inches.

"Sorry, sir."

"Don't mention it," replied Peter affably. "A miss is as good as a mile. Anything for me? You're early this afternoon."

"A telegram for you, sir; postmaster he sent me with it, seeing it's on my way home and there'll not be a lad at t'office."

Peter took the orange-coloured envelope and opened it. Within was a form bearing the words:

"Report for duty at Rosyth immediately."

"No answer," said Peter shortly; then "You might put this in the post for me," handing the man the stamped envelope.

Barcroft Senior retraced his steps. Dashed to the ground were the castles in the air he was building concerning Billy's programme. "Jolly rough luck," he decided, that a youngster's leave should be curtailed in that off-hand manner.

Then he realised that there was a higher claim. His son was wanted— urgently. Personal considerations were nothing compared with the exigencies of the Senior Service in wartime.

"It shows Billy is of some importance," he decided proudly. "They wouldn't trouble to recall him if he were otherwise. Hang it all! if he doesn't turn up within the next half-hour he'll miss the 4.45 from Tarleigh, and that will put him in the cart as far as the Scotch express is concerned. I'll go and meet him and hurry him along."

Peter Barcroft was not usually given to changing his mind in this erratic fashion, but perhaps present circumstances were sufficient excuse. He had not seen his son for some twelve months previous to Billy's belated arrival at Ladybird Fold fourteen hours ago. Of that fourteen hours six had been employed by making up arrears of sleep, and another five by Peter's own act of sending his son into Barborough. Of the remaining time father and son had spent hardly an hour alone—and there were such a lot of things that Peter wanted to tell his boy. Then, as a coping-stone to the series of disappointments, Billy had not seen his mother, as Mrs. Barcroft was not expected home until the evening.

While Peter was walking along the high road, Billy on his homeward journey took the path across the fields, and on the former's return was sitting comfortably in front of the fire.

"Hullo! how did I miss you?" was Peter's greeting. He was considerably puzzled as to how Billy had contrived to reach home with the donkey without passing him on the road. "I've a telegram for you."

"About Fuller?" asked the flight-sub eagerly.

"No," replied Mr. Barcroft. "Why should he want to wire? It's your recall, my boy; and it's too late for the train that catches the Scotch express. She's leaving Tarleigh station now."

"Something in the wind, I'll swear," declared Billy, searching in vain for a time-table. "Fuller's missing. You've heard me mention him several times. Went after one of the returning Zeppelins and hasn't been seen since. Only the other day——"

"What are you disarranging my desk for?" interrupted his father. "A time-table? Here you are. Next train from Tarleigh is at 7.5. That will catch a connection at Barborough and land you at Edinburgh about 4 A.M. How much further to Rosyth?"

"About an hour," replied Billy. "Might do it in time."

"No use worrying about it: that won't help matters," said his father philosophically. "You'll be able to see your mother. She arrives by the same train you leave by. It will only be for a couple of minutes. Better luck next time." Tea over, Billy began his preparations for the journey north. With the assistance of Mrs. Carter his greatcoat was made sufficiently presentable until he could borrow a uniform from an obliging shipmate.

At the station the flight-sub's meeting with his mother was, as Peter had predicted, only of a brief duration, delayed until the guard's in patient exhortation of "Take your seat, sir, if you're going," brought it to a close.

"Good-bye, my boy!" said Barcroft Senior as his son lowered the window of the now closed door.

"I say, pater!" exclaimed Billy, suddenly remembering something in his pocket. "Here, take this. It will interest you. Forgot all about it before this."

Peter took the proffered paper—a copy of the document found on the body of the dead German airman, setting a price upon Barcroft Senior's head.

The train was on the move. Billy, with his head and shoulders still protruding through the window, waved farewells to his parents, then— —

"Dash it all!" he shouted. "Butterfly—the donkey—ran away. Clean forgot to mention it."

But Peter merely shook his head. The rumble of the train made the words quite inaudible.

It was nearly seven in the morning when Flight-sub-lieutenant Barcroft arrived at Rosyth, after a long and tedious journey. Mists were hanging over the waters of the Firth of Forth. Even the lofty structure of the Forth Bridge was hidden by the grey bank of vapour. Service craft of all sizes and descriptions were feeling their way up and down the broad estuary, making the welkin ring with the discordant braying on their syrens and foghorns.

"Have you seen anything of the 'Hippodrome's' boat?" inquired Billy of a petty officer on duty on the jetty.

"'Hippodrome's' boat, sir?" repeated the man. "Why, the 'Hippodrome' got under way a couple of hours ago, along with the Seventh Destroyer Division, The Ninth's just off, sir."

Barcroft rapidly reviewed the situation. Experience had taught him that there are often two ways of doing things in the Service—the official and the non-official. To be strictly in accord with the precedent he should have reported himself to the Admiral, giving his reasons why he missed his ship and getting a smart "rap over the knuckles." On the other hand he might be able to enlist the sympathies of one of the officers of the Ninth Destroyer Division and get a passage—provided the boats were proceeding to the same rendezvous. He resolved to put the latter proposition into effect; failing that, he would have to fall back upon the official routine.

His luck was in. As he hurried across the caisson on his way to the jetty where the destroyers were berthed he overtook a lieutenant commander, whom he recognised as Terence Aubyn, a particular friend of Flight-lieutenant Fuller.

"By all means," replied Aubyn when Barcroft had explained the circumstances and requested a passage. "We're pretty certain to fall in with the 'Hippodrome,' although I have as yet no idea of the position of the rendezvous. In fact, I have a couple of her men on board now. They got adrift in a copper punt last night, and were only picked up after the ship had left."

"No further news of Fuller, I'm afraid?" remarked Barcroft.

"Not a whisper," replied the lieutenant-commander as he ran briskly up the steeply sloping "brow" to the quarter-deck of the destroyer "Audax."

And thus Flight-sub-lieutenant Barcroft found himself on board one of the newest type of destroyers bound for an unknown rendezvous somewhere in the North Sea.

CHAPTER XVI
CAPTIVES IN A SUBMARINE

ON being hauled on board the German submarine Fuller and Kirkwood were sternly ordered to go below, their captors indicating a small hatchway fifteen feet for'ard of the conning-tower.

The prisoners had no option. They descended the almost vertical steel ladder and found themselves in practically the bow compartment of the vessel. It was the crew space of the submarine mine-layer, for the craft, on which was painted the number UC49, was not fitted with torpedo tubes, nor did she carry guns of the "disappearing mountings" type. Her part was to sneak out of the Elbe, cruise on the surface whenever practicable, diving only when any strange vessel hove in sight. Her cargo had consisted of forty metal cylinders stowed aft—mines of the most recent type—but having sown her harvest of death and destruction, regardless whether an enemy or a neutral vessel fell a victim to the deadly peril, she was on her way back to the Fatherland.

The compartment in which Fuller and his companion found themselves was about thirty feet in length and fifteen at its maximum diameter, which was at the after end. For'ard it tapered, at first gradually, then sharply, until it terminated at a bulkhead close to the bows. In the lower part of the recess were the anchors and cables, capable of being lowered or hauled by means of elaborate mechanism which was controlled from within. The upper portion of the bow compartment consisted of a large fresh-water tank. Round the crew space were lockers that served a double purpose: besides containing the effects of the men they were used as seats. Hooks were bolted to the cambered deck-beams in order to sling hammocks—in fact, half a dozen hammocks were at that time occupied—and mess-tables.

Against the after bulkhead was a small partitioned-off place that served as the cook's galley, the stove being heated by electricity. While running awash the fumes were carried off by means of a funnel that projected a few inches above the deck, which was fitted with a watertight cover that could be operated from the conning-tower when the submarine was trimmed for diving. Yet in spite of the ventilation the place reeked vilely of a variety of odours. Fuller wondered what the atmosphere must be like when UC49 was submerged.

In addition to the sleeping occupants of the hammocks, who by their restlessness even in slumber showed signs of the mental strain, the crew space was occupied by three fairhaired, fresh-featured Frisians, who regarded the captives with scant curiosity and, after the first five minutes, seemed to ignore the Englishmen entirely.

"May as well make the best of things," remarked Fuller. "I know the ropes a bit—been through it before. Take your wet clothes off, old man. Keep a tight hold of your personal gear. We'll see if we can't persuade that fat chap in the galley to put our things to dry."

"They would dry on us in this hot show," observed Kirkwood. "Suppose we are sent for?"

"Then we are," added the flight-lieutenant grimly. "We'll have to grin and bear it. All the same, I'm not going to act as a human clothes horse while my gear is drying, so here goes."

The German cook seemed anxious to oblige, in spite of a muttered protest from one of the crew.

"My broder on der 'Blucher' vos," he explained. "Englische him pick up and well treat. Him write an' tell me so. Thus your clothes make dry."

Although the hatchway was closed and secured the submarine was still running awash, lifting sluggishly as she forged ahead at a modest fifteen knots. A couple of hours passed, and no attempt was made on the part of the vessel's officers to interrogate their prisoners.

"For one thing we are clothed and, let us hope, in our right minds," observed Fuller as the pair redressed in their now dry clothing, dispensing, however, with their leather jackets, which were as stiff as a board and white with sea-salt.

"Much more of this would drive me out of my mind," protested Kirkwood. "Give me the freedom of the air any day. Suppose this old hooker bumps into a mine?"

"Pull yourself together, man," said the flight-lieutenant sharply. "It's all one big risk, I admit, but for heaven's sake don't give these fellows a chance to think we've cold feet!"

The A.P. stiffened his upper lip.

"By Jove, I won't!" he exclaimed.

"The youngster has good cause for concern," soliloquised Fuller. "This old tub wouldn't stand a cat's chance if anything went wrong. She's one of those craft that's made by the fathom and cut off where required, I should imagine. Never saw such rough work in all my life. And no sign of air-locks or any lifesaving devices. I suppose such details don't worry the German Admiralty. Those leaking joints remind me of the old Tower Hill subway. A coat of whitewash and gas jets instead of the electric light would make the illusion complete."

His reveries were interrupted by a sliding door in the after bulkhead being opened. The German seamen sprang to their feet and stood rigidly at attention as a young, heavily-built unter-leutnant appeared and beckoned the prisoners to follow him.

Stepping over the sill of the watertight door Fuller and his companion found themselves in the officers' quarters—a compartment extending the whole width of the vessel, and separated from the engine-room by another bulkhead. The cabin was plainly furnished but with a certain degree of comfort. On either side were two curtained bunks. A swinging table occupied the centre of the floor, with four revolving arm-chairs, the feet of which were clamped to prevent them being capsized in heavy weather. Against the after bulkhead were two bookshelves and a folding wash-basin, while between them was a ladder communicating with the conning-tower. On the for'ard bulkhead were voice-tubes and telephones for conveying orders to various parts of the vessel, also gauges of various descriptions similar to those in the conning-tower, so that the commander, when not on duty, could know what was going on without having to hail the navigating officer. In the arched ceiling was an illuminated tell-tale compass.

"North 88 east," said Fuller to himself, as he read the magnetic bearing. "She's making for the Elbe or the Weser, I'll swear."

"There is no need for you to trouble about the course," said a broad-shouldered officer dressed in the uniform of a kapitan- leutnant of the Imperial German Navy. "That is our affair. Now, tell me—no lies, mind—what is your name?"

Fuller met the penetrating eye of his examiner without flinching, yet he realised he was "up against" a sharp Teuton, who, by his command of the English language, had evidently an intimate and first-hand knowledge of his enemy's country.

It was, Fuller knew, futile to dissemble. The fact that Kirkwood and he were missing would be revealed by the British Admiralty casualty list. Neither would any good purpose be attained by refusing to reply to any questions that could be answered without giving useful information to the Huns.

"John Fuller, flight-lieutenant, H.M.S. 'Hippodrome,'" he replied promptly.

"So? Then let me offer my congratulations at you again becoming the guest of the Imperial German Government," rejoined the kapitan-leutnant sarcastically. "I do not think you will escape again, Mr. Fuller. Since Sylt was too easy a place of captivity you will most a certainly be sent inland when we arrive in harbour—somewhere a very long way from the convenient neutral port of Esbjerg. Now, I suppose it is of no use asking you under what circumstances you were brought down?"

"Engine failure owing to the petrol tank being perforated."

"Ach! How far from the coast? And what part of the coast? Did you ascend from a ship or from a harbour?"

Fuller shook his head.

"I cannot say," he replied.

The German took the refusal quite in good part.

"I do not blame you for refusing," he remarked. "Any brave man, be he German or English, would do the same. Now, sir, am I to have any better luck with you? Your name?"

The A.P. told him his name and rank, but resolutely declined to commit himself on other points. His captor merely grunted with the air of a man who has been given information of little or no interest. Kirkwood had not broken out of a German prison. Compared with the redoubtable Fuller he was a nonentity in the eyes of the kapitan-leutnant.

A gong clanged noisily in the conning-tower, its verberations outvoicing the pulsations of the oil-fed motors. Without a word the submarine's commander sprang to the ladder and, ascending, left Fuller and his companion in misfortune standing at the foot of the table.

A hoarse order, followed by the heavy pattering of sea,—boots upon the deck and the metallic clash of water-tight hatches being closed, denoted that UC49 was being trimmed for diving.

Fuller felt a hand tap him on the shoulder.

"Get you outside!" ordered the young unter-leutnant, indicating the for'ard compartment.

Barely had the prisoners regained their place of confinement than the bulkhead door was shut, a slight yet distinctly perceptible list announcing that the submarine was diving. The fore-peak was now uncomfortably crowded, for the "watch on deck," unable to remain any longer on deck, had come below at the order to trim ship for diving. One and all looked drawn and anxious. Unlike their brethren in the non-mine-laying submarines they had practically nothing to do. The excitement of being able to launch a torpedo at a British ship, be she naval vessel or merchantman, was denied them. They were, in fact, nothing more than passive individuals cooped up in the shell of a submerged craft, unable to see what was going on without, and helpless to save themselves in the event of the submarine being rammed.

For quite a minute the obliquely downward plunge was maintained, the vessel the while turning sharply to starboard. Then, pitching slightly to the violent displacement of a volume of water, she resumed her normal trim at a depth of ten fathoms beneath the surface.

The action of porting helm had undoubtedly saved the mine-laying submarine. An alert British patrol boat had sighted her from afar, and at a rate resembling that of a train had charged down upon the spot where UC49 had disappeared, while trailing astern at the end of an insulated cable was an explosive grapnel of sufficient power to shatter the submarine's hull like an egg-shell.

The skipper of the patrol boat had made due calculations to ensure, as he thought, the destruction of his prey, but he had not reckoned upon the UC49 changing course as she dived. As it was, the explosive grapnel passed within a couple of yards of the submerged vessel's beam.

Of this Fuller and his companion knew nothing. Perhaps, for their state of mind, it was as well. A man will bravely face death at the hands of his foe, but he will jib at the idea of being "snuffed out" by his own side.

Slowly the minutes passed. UC49 was still running submerged, increasing the depth to twenty fathoms and maintaining a zig-zag course in order to baffle her pursuer. The German seamen were beginning to breathe more freely. The worst part of the business—the great risk of being rammed as she dived—was over, and although under the enormous pressure jets of water were hissing through the faulty joints the men realised that they stood more than a fighting chance of evading destruction.

For perhaps five hours UC49 blindly made her way under the waves. The captives had lost all count of time. Their watches had stopped owing to their immersion when the seaplane was sunk; there was no clock in the fore compartment nor were the bells struck in the customary style on board. But at length, after a seemingly interminable interval, the order was given to empty the auxiliary water ballast tanks. Simultaneously the floor assumed a list—this time in a contrary direction.

Then, without warning, the fairly regular throb of the electric motors gave place to a discordant jar that shook the hull from end to end.

"Main shaft gone, for a dead cert," exclaimed Kirkwood. "I remember the same thing occurring on the 'Tremendous's' picket-boat Yes, they're switching off."

The mine-layer was helpless. Without means of propulsion there were only two courses open to her—to float or sink to the bottom. It was impossible to keep submerged to a certain depth simply by means of admitting a certain quantity of water ballast. Once the reserve of buoyancy was overcome she would sink to the bed of the North Sea, in all probability collapsing under the terrific pressure on her hull long before she arrived there. It is only by means of the diving rudders acting in conjunction with her diving trim that a submarine can remain submerged to a required depth; and since the kapitan-leutnant of UC49 had no desire to make the acquaintance of the floor of the ocean other than by means of an "armed" lead-line, he chose the other alternative and rose to the surface.

The moment the fore hatch was removed the watch rushed on deck. There was a lot of scuffling and shouting of orders, accompanied by the clanking of the auxiliary motors actuating the bilge pumps. When the main shaft fractured—the submarine had only one "screw"—the propeller had flown off, taking with it the broken tail shaft and straining the stuffing-box to such an extent that water poured through the glands. The pumps were just able to cope with the inrush. Should they choke or otherwise get out of order the vessel would promptly founder.

Another order was given. Those of the crew who still remained below hurriedly collected their personal belongings and went on deck, while their place was taken by their companions who, following their example, set to work to "pack up" their scanty bundles. In five minutes the crew space was untenanted save by Fuller and Kirkwood.

"It strikes me very forcibly that we had better be clearing out of this rat-hole," suggested the former, "If we don't we'll be overlooked, and I don't suppose the Huns will mind that."

The two chums ascended the ladder and gained the platform in front of the conning-tower. Here were about a dozen of the crew, a similar number being stationed aft. The officers were grouped amidships, their attention fixed upon some distant object which they were examining through their glasses. The chug-chug of the pumps continued, showing that some of the engine-room staff were still standing by the auxiliary machinery.

"Hurrah!" exclaimed Kirkwood. "A couple of our destroyers. No German prison for us this trip."

Several of the German seamen hearing the exclamation regarded the A.P. angrily; otherwise they offered no objection to the prisoners being on deck. The kapitan-leutnant, also overhearing Bobby's expression of satisfaction, lowered his binoculars and glared at the irrepressible Briton. Then he raised the glasses again and scanned the horizon, finishing up his scrutiny by keeping the on-coming craft under observation.

For half a minute he looked steadfastly at the approaching destroyers, then he gave an order to a man standing by the diminutive mast.

Promptly the sailor hoisted the Black Cross Ensign, but whether as a token of defiance or otherwise the British officers were unable to decide. But they were not long left in ignorance.

"You are a little too hasty in your surmise, Mr. Englishman," sneered the kapitan-leutnant. "You will yet sample the joys of a German prison. These are two of our torpedo-boats."

CHAPTER XVII
THE MIDDLE WATCH

A DULL, reverberating crash roused Flight-sub-lieutenant Barcroft from his temporary bunk on board H.M. torpedo-boat destroyer "Audax."

"Eight bells," midnight, had just gone—silently, for the destroyer was ploughing through the waves at break-neck speed, without navigation lights and as steadily as possible. So well were her oil-fed furnaces tended that no tell-tale sparks escaped from her four squat funnels. In spite of the heavy seas she was cleared for action; life-lines took the place of the stanchion rails and afforded the only means of preventing the bluejackets being swept overboard by the green seas that poured completely over the raised fo'c'sle. Around the four-inch guns men hung on, ready at the first alarm to open fire, while the deadly torpedoes had been launched into their tubes to be let loose at the word of command upon the first unit of the German Navy—be she large or small—that had the temerity to try conclusions with the alert British destroyer.

There had been signs of activity in Hun naval circles—activity forced upon them by prompt and vigorous measures of the sea-dogs under the White Ensign. Zeebrugge was getting too hot to hold the German torpedo-boat flotillas that for months had existed under nerve-racking conditions in that Belgian port. Constant bombardments from the sea and from the air had made the Huns' new base so insecure that the German ocean-going torpedo-boats (craft that compare in point of size with destroyers, although the term destroyer does not figure in Hun naval reports) had been compelled to make a dash for the neutral defences of the Elbe, Weser and Jade. Existing conditions made it undesirable to sneak through Dutch territorial waters, and the only other way was by a circuitous course rendered necessary by the presence of a vast British minefield.

The British Admiralty, out of consideration for neutral shipping, had advertised the limits of the danger zone, which was an aggressive minefield rather than a defensive one—in other words its base was situated close to the German coast, while its apex stretched westward far across the North Sea. Round this apex the German torpedo craft had to make their way.

Knowledge of the attempted dash had reached the ears of the British Commander-in-Chief, and strong flotillas of destroyers were patrolling the length and breadth of the North Sea, their search assisted in broad daylight by seaplanes sent up from attendant parent ships. At night the difficulty of maintaining the cordon was enormously increased. A German boat might slip through in the darkness, while, even if discovered, her attackers would be under the disadvantage of making sure that she was not one of their consorts before opening fire.

The "Audax" was operating in the high latitudes of the North Sea. In fact, if she held on the course for another five hours she would run ashore somewhere in the close proximity of The Naze of Norway.

Two miles ahead and astern of her were other vessels of the same class, the line being continued until the chain of destroyers stretched across the North Sea from Scotland almost to Scandinavia. The Straits of Dover were similarly patrolled, while auxiliary destroyers swept the seas between the northern and southern limits, ready to head off the fugitives or bring them to action.

Rolling fully dressed out of his bunk—for under these conditions it would be folly to turn in otherwise—Billy dashed on deck, followed by the Engineer-lieutenant, who happened to be the only officer in the ward-room not on watch.

Wriggling through the partly-closed hatchway, dubbed by courtesy the "companion," and receiving a greeting in the form of a cold douche—the tail end of a particularly vicious comber—Barcroft stood still until his eyes grew accustomed to the darkness. Then, grasping the life-line, he made his way for'ard, often knee-deep in water, until he gained the doubtful shelter afforded by the rise of the fo'c'sle. Here, clustered round the two guns abreast the for'ard funnel, were a dozen men in "lammy" suits, oilskins and sou'-westers, all peering through the darkness in the direction in which the "Audax" was now proceeding.

"What was the explosion, Mr. Black?" inquired Barcroft of the gunner.

"We don't know, sir," replied the warrant officer. "A mighty big flash and a brute of a report. We've wirelessed the commodore to ask permission to investigate, and now we're off to see, judging by the alteration of course."

The young officer thanked him for the information, vague though it might be, and ascending the bridge ladder took up his stand in front of the after guard-rail of the bridge.

Lieutenant-commander Aubyn and three of his officers were standing with their backs turned to him, oblivious of his presence. Actually Barcroft had no right there, save on sufferance and by the courtesy of the skipper. The executive officers were crouching behind the storm-dodgers—the force of the wind and the sting of the icy spray made it impossible to withstand the full force of the elements unless protected by these canvas screens—and were directing their attention mainly on some as yet invisible object dead ahead. At intervals one or other of the officers would scan the seas abeam, as if expecting to see a dark and swiftly-moving vessel—to wit, an enemy craft pelt through the blackness of the night on her dash for safety.

The skipper remained as rigid as a statue, the personification of silent alertness; but the lieutenant and sub of the "Audax" were conversing, raising their voices in order to make themselves understood above the roar of the wind and the crashing of the waves as they flew over the fore-deck of the destroyer and hurtled against the bridge. Scraps of the discussion wafted to Barcroft's ears.

"A neutral, I think," remarked the sub. "Swede or Norwegian.... Bumped on a mine."

"Torpedo," declared the lieutenant. "I distinctly saw one flash ... before the big blaze... second explosion; yet, it points to it."

Billy caught enough of the conversation to read the lieutenant's theory. Evidently he believed that the victim was one of the British armed liners patrolling this section of the North Sea. Torpedoed, in the darkness and in spite of the heavy seas, she had been blown up by the detonation of her magazine.

Suddenly Aubyn straightened himself and sprang to the telegraph indicator communicating with the engine-room.

Following the double clang of the bell the destroyer's engines were promptly stopped and quickly reversed. The skipper's keen eye had discerned a raft crowded with men as the "Audax" swept past at a distance of less than twenty yards.

Aubyn gave a brief glance at the raging seas and held up his hand. The gesture was understood by the men already standing in expectancy at the falls. It meant "Stand fast." No boat could live in such a turmoil of angry waves, yet there were heroes ready and willing to risk their lives in a vain attempt at rescue.

The "Audax" was about to make an effort by other means, but first the raft had to be found again, for before way had been taken off the destroyer the handful of survivors of the ill-fated ship were lost in the darkness and in the wash of water astern.

Nor could the searchlights be switched on without grave risk to the all-important task of rounding-up the German torpedo-boats. The "Audax" had to grope round like a blind man in the hope of falling in with the drifting raft.

"Shoutin' dead to wind'ard, sir, right on the starboard beam," shouted half a dozen voices. "There they are, sir, a cable's length off."

In a patch of phosphorescent foam, as it lifted dizzily on the crest of a broken wave, could be discerned the object of the search. The next instant it had vanished in the trough of the seas.

"Hard a-port!" roared the skipper.

"Hard a-port, sir," repeated the quartermaster,

Turning, the "Audax" slowed down, coming to a standstill, save for the motion created by the scend of the seas and the leeward drift caused by the strong wind, at a few yards to windward of the raft, which on nearer acquaintance proved to be a number of deck planks still adhering to the fractured beams.

Under the lee of the destroyer the raft floated in comparatively smooth water, and the work of transferring the handful of well-nigh exhausted men commenced. Five or six were hauled on board by means of bowlines; three were incapable of stirring a hand to help themselves, and since their comrades made no effort to assist in their rescue several of the destroyer's hands went overboard and, grasping the unconscious men, were heaved back with no greater damage than bruised knuckles and grazed shins.

"Wot are we to do with these 'ere blokes, Sir?" inquired a seaman of the destroyer's lieutenant, who had temporarily quitted the bridge to superintend the work of rescue. "Our mess deck's flooded out."

"They want warmth. Pass the word to the engineer commander to ask if he has room for nine men in the stokehold."

"Me from Danmark sheep," volubly asserted one man as he was being led below.

"All right, my man," replied the lieutenant, "We'll hear your story later. Hullo, Barcroft, you on deck? Make yourself useful, old boy, and find out what happened to these fellows. I must be hopping back to my perch. Thank your lucky stars it isn't your watch."

Refraining from remarking that he had already had a voluntary trick on the sprayswept bridge Billy followed the survivors of the lost vessel into the hot, steam-laden atmosphere of the stokehold. The foreigners who were in possession of their faculties had "stripped to the buff" and were being rubbed down by sympathising British stokers, while heir clothes were being dried in front of the furnaces.

The rescued men seemed extraordinarily anxious to assert that they belonged to a Danish vessel, almost overwhelming Barcroft in their eagerness to emphasise the point. None of them spoke English, and as the flight-sub knew hardly a word of Danish his attempt to gain information seemed hopeless. He tried speaking in German, with no better results, except for a reiterated chorus of "Me from Danmark."

"It's strange that they don't jabber to each other in their own lingo, sir," remarked a leading stoker, who was kneeling over one of the unconscious seamen and methodically pressing his ribs according to the precepts laid down in the *Manual of Seamanship* for the treatment of persons apparently drowned.

The patient was a powerfully built, hugelimbed young giant, by appearance of far better physique than the others, yet he seemed to be the worst off from the effects of exposure. External examination revealed no signs of an injury, although two of the other men had been badly battered by flying debris from the explosion.

Just then the man stirred, gasped, and endeavoured to free himself from the attentions of the humane leading stoker.

"Then I am still alive?" he asked feebly. "A prisoner on an English ship. 'Well, I am not sorry. I am tired of the war."

"Wot's 'e a-sayin', sir?" inquired the leading stoker.

"Quite enough to give the show away," replied Barcroft, fixing with his eyes the other foreigners, who were now showing every symptom of consternation, for the man had spoken in German and his comrades had understood every word.

"So you are from a German ship?" demanded the young officer, addressing the group of survivors.

The men freely admitted that the game was up, and finding that their good treatment was not modified they became quite communicative.

They were, they announced, some of the crew of the armed commerce-raider "Volksdorf," a converted liner that had left the port of Swinemunde two days previously. Hugging the Norwegian coast she had sighted two British patrol ships, and turning southward had shaken off pursuit in hazy weather. Apparently the "Volksdorf's" attempt was-timed to take place simultaneously with the German activity in the North Sea, and by keeping slightly to the northward of the screen of British destroyers she stood a fair chance of gaining the Atlantic. Unfortunately for her she came within easy torpedo range of a U-boat, and the pirate, not knowing that she was of the same nationality and utterly indifferent as to whether she destroyed enemy or neutral ships without warning, promptly discharged a torpedo. The missile struck home, causing a second explosion, as the after magazine of the raider blew up, causing the ship to sink in less than thirty seconds.

Billy went on deck to find the "Audax" still cruising about in the hope of finding more survivors, but without success. Making his way to the bridge he informed Aubyn of his discovery.

"That's great," declared the youthful skipper. "Fritz committing frightfulness upon his own pals requires some beating. It must have been a strafed U-boat, since I know for a dead cert that none of our submarines are taking part in the present operations. Keeping Middle Watch, Mr. Barcroft? I'd turn in while I had the chance, if I were you. We're in touch with the 'Hippodrome.' Picked up a wireless call not five minutes ago. We'll put you on board before many hours, I dare say, but we don't want to hand you over looking like a sleepy owl; so down below you go."

"Thanks, sir, I will," replied the flight-sub, who after the heated atmosphere of the stoke-hold was feeling the cold acutely.

And carrying out the genial lieutenant-commander's advice Billy went below, pulled off his sea-boots, divested himself of his oil skins, or, rather, those of the engineer-sub who had insisted on lending them, and flopped into his bunk. He was dimly conscious of thrusting his back hard against the partition, gripping the edge of the bunk with both hands and drawing up his knees to wedge himself in—matters of precaution owing to the erratic motion of the destroyer—and in ten seconds he was in a sound, dreamless slumber.

CHAPTER XVIII
AN OCEAN DUEL

"ACTION Stations!"

Billy Barcroft leapt from his bunk, labouring under the delusion that he had turned in only a few minutes before.

The deadlights screwed to the brass rims of the scuttles and the electric lights in the wardroom gave him the impression that it was still night, and it was not until he scrambled on deck that he was aware that grey dawn was breaking.

The wind had piped down considerably. The seas, still running high, no longer showed their teeth in the form of vicious, foam-crested breakers. Yet the decks of the "Audax" were at regular intervals ankle-deep in water, as the destroyer cut through the billows.

A cloud of steam, caused by showers of spray striking the hot, salt-encrusted funnel casings, drifted aft, temporarily obscuring the flight-sub's range of vision. As it cleared he could discern the greatcoated figures of Aubyn and his brother-officers on the bridge, and the indistinct forms of the men as they passed ammunition from the shell-hoists to the guns.

"Got her this time, sir," remarked a burly petty officer, the rotundity of whose figure was still further accentuated by the prodigious quantity of clothing he wore.

He pointed to a dark grey, indistinct object almost dead ahead, her outlines rendered almost invisible by the trailing clouds of smoke that poured from her funnels. Barcroft estimated her distance at two thousand yards. It was impossible to see whether she flew her ensign.

The vessel was a German ocean-going torpedo-boat, one of the nine which had stolen out of Zeebrugge. By sheer good luck she had gone northward over practically the extreme length of the North Sea without being sighted by the British patrols. An hour, or even half an hour earlier she might have slipped unobserved past the "Audax" without being seen by the latter. As it was, one of the British destroyer's look-out men "spotted" the strange craft in the deceptive half-light of the late autumnal dawn.

The "Audax" threw out her private signal by means of a flash lamp from the bridge. The stranger replied by an unintelligible jumble of long and short flashes.

"Either that is a Hun or her signalman is three sheets in the wind," declared Lieutenant-commander Aubyn. "Tell her to make her number, or we'll open fire. And wireless the 'Antipas'; give her our position, and say we are in touch with a suspicious craft."

Aubyn, though brave as a lion, was of a discreet and cautious nature. Dearly would he have liked to engage in an ocean duel with the hostile craft, for such, he now felt convinced she would prove to be. Both vessels were equally matched in the matter of armament, tonnage and number of complement: it was necessary only to again prove the moral and physical superiority of Jack Tar over Hans and Fritz, unless something in the nature of sheer ill-luck allowed the coveted prize to slip through his fingers. It was against the possibility that Aubyn had to guard. The fight had to end in only one way—annihilation to the foe. Hence the call to the destroyer "Antipas" to eliminate that element of chance.

"Let her have it!" shouted the skipper of the "Audax," just as Barcroft gained the bridge.

The four-inch gun on the fo'c'sle barked. It was still dark enough for the flash to cast a lurid glow upon the set faces of the British officers, who stood by with their glasses ready to bear upon the flying torpedo-boat the moment the acrid fumes from the burnt cordite drifted clear of the bridge.

The first shell struck the water close to the German vessel's port side, throwing up a column of water fifty feet in the air as it ricochetted and finally disappeared beneath the waves a mile or so ahead of the target.

Fritz replied promptly. He must have fired; directly the flash of the "Audax's" bow gun was observed. The projectile screeched above the heads of the men on the bridge, seemingly so close that Barcroft involuntarily ducked. It was quite a different sensation from being potted at by "Archibalds." Up aloft the roar of the seaplane's engines and the rush of the wind practically overwhelmed the crash of the bursting shrapnel. This weird moaning, as the four-inch shell flew by, was somewhat disconcerting as far as Billy was concerned, while to heighten the effect a rending crash accompanied the passing of the projectile.

"Our wireless top-hamper, dash it all!" exclaimed Aubyn, turning his head for a brief instant. "Starboard a little, quartermaster."

The slight alteration of helm enabled the midship quick-firer on the starboard side to bear upon the enemy. The latter, evidently with the idea of dazzling the British destroyer, had switched on a searchlight mounted on a raised platform aft. Probably the Huns might have derived advantage from the rays, that still held their own against the increasing dawn, had not a well-directed shell from the "Audax" fo'c'sle gun blown searchlight, platform, and half a dozen men to smithereens.

For the next ten minutes the adversaries were at it hammer and tongs. More than one shell got home on board the British craft, playing havoc with the after-funnel and deckfittings, while three badly wounded but still irrepressibly cheerful seamen were taken down below.

The German craft was being severely punished. The speed had fallen off considerably, while she was on fire fore and aft, although the for'ard conflagration was quickly got under by her crew. By this time she bore broad on the British destroyer's bow, the range having decreased to 1,500 yards.

Suddenly the Hun put her helm hard down. Either she saw that flight was no longer possible, or else her stern quick-firers had been knocked out, and she wished to bring her as yet unused guns to bear upon her foe.

As she turned Aubyn saw through his binoculars a gleaming object shoot over the German craft's side, quickly followed by another. Both disappeared in a smother of foam beneath the waves. "Hard a-port!" he shouted, knowing full well that at that moment a couple of powerful Schwarzkopft torpedoes, propelled by superheated compressed air, were heading towards the "Audax" at a rate of forty to fifty miles an hour.

Round swung the destroyer, listing under excessive helm until the deck on the starboard side dipped beneath the water. As she did so the two torpedoes could be distinctly seen, as, adjusted to their minimum depth to prevent them passing under the lightly draughted objective, they appeared betwixt the crests of the waves.

One passed fifty yards away; the other almost scraped the destroyer's quarter. Had the "Audax" not promptly answered to her helm both torpedoes would have "got home." Yet, not in the least perturbed, the British seamen continued their grim task of battering the Hun out of recognition. They worked almost in silence. Each man knew his particular job and did it. Time for shouting when the business was finished to their satisfaction.

Yet there was a regular pandemonium of noise. The hiss of escaping steam; the vicious thuds of the waves as the "Audax," at twenty eight point something knots, tore through the water under the action of engines of 14,000 horse-power; the rapid barking of the quick-firers; the sharp clang of the breech-blocks and the clatter of the ejected shell-cases upon the slippery decks—all combined to bear testimony to the stress and strain of a destroyer action. The "Audax" was the latest embodiment of naval science in that class of boat, yet without the intrepid energies of the men behind the guns, aided by the strenuous efforts of their mess-mates in the engine-room stokehold, that science would be of little avail in gaining the victory. Man-power still counts as much as it ever did, provided an efficient fighting machine is at their disposal. British Hearts of Oak are much the same as in Nelson's day— and yet the average pay of the Lower Deck ratings is about three shillings a day with no eight-hour shifts, risking life and limb for a wage at which a navvy would sneer.

And why? It is the call of the sea—a call that appeals to Britons more than to any other nation under the sun. In the piping times of peace the Navy offers unrivalled facilities for poor men to travel and see the world, it responds to their love of adventure. In wartime it calls for hard and often unappreciated work with the chance of a glorious scrap thrown in; and right loyally the Navy answers to the call to maintain the freedom of the seas and to guard our shores against the King's enemies.

By the time that the opposing vessels had steadied on their respective helms the "Audax" was steaming obliquely on her foe's broadside, sufficiently to enable three of her four guns to bear.

The Hun's fire was now slackening, and in spite of the shortness of the range, decidedly erratic. Her hull was perforated in several places, her funnels were riddled to such an extent that it seemed remarkable that they had not already collapsed. Her masts had vanished, also a portion of her bridge, while her deck was littered with smoking debris.

"Cease fire!" ordered Lieutenant-commander Aubyn as the German no longer replied to her severe punishment. What was more, her Black Cross ensign, which she had hoisted after the commencement of the engagement, was no longer visible.

Aubyn's chivalrous instincts were ill-repaid, for a couple of shells screeched through the air from the vessel which he thought had surrendered. One went wide; the other penetrated the ward-room of the "Audax," fortunately without exploding. Simultaneously a German bluejacket held aloft the tattered Black Cross emblem of unholy kultur.

In an instant the British tars reopened fire; while to make matters worse for the Huns, the "Antipas," racing up under forced draught, let fly a salvo from the three guns that could be brought to bear ahead. That settled the business. The hostile craft, literally battered out of recognition, began to founder.

"Cease fire!" Aubyn ordered for the second time within two minutes. Then, "Out boats."

It was an easy matter to order the boats away, but a most difficult task to carry the instructions into effect. The gig had been completely pulverised, while the other boats were in a more or less unseaworthy condition.

"Look alive, lads!" exclaimed a petty officer of the carpenters' crew. "T'other blokes'll be there first if we don't look out."

Hastily the holes in the bottom strakes of that particular boat were plugged, and, quickly manned, the leaky craft pushed off, the men urged by her coxswain to "pull like blazes an' get them chaps out o' the bloomin' ditch."

By this time the German torpedo-boat had vanished beneath the waves, leaving a rapidly-dispersing cloud of smoke and steam to mark the spot where she had disappeared and the heads of about twenty swimmers—the survivors of her complement.

In twos and threes the war-scarred and nerve-shattered Huns were hauled into safety, for other help from both destroyers was now upon the scene, and deeply laden the boats returned to their respective parents.

Suddenly Barcroft, who was watching the arrival of the sorry-looking crowd of German prisoners, gave vent to an uncontrolled shout of joyous surprise, for huddled in the stern sheets of the whaler were Flight-lieutenant-John Fuller and his comrade in peril, Bobby Kirkwood.

"There's precious little of report," said Fuller in reply to the skipper of the "Audax", when the two rescued officers were snugly berthed in the ward-room—warm in spite of the additional ventilation in the shape of a couple of neatly-drilled holes marking the place of entry and the point of departure of the ill-advised German "dud" shell. "We had to make a forced descent, got collared by a strafed U-boat just as we had effected repairs. The U-boat rattled herself to bits, so to speak, and had to be abandoned. I've had quite enough submarining, thank you. Give me a seaplane any day of the week, Sunday included. Then that torpedo-boat—V198's her designation— picked us up. They stowed us in the forehold and forgot to let us out when she went under. Suppose they had quite enough on their hands and clean forgot about us," he added generously, giving the kapitan-leutnant of the V198 the benefit of the doubt.

"Anyhow, there we were," continued the flight-lieutenant. "We knew the rotten packet was going, and although we yelled the racket on board prevented them hearing us, I suppose. Still, our luck was in, for a shell burst in her fo'c'sle, ripping up the deck and bursting the cable-tier bulkhead. It was pretty thick with the smoke, but we groped for'ard — —"

"You hauled me for'ard, you mean," interrupted the A.P.

"Shut up!" said Fuller reprovingly. "Well, by standing on the edge of the manger we managed to haul ourselves on to the mess-deck. There we stuck till the firing ceased, and the boat's stern was well under water. Then—it was quite time for us to go, and we dived overboard. The rest you know."

"And what might you be doing on board, old bird?" asked Kirkwood addressing the overjoyed Billy.

"Passenger for the 'Hippodrome,'" replied the flight-sub.

"And it strikes me very forcibly," added Aubyn, "that at this rate I'll find all the 'Hippodrome's' birds on board this hooker. The trouble now is: how can I deliver the goods? We'll have to ask permission to quit station and return for repairs and overhaul. Another three weeks in dockyard hands, I suppose, and the fun only just beginning. Just my luck."

The skipper went on deck. There was much to be done. Although the "butcher's bill" was light, and the destroyer had sustained no serious damage to her hull—thanks to the defective German shells—the loss of the tophamper was considerable. In her present state she was unable to carry out her duties as an efficient patrol boat. With her wireless out of action she was impotent to perform the vital function of communicating with her invisible consorts. For centuries the British Navy had done very well without the aid of wireless telegraphy, but, like many other things, Marconi's discovery had come to stay. Its use enabled fewer vessels to effectually do the work that hitherto required more to perform, owing to the necessity of keeping within visible signalling distance; and a destroyer without wireless was a "dead end," in modern naval warfare.

But Lieutenant-commander Aubyn was not a man who would willingly miss the opportunity of doing his friends a good turn, provided the exigencies of the Service permitted.

Before parting company he signalled the "Antipas," which was still standing by the injured destroyer, with the result that a boat put off from the latter and came alongside.

"Look alive, you fellows!" shouted Aubyn down the ward-room companion. "If you want to get on board the 'Hippodrome' within the next few hours now's your chance. Tressidar, of the 'Antipas,' will give you a passage. That's all right: stick to that gear till you find the old 'Hippo.' I've had to borrow a kit myself before to-day."

CHAPTER XIX
HELD UP IN THE NORTH SEA

"BEHOLD US, Tress old boy!" exclaimed Fuller, when in the privacy of Lieutenant-commander Ronald Tressidar's cabin the old chums could forget the slight differences in their respective ranks. "Three stormy petrels; nobody loves us. Kind of social pariahs, don't you know. Even the Huns wouldn't have us on two of their packets, after little Seaplane 445B slung us out. And, worse, that blighter Aubyn washed his hands of us. Suppose you'll be slinging us out next, Tress?"

"I shall be delighted," replied Tressidar. "The moment——"

"Surly old cave-dweller!" continued the flight-lieutenant. "That's what comes of being shipmates with a mouldy bird in a captive balloon. You will be delighted to—what were you saying?"

"Delighted to feed, partly clothe and certainly educate you, my festive, until we fall in with the 'Hippodrome.' This last condition doesn't apply to your companions," proceeded Tressidar. "But when or where we fall in with the 'Hippo' is a matter for sheer conjecture. I believe now this duck hunt is over (the rest of the Hun torpedo-craft bar two have been accounted for: I suppose you heard that?) the three seaplane carriers are off south to tackle this Zeebrugge business again. However, trust to luck and don't whine if it kicks you. Them's my sentiments, my dear old pal."

It was the "bar two" that kept the "Antipas" and the rest of her consorts patrolling the wild North Sea, until news had been definitely received to the effect that the forlorn pair of Hun boats had done one of three things— had been sunk, captured or had contrived to slip through the cordon into a home or neutral port.

For the next twenty-four hours nothing of incident occurred. The destroyer, maintaining her course within set limits as stolidly as a policeman on his beat, encountered little to attract the attention of her look-out. Every two hours she was in touch with her "next on station," and receiving the information that all was well and nothing doing she would starboard helm and retrace her course.

"Yes, pretty tame," commented Tressidar in reply to a remark of Barcroft's, "but we are getting quite used to it. Yesterday's scrap came as a little tonic, although we didn't have so very much to do. Aubyn had the bounder well in hand already when we came up."

"This youth," remarked Fuller, indicating the flight-sub, "is an optimist of the deepest dye. What d'ye think is his idea of penultimate bliss? Having dinner at a swagger hotel somewhere on the East Coast, with the blinds up and every available electric light switched on."

"That shows, Mr. Barcroft," said the lieutenant-commander, "that you have a pretty firm belief in the fact that the war will be over some day— unless you are prepared to shell out to the tune of fifty pounds for an offence against the Defence of the Realm Act."

"Heaven forbid, sir!" replied Barcroft. "But, personally speaking, I'm fed up with having to hang about ashore in utter darkness. It's necessary, of course."

"Of course," echoed Tressidar. "It's part of the mess of pottage we received when we sold our birthright on that memorable morning when Blériot flew across the Channel. From that hour our insular superiority was threatened not by La Belle France, though. Only the other day— —"

A knock upon the door of the cabin, followed by the appearance of a messenger, interrupted the lieutenant-commander's narrative.

"Orficer of the watch's compliments, sir," reported the man, "an' there's a Danish vessel; making to the nor'-west, distant three miles."

"Very good—carry on," replied the skipper, and snatching up his cap he hurried on deck, followed by the trio of naval airmen.

The Dane proved to be a two-funnelled, twomasted craft of about 3,000 tons. On the foremost funnel and along her sides were painted her national colours, while to leave no doubt as to her identity the words "Trone— Danmark" appeared amidships in letters six feet in height.

"I've signalled to her to stop, sir," reported the officer of the watch. "Ah, there she goes—well, signalman?"

The "bunting-tosser," with his telescope glued to his eye, called out the letters of a string of bunting that rose to the "Trone's" mast head. His mate, having written various cabalistic signs on a signal-pad (the numbed state of his hands prevented his making any legible letters), hurried off to consult the International Code Book..

"Is it necessary for me to heave-to?" was the significance of the Jane's signal. "I have been examined twice already."

"Then three for luck, you bounder!" chuckled Tressidar. "Signalman, hoist the International 'I D'."

I D—signifying the peremptory order, "Heave-to or I will fire into you," was a message not to be ignored. Patches of foam under the vessel's counter and streaming for'ard past her water-line announced that her engines were going astern in order to check her way.

"Like a trip in the boat, Mr. Barcroft?" asked Tressidar, as he noticed the flight-sub regarding the boarding party with studied interest. "Very good; you may learn a few tricks of the trade."

With her guns trained upon the suspect—for experience had taught British officers that Hun raiders do not scruple to sail under neutral colours—the "Antipas" circled round the now stationary "Trone," the while maintaining a sharp look-out for hostile submarines that have a habit of keeping in touch with ships liable to examination much in the same manner as a pilot fish attends upon a shark.

"She looks quite a mild cuss," observed the sub of the duty boat to Billy, "but one never knows. A few weeks back I was boarding some old hooker. Pitch dark night and raining like blue blazes. We'd just run alongside when the blighters heaved something overboard—looked like an elephant by the size of it. Anyway, it missed us by a yard and gave us all a sousing, which we didn't mind as we were pretty wet already. Then she pushed off for all she was worth, thinking that our skipper would have to moon about and pick us up. He did," added the young officer grimly, "—after he had squared accounts with the brute—another would-be 'Moewe.' A torpedo at five hundred yards settled her. In bow!"

The bowman boated his oars, and balancing himself in the plunging bows of the little craft, dexterously secured the end of a coil of rope that was thrown from the "Trone's" deck.

Up the swaying "monkey-ladder" swarmed the British officers and men, and gaining the Dane's deck were received by the dapper, clean-shaven skipper.

"Of course, of course, I understand," replied the Dane in excellent English when the sub apologised for having had to compel him to heave-to. "Our papers are here. We are from Esbjerg to Newcastle with passengers and general cargo."

"Very good," replied the sub in charge of the boarding-party. "I'll have a squint at your papers. Say, Barcroft, would you mind examining the passengers? Try a few words of German on 'em unawares. That generally fetches the black-listers."

The civilians, to the number of nineteen, were formed upon the poop. A few bore the appearance of being respectable, the others looked utterly out-and-out scarecrows..

The "Trone's" second mate appeared with the passenger list. To Billy's surprise ten of the men were English.

"Yes; men sent back from Germany," declared the mate, who, like his skipper, spoke English fluently. "They were exchanged, and were to have travelled through Holland, but the Dutch steamers are temporarily stopped, so they came through Denmark instead."

The scarecrows greeted Barcroft with cheerful smiles as he approached. In spite of their rags, the torments of hunger and degradation that they had undergone, they were British to the core—men over sixty years of age who, deemed to be useless by the Germans, had been repatriated: living examples of the gentle and humane treatment afforded to the unfortunate captives who had the ill-luck to fall into the hands of the apostles of kultur.

Billy interrogated the men one by one. No need to doubt their words. One and all were unanimous in their story of the horrors of the famine-prisons of Germany.

"I won't ever turn up my nose at a dogbiscuit after this, sir," said one old veteran of seventy-two.

"William McDonald—where's William McDonald?" inquired Barcroft reading the names from the list.

"Here, sir."

The speaker was of different appearance from the nine. Although dressed in rough clothes his garments bore the appearance of being practically new, nor did his features betray the traces of months of semi-starvation.

"Not much to complain about," he replied in answer to the flight-sub's question. "I was at Eylau. Fair amount of food and of good quality."

"You are not sixty, by any means," said Barcroft.

"No, not fifty yet. Heart trouble—fit for nothing, so they sent me back to England."

"H'm," muttered the flight-sub.

"He's one of a few that drew a lucky number, I'm thinking, sir," remarked the man who stood next to him. "Fair slave-driven, that's what we were. But that's all over now, thank God."

The rest of the passengers passed muster. They were Danish subjects—merchants and farmers, brought over at the instance of the British

Government to assist in certain transactions between Great Britain and Denmark.

"A clean bill of health," reported Billy as the destroyer's sub rejoined him.

"And all serene down below," rejoined the latter. "We'll shove off. Thanks, captain, for your assistance; sorry we had to hold you up, but we're at war, you know."

"Yes," added the Dane, "and you have our moral support. I wish that we were a bigger nation. We, too, have old scores to wipe off—my family lived at Flensburg for years until '66. Flensburg is in Germany now, but some day—who knows?"

"A good sort," announced the sub, as the boat made her way back to the "Antipas." "These Danes remember Schleswig-Holstein almost if not quite as much as the French do Alsace Lorraine. I shouldn't be surprised if they chip in just before the end, if only to get their lost provinces back. How about Denmark extending frontiers to the Kiel Canal, and making that artificial waterway an international concern, eh?"

The sight of the destroyer dipping her ensign caused both officers to turn their heads and look at the "Trone." The latter was again under way and had just rehoisted her ensign after saluting the British warship.

"I feel downright sorry for those ten Britishers," thought Billy. "Their experiences have put years on to their lives."

But, had he known, he might have made an exception; for, holding aloof from his companions, Mr. William McDonald was thanking his lucky stars that he had again bluffed the inspecting officer. Within the next twelve hours William hoped to reassume the name of Andrew Norton, trusting to his natural cunning to explain satisfactorily the reason why he left the neighbourhood of Barborough so suddenly on the night of the raid.

Evidently Siegfried von Eitelwurmer, *alias* Andrew Norton, otherwise McDonald, had strong reasons for leaving his Fatherland in order to risk his life in the British Isles.

CHAPTER XX
INVESTIGATIONS

"To come straight to the point, my dear Entwistle," said Peter Barcroft. "I may say that I have two reasons for looking you up. The first is purely a matter of form—to inquire after your injured ankle. Judging by the way in which you crossed the room I think I am right in concluding that your recovery has been rapid and, I hope, permanent. No, don't limp, old man. That won't do. The second is to make inquiries respecting a donkey—to wit, one Butterfly."

"Oh!" remarked Entwistle. "Anything wrong? What are the symptoms?"

"A bad form of absentitis," replied Peter grimly. "Don't you know?"

The vet shook his head.

"Continue," he said, as he handed his tobacco-pouch to his caller.

"The brute never came back. In his hurry my son forgot to mention it—he was recalled by wire, and the young bounder never even dropped me a postcard. Now I'm on Butterfly's track. Can you assist me in my quest?"

"Sorry," replied Entwistle, taking the pouch and deliberately filling his briar. "Stay. I did mention to Billy that the animal ought to be shod. Why not inquire of the various blacksmiths on the way to Tarleigh? Let me see: there's Schofield's in Cook Street, Barnes's in Forge Lane, and Thomas's in Dyke Street—they are all just off Chumley Old Road. How did you come into Barborough—by train?"

"No, I walked as far as the tram terminus," replied Barcroft Senior.

"If you like I'll run you back in my car," suggested the vet. "We'll look the blacksmiths up on our way. Any news of your friend Norton?"

"Not a sign or a word."

"H'm!"

Entwistle shrugged his shoulders. Peter looked at him keenly.

"Why that 'h'm'?" he asked.

"Only—by the bye, have the police been informed?"

Barcroft shook his head.

"Not by me," he replied. "I'm inclined to think that he'll turn up again in a day or two. It may be a form of eccentricity encouraged by the excitement of the raid."

"Yes," agreed the vet. "Three days ago. Yes, it is quite about time he put in an appearance. Well, excuse me a moment. I'll tell Jarvis to bring the car round."

"Sure I'm not putting you out?" asked Peter.

"On the contrary—delighted. As a matter of fact, I have to see a horse belonging to a farmer over Windyhill way, so it will be killing two birds with one stone. Now for this bad case of absentitis."

Inquiries at two blacksmiths were without satisfactory result. The third, who happened to be the man who had shod the refractory Butterfly, could only state that the last he saw of the animal was that it was scampering along Jumbles Lane, and that the trap still remained in a shed in his yard.

"Th' oughtn't ta' be much trouble to trace yon animal," concluded the smith. "A champion she were—a right down champion, mark you. They may clip her coat or dock her tail or change her colour, but 'tis her size as they can't alter. Meantimes I'll keep a look-out, master, and if I hears aught——"

"Going to report the matter to the police?" asked Entwistle, as the pair re-entered the car.

"I think not," replied Peter. "It might end in the representative of the law running in every itinerant donkey owner on sight. I think I'll enlist the services of the Press to the tune of an eighteenpenny advertisement."

Outside the newspaper offices a crowd had collected to read the latest bulletin:

"Destroyer Action in the North Sea. German torpedo-boats destroyed. British Naval Airmen rescued from sinking enemy craft."

Making his way through the throng Peter entered the office, gave in his advertisement and bought a paper.

"That's great!" he ejaculated as he read the brief report. "Billy's pals, Fuller and Kirkwood, saved by one of our destroyers. By Jove, Entwistle, who says that the British Navy is sitting tight in harbour? Whenever there's an opportunity our lads in navy blue are on it."

"Then why the deuce confine the facts to a few bald lines?" asked the vet. "The job's done properly, and a stirring story it would make! Something to buck up people at home. Instead, you have to rely upon your imagination, which is apt to let you down."

"Give it up," said Peter the optimist. "All I know is that we are top dog, and everything will pan out all right in the end."

"Granted," agreed Entwistle. "The Navy's all right; the New Army is splendid—we'll muddle through somehow, in spite of the miserable legacy of the Wait and See crowd. There's a hymn beginning 'A people who in darkness sat.' That sums up the whole state of the civil population of Great Britain. To my mind the nation resembles a mass of iron filings spread out on a sheet of paper—all sixes and sevens. A magnet will instantly cause those particular pieces of metal to fly into orderly formation following the lines of magnetic force: a Man will be able to do the same with the nation, only, unfortunately, we haven't yet found the Man. We as Britons trust too much to chance—to a sort of voluntary organisation of labour. Result, every man is asking why some one else doesn't do his bit and tries to persuade himself that he is a sort of indispensable himself, I shouldn't be surprised if the war ends in a patched-up peace."

"No fear," asserted Barcroft firmly—so emphatically that Entwistle almost relaxed his grip upon the steering wheel and narrowly avoided collision with a brewer's dray. "There'll be nothing of the sort. The men who are now fighting mean to see the business through and not leave the horrors of war to be repeated with triple violence as a legacy to their children and their children's children. It's got to be done—and done it will be, even if it takes another two years."

When in due course the car arrived at the narrow lane leading to Ladybird Fold, Entwistle, somewhat to his companion's astonishment, insisted upon driving right up to the house.

"No hurry," commented the vet. "I like taking a car along a tricky path. Hullo! there are your dogs, Barcroft. They seem to know that I'm something in the animal line, and wish to be run over in order to give me a job."

The car came to a standstill at the house. Peter descended, to be overwhelmed with the noisy and frantic attentions of Ponto and Nan.

"Come in," he said, "May as well have tea with us."

"Thanks, I will," replied Entwistle; then pointing in the direction of "The Croft," the tiled roof of which was just visible above the ridge of a hill, "Is that where Norton hangs out? I've heard of the place. What sort of a show is it?"

"Come and see for yourself," said Barcroft. "There'll be time for a stroll before tea. I have the key, thanks to the magnificent condescension of Mrs. What's-her-name, Norton's generalissimo and domestic help. Why are you anxious to see the place? Thinking of renting it and being my nearest neighbour if Norton fails to return?"

"Perhaps," laughed Philip Entwistle. "When I retire, and I cannot see myself doing that yet."

"I wouldn't," said Peter gravely. "Retirement is a rotten state for a professional man to enter into. Sudden dislocation of his routine, nothing to occupy his mind—result, he generally pegs out in a couple of years. I've noticed it scores of times."

"It's all very well for you literary fellows to talk," protested Entwistle. "You can never complain of overwork."

"There you are mistaken," said Barcroft. "I admit I slack off a little now, but at one time I dare not. It may seem easy for a fellow to knock off a couple of thousand words a day, but try it for a year and see how it feels. Remember, it isn't the actual work of putting pen to paper. One has to think, and think jolly hard. Do you remember some years ago a man tried to cover a thousand miles in a thousand consecutive hours? One mile an hour day and night. Doesn't seem much, but imagine what it means."

"You seem to have done pretty well out of it," remarked Entwistle.

"It took some doing," confessed Peter. "I can recall a certain Christmas Eve when, with two other congenial spirits, I sat in a fireless attic in Town. We were literally on our beam ends—too jolly proud to sample the fatted calf that awaited us in our respective parents' homes. I think we had sevenpence halfpenny between us."

"Sounds cheerful."

"Precisely. However, being fresh-air fiends even in those days, we had left the window open——"

"And some philanthrophic soul threw in a big parcel of provender?"

"Into the attic window of a six-storeyed house? Hardly. No; a pigeon flew in. It never flew out again, for in less than twenty minutes it was roasting in front of the landlady's kitchen fire. That same evening one of my companions in distress received an unexpected guinea for a pot-boiler, and there was no longer famine in the land."

The two men had now climbed the hill and were outside the front door of The Croft. The house was considerably smaller than Ladybird Fold, although built on the same principle. At one time it had been a farm house, but most of the outbuildings had been removed. Standing on higher ground it commanded even a more extensive outlook than that enjoyed by the Barcrofts; in fact, almost the whole of Barborough could be discerned.

Within, the place was plainly furnished. The ground floor consisted of stone flags on which were spread large mats. The fireplace was large and at one time boasted of a chimney corner and settle. In the grate a fire had been laid in anticipation of Mr. Norton's return.

"I'm just going upstairs to shut those windows," said Peter. "I suppose Norton's D.T. forgot to close them. Do you want to have a look round the upper rooms?"

"Not with this ankle. It feels a bit painful," replied Entwistle. "If you don't mind I'll wait here."

Directly he heard the sound of Barcroft's footsteps through the raftered ceiling Entwistle stole softly to the desk that stood in the corner of the room. Slipping on a pair of thin gloves and producing a bundle of keys from his trouser's pocket he set deliberately to work to open the locked drawers, for in contrast to Peter Barcroft's easy-going methods Andrew Norton had locked everything up, notwithstanding his supposedly temporary visit to Ladybird Fold on the night of the raid.

In less than thirty seconds Entwistle had the desk open. Deftly he went through a pile of papers, as brazenly as Andrew Norton had examined the manuscript on Peter's bureau. In quantity there was very little: a small batch of tradesmen's receipts, a notebook half filled with calculations evidently referring to electrical problems, a few letters that seemed of no interest except to the writers and their recipient, and an unfinished manuscript written on two sheets of foolscap, the opening sentences of which were as follows:

> "Whenever you have an opportunity of visiting Dartmoor I should strongly advise you to take it. It is fairly easy to reach from Plymouth. Even in the depth of winter the rugged uplands have their charm. When last in that neighbourhood I took coach to Totnes: Every few hours a boat runs to Dartmouth. If tide permits, I ought to add. The Dart is a charmingly picturesque river. In the town itself there is much to be seen. Several of the old houses, especially in the Butter-walk, are worthy of close inspection. The castle is open to visitors. Every facility for tourists and visitors in the town. Some fishing to be had in the river. Better hauls are to be obtained in Start Bay. It is advisable to take a professional

boatman, as the tide is tricky and at times dangerous. Sailing boats can be hired by the day or hour. Zealous devotees of the piscatorial art will have no cause to regret their choice of this fishing centre. Up the river, above Totnes, trout abound. Rules and regulations relating to the close seasons are by no means drastic."

Philip Entwistle chuckled as he perused this document.

"Sort of thing that would easily pass the Press Censor," he said to himself, "At first sight a kind of extract from a guide book to Devonshire. Quite harmless—I think not. *Now let me jot down the first letter of each sentence*: WIE (that's promising) WEIT (better) IST (better still) ES (now we begin to see light. German for a dead cert) BIS ZUR KLIPPEN HOHE, which, translated, means, 'What is the distance to the summit of the cliffs?' That's good enough. I'll take the liberty of borrowing this document. I must risk friend Norton returning before to-morrow."

Carefully refolding the papers the vet, placed them in his inside coat-pocket, then having slipped the catch of the window, he awaited Peter's return.

"Hope I haven't kept you?" inquired Barcroft.

"Not at all," was the prompt reply.

"By the bye," remarked Peter as the pair retraced their steps to Ladybird Fold, "this might interest you. I meant to have shown it you before, but somehow I forgot."

He handed Entwistle a copy of the document that had been found on the body of the German airman.

Philip Entwistle read it carefully.

"Ha! A price on your head, eh?" he remarked.

"I don't take it seriously," said Peter. "It may be genuine. Billy handed it to me just as the train was leaving the station. He had no time to explain. Usual family failing, I suppose—leaving things to the last minute."

Entwistle made no reply to his companion's remarks. He was thinking deeply, trying to piece together certain items that had already been brought to his notice.

"I won't tell him just yet," he soliloquised. "Must make sure of my ground first."

After tea Entwistle drove away, ostensibly to visit a farmer at Windyhill. As a matter of fact he stopped at the Waterloo Hotel, retired to a private room and made a careful copy of the document he had annexed from The Croft.

"So that's how they communicate with him," he mused. "Simple solution when you've been given the tip. The next point is: how does he convey his information to them?" Late that night Entwistle returned from Windyhill by a loop route that passed within half a mile of The Croft. Driving his car off the road and on to a patch of waste land he extinguished the lights. This done he walked over the moor to The Croft, opened the unlatched window, entered the house and replaced the borrowed document.

Then, conscious of a good day's work accomplished, he went home, to gather up the tangled skeins of the complicated task in hand.

CHAPTER XXI
ON THE TRAIL

AT ten o'clock the following morning Peter Barcroft had a visitor. The announcement, delivered by Mrs. Carter, was greeted with a flow of forcible language.

"Tell the blithering idiot I can't see him now," shouted Mr. Barcroft. "I'm busy. He must call again in an hour's time."

The Little Liver Pill departed with the message, to return with the information that the caller came with news of "that there moke."

"In that case, show him in," decided Peter.

The informant was a short, thick-set, bowlegged man, with features that had cunning stamped indelibly on every line. His watery blue eyes and stubbly grey moustache contrasted vividly with his reddish complexion, the colour of which reached its maximum intensity at the tip of his turned-up nose. "The straight tip, guv'ner, an' no questions axed," began the man, winking solemnly.

"What d'ye mean?" demanded Peter.

"Wot I says," replied the slightly inebriated one. "You offers in this 'ere paper a bloomin' quid to any bloke as gives information about your moke. 'Ere's the bloke—me. Na, 'ow abaht it?"

"Can you produce the animal?" asked Barcroft.

"Wot! Tike me fer a bloomin' conjurer? D'ye fink as 'ow I can make a bloomin' moke come outer me 'at like a rabbit?"

"In that case I don't think I'll trouble you any further," said Peter, placing his hand on the bell.

"'Old 'ard, guv'ner!" interrupted the man. "You mistakes my meanin.' Wot I says is this, if you'll pardon my manner o' speech. I knows where your donkey is. A chap wot I owes a grudge to 'as pinched it. You pay me the quid, I'll give you the straight tip, s'long as you don't bring my name inter it, an' there you are. You gets yer moke back agen an' it's a jimmy o' goblin well spent."

Peter considered the points raised. He felt disinclined to treat with the rascal. He might have telephoned for the police, but it was hardly a case of blackmail. Quite possibly at the threat of the law the fellow might be cowed; on the other hand he might shut up like an oyster. Again, the whole story might be a cock-and-bull yarn with the idea of getting money.

"Very well," said Barcroft at length. "I agree. Now tell me where the animal is."

"Steady on, guv'ner," protested the man. "'Ow abaht it?—the quid, I means."

"I've promised," said Peter. "My word is your bond."

"Sooner 'ave the brass."

"When I regain possession of the animal," decided the lawful owner firmly. "You give me your name and address and directly I recover my property I will send you the money. You cannot reasonably expect me to trust you, an utter stranger, with a sovereign on the off-chance that I may get the animal back on the strength of your information. In fact, rather than do so, I would let the donkey go. Now, make up your mind quickly. My time is precious."

The informer scratched the back of his head. "Look 'ere, guv'ner," he began. "I don't want to be 'ard on yer——"

"You won't, my man," interrupted Peter grimly. "Now, yes or no: which is it to be?"

"Orl right," exclaimed the man in a tone of virtuous resignation. "I'll tell, only you might 'ave parted with that there quid on the nail. I won't give yer me name, but p'raps you won't object ter me a-comin' round an' collectin' the brass when you've got the moke back?"

To this Peter assented.

"You'll find the donkey at Bigthorpe," continued the fellow. "Third archway of the viaduct across Thorpe Beck—Stigler's the name o' the bloke wot pinched 'er, although she trotted into 'is father's place down in Barborough. Stigler's a bad 'un, so yer wants to be pretty fly or 'e'll be sellin' 'er to some one. That's the straight tip, guv'ner, an' don't you ferget it— third archway o' Thorpe Beck Viaduct. Supposin' I looks in fer that quid this day week?"

"Very good," agreed Peter, as he showed his visitor to the door. "By the bye, what sort of man is this Mr. Stigler?"

"I reckon as 'ow 'e's a bit of a bruiser," was the not unexpected reply.

When his caller had taken his departure Barcroft reviewed the situation. Bruiser or no bruiser Mr. Stigler had to be tackled, and Peter was not a man to be intimidated. He would go at once to Bigthorpe. But perhaps it would be as well to have some one with him. He thought of Philip Entwistle; he remembered his new-found friend remarking that he was not particularly busy.

Although he detested having to use the telephone—he would much rather have taken the trouble to go into Barborough to broach the matter, only time was of importance—Peter rang up the vet. The reply was to the effect that Mr. Entwistle was away from home and was not expected back until to-morrow.

"That's done it," muttered Barcroft, "I'll go alone."

It was normally a two hours' railway journey to Bigthorpe, a fairly large town in the East Riding of Yorkshire, but owing to various unforeseen delays the clocks were striking four when Peter reached his destination.

Having obtained direction from a porter as to the nearest way to Thorpe Beck Viaduct Peter walked out of the station, and to his surprise ran into the missing Andrew Norton.

"Hullo!" exclaimed the spy, somewhat guardedly, for he had to feel his ground. "I hardly expected to see you here."

"Nor did I," replied Peter extending his hand, which the other grasped with well-assumed cordiality.

"You've heard?"

"I've heard nothing."

"I wired to my housekeeper yesterday," explained the *soi-disant* Norton. "Had a sort of nervous breakdown—complete loss of memory."

"The Zep. raid, I suppose?" asked Peter sympathetically.

"Yes, yes, precisely—the Zep. raid, confound it!" said the German hurriedly. "I remember the bombs dropping, and I ran, goodness knows where. Must have wandered about all night. Have some recollection of finding myself at a strange railway station. Eventually I arrived at Bigthorpe, not even remembering my name and address until I found my registration card in my pocket. Deuced useful things those cards. However, since I was at Bigthorpe, I thought I would stay there a couple of days or so to restore my shattered nerves. Just back by the 4.38."

"Can you postpone your return for another day?" asked Peter. "I'm returning to-morrow. But perhaps I oughtn't to detain you, although everything's all right at The Croft."

"Is it?" asked the spy. "Thanks awfully. No. I'm afraid I can't stop here any longer."

"In that case I'll see you anon," said Peter. "Oh, while I think of it: where were you staying here? I know nothing about the place and must get a room at a comfortable hotel."

Von Eitelwurmer considered for a moment. He was not altogether sure that Barcroft was not "pulling his leg." Early that morning the "Trone" had arrived at a British port, and on landing the spy had successfully maintained the role of McDonald the repatriated prisoner from Eylau. He was now returning to Barborough, with a view to making careful inquiries as to whether it would be quite safe to return to his house at Tarleigh.

"Where was I staying?" repeated the spy. "At the 'Antelope.' Wouldn't advise you, though. Not at all comfortable—catering rotten, rooms wretchedly cold and draughty. Well, *au revoir*, Barcroft. May look you up to-morrow night."

"Do," replied Peter cordially. "You know the time."

The question as to how he was to get the donkey home in the event of Butterfly being found had hardly occurred to her owner until Peter was in the train. In any case he could not hope to return that night. To-morrow he might make arrangements with the railway company. Meanwhile he must secure quarters at an hotel.

"I'll try the 'Antelope,'" he decided. "What's good enough for Norton ought to suit me. Fortunately I am not altogether unaccustomed to discomforts."

The exterior of the hotel rather belied his friend's disparaging remarks; the interior even more so. The place seemed replete with modern conveniences.

"I've been recommended by Mr. Andrew Norton, who has been staying here for the last three or four days," announced Peter. "I require a room."

"No gentleman of that name has been staying here, sir," replied the hotel clerk. "At least, not recently. Yes, sir, this is the only 'Antelope.' Perhaps you would like to see the registration papers?"

Peter examined the documents. None were made out in the name of Andrew Norton, nor were any filled in in his handwriting.

"Perhaps I have made a mistake," he said. "But that is of little consequence. If you will let me have a room— —"

Ten minutes later Barcroft was on his way to Thorpe Beck Viaduct. Altogether he could not form a satisfying solution to Norton's statement, until he came to the conclusion that in his excitable state of mind his friend had muddled up the names of two or more hotels.

"By Jove! I will take the rise out of him when I see him again," he chuckled. "Fancy putting up at the 'Pig and Whistle,' most likely, and imagining he was at the 'Antelope.' That's a great jape."

Presently he came in sight of the viaduct, the spaces between the lofty granite arches of which were utilised as cow-sheds and stables.

No, Mr. Stigler was not there, so a halfwitted, deformed lad informed him. A donkey? Yes, there had been a donkey there. Mr. Stigler had sold it that afternoon to a pedlar living at Scarby. Where was Scarby? A matter of about ten miles and right on the coast. Anybody at Scarby would tell him where old Joe Pattercough lived.

Peter Barcroft rose to the occasion. Added difficulties only increased his determination to see the thing through. He decided to cancel his room at the "Antelope" and proceed by the first train to Tongby, the nearest station to the seaside hamlet of Scarby.

CHAPTER XXII
THE STRUGGLE ON THE CLIFFS

"A MATTER O' fower moiles, sir," replied an old fisherman in answer to Peter's inquiry as to the way to Scarby. "That is, if you'll be taking t' cliff path, which I wouldn't advise you, seeing as 'ow you'm a stranger. 'Tain't pertickler safe is yon path. Follow the righthand road. 'Tis a bit roughish in parts, but main passable."

Mr. Barcroft thanked the man for his information and set out briskly upon his way. Twilight had already set in, to add to the difficulties of the last stage of the journey of the intrepid Peter. Ahead rose the steep hill terminating in a frowning cliff—the first of three such ridges that lay betwixt him and Scarby. Away on his left he could discern a momentary glimpse of the North Sea, now grey and sullen and mottled by patches of fog that drifted slowly with the faint westerly breeze.

At a mile from Tongby railway station he struck the fork roads. The one to the left was the cliff-path, an almost grass-grown track, marked at regular intervals by whitewashed stones—necessary guides for the coastguards on a pitch-black night when a false step might hurl the incautious pedestrian to his death over the brink of a three-hundred-foot cliff. The right-hand way was a little *better*, although, judging by its condition, rarely used except by country carts. On either side the ground was rugged and thickly covered with gorse.

Wilder grew the countryside as Peter breasted the first of the three hills. Stunted trees, standing out against the crimson afterglow of the sky, assumed weird and fantastic shapes. To the faint moaning of the wind and the murmur of the sea came an accompaniment in the form of the cries of countless seabirds that find a nesting-place in the frowning face of those almost perpendicular cliffs.

Inland all was darkness. The narrow valleys contained human habitations, no doubt, but there was not a sign of their presence.

Peter's thoughts turned to his son as he looked seaward. Somewhere out there—it might be a matter of a few miles or of hundreds—Billy was serving King and country, perhaps snugly sheltered in the "Hippodrome's" wardroom, or, on the other hand, cutting through the darkness at an altitude of several hundred feet. It was not a pleasant task on a late autumnal night. With his trained imagination Peter could picture his boy out there—simply because of the German Emperor's insane ambition.

"Not content to let well alone," soliloquised Peter, "even when the German Empire was on the high road to commercial success and internal prosperity, the All Highest must butt in and try to upset everything. Incidentally Wilhelm has done the British Empire a lasting service. He has cemented it far more effectively than centuries of legislation. He has welded it into a homogeneous whole; he has awakened every Briton worthy of the name to a sense of his individual responsibility to the colossal task that confronts him. And, by Jove, we mean to see this business through. No half measures. A lasting peace built upon the ruins of German militarism."

Peter's reveries were suddenly interrupted by the sound of creaking cart-wheels and the steady patter of a beast of burden.

"Wonder if that is Butterfly?" he thought. "Now, if Mr. Pattercough is of the same type as friend Stigler and a bit of a tough customer I'd best lie low. Somehow I hardly like to argue the point about the lawful ownership of a donkey in this desolate spot."

There were plenty of places of concealment. Barcroft selected the shelter afforded by a gorse-bush close to the left hand side of the road. Immediately opposite was a beaten track that evidently effected a junction with the cliff path. At any rate, it wound in that direction, following the steeply sloping sides of a narrow, rugged valley.

The cart approached slowly. The driver seemed in no hurry, for he made no attempt either by word of mouth or by the application of his whip to hasten the animal. Only when the vehicle was opposite Peter's place of concealment did the man utter a subdued "Woa."

The donkey—for such it was—made no attempt to stop. "That's Butterfly for a dead cert," commented Peter.

The man uttered an imprecation, jumped from the cart and tugged viciously at the animal's bridle. Then, by main force, he backed the donkey a short distance along the side track.

"Plenty o' time," Barcroft heard him remark. "Better an hour too early than five minutes too late."

"Awkward habit, expressing one's thoughts aloud," mused Peter. "I do it myself occasionally, and I know. Now, what are you doing with a loaded cart on this unfrequented road at this time of night? I scent a mystery. I'll wait an hour and see what happens. If nothing, then I will kick myself for being an inquisitive ass."

The pedlar was not going to be inactive. Unharnessing the donkey—Peter was now absolutely convinced that it was Butterfly—he led the animal to a patch of grass-land hidden from the road by the bushes, a task requiring considerable physical strength. This done he backed the cart from the path until the gorse hid it from the watcher's sight.

Ten long minutes passed. The pedlar, swinging his arms vigorously, for the night air was chilly, made no attempt to look up or down the road. The person or persons he expected were evidently not approaching from that direction. Presently he walked to the cart, removed something from under the tarpaulin—it was too dark to see what the article was—and set off along the side track.

At fifty yards he surmounted a steep rise and disappeared the other side. The sound of his footsteps, deadened by the nature of the soil, quickly died away.

"Now I'll investigate," decided Barcroft. "If he returns in a hurry there'll be trouble. Friend Pattercough looks like a quarrelsome card. However, I'll risk it."

He stole cautiously to the place where the donkey and cart stood. Butterfly, indifferent to the attentions of her lawful master, browsed steadily at the scanty herbage. The cart, although inanimate, was far more interesting. It was piled high with faggots and bundles of brushwood, a tarpaulin being tightly lashed over the top of the load. Mingled with the scent of the newly-cut wood was the faint odour of petrol.

Without the slightest hesitation Barcroft probed the load with his stick. The ferrule grated against metal—the side of a tin. Again and again he tried; the bottom of the cart was packed with petrol-cans.

"Now, if I set fire to this little lot who would stand the racket?" inquired Peter. "This is obviously intended to be used illicitly—for supplying German submarines, although I can't be sure on that point. On the other hand, how would I stand under the Defence of the Realm regulations if I started a gorgeous bonfire? An hour too soon, he said; well, there's a quarter of an hour or twenty minutes gone, I should imagine. Remains enough time for me to get to Scarby, rout out the coastguards and put a stopper on this little game."

With this praiseworthy resolution Barcroft hurried off, keeping to the grassy ground in order to deaden the sound of his footsteps. His prowess as a long-distance runner had not entirely departed, although lack of training tried his wind sorely.

At the outskirts of the darkened village he came to a row of grey lime-washed cottages in front of which a tall flagstaff loomed up against the misty starlight.

"Halt!" exclaimed a hoarse voice peremptorily.

Peter halted. Confronting him was a greatcoated, gaitered, bearded man in seaman's uniform.

"'Gainst orders to use this path after dark," quoth the coastguardsman. "What's your name? And what are you doing running like this at this time o' night?"

"How many men have you at the station?" asked Barcroft breathlessly.

"Eh? What do you want this information for?" demanded the man suspiciously. "You'd best come along with me an' give no trouble. Strikes me there's something that ain't proper jonnick."

Barcroft preceded the seaman up the shingled path leading to the watch house.

"Look here, my man," he said authoritatively. "You had better inform your chief officer and turn out the detachment. I've hurried here expressly to tell you that a man from the village, Pattercough by name, is running a cargo of petrol. Barcroft's my name. I have documents to prove it. Also I have a son a commissioned officer in the Service, as you will find if you refer to a Navy List."

"In that case I ask your pardon," replied the coastguard, whose badges proclaimed him to be a chief petty officer. "I'm in charge, sir. This station is partly closed down since the war. I've only a few Boy Scouts to give you a hand—an' smart, plucky youngsters they are, too."

"Any special constables in the village?"

"Not one, sir; in fact, there ain't what one might call an able-bodied man in the place, barring this Pattercough. Tribunal exempted him 'evings only knows what for."

"Then turn out the Scouts," said Peter. "They'll come in jolly useful. There's no time to be lost."

Quickly half a dozen of the lads were on the spot, falling in at the word of command from the patrol leader. In a few words Barcroft explained the situation, enjoining silence until the petty officer gave the word for action.

"I'll just telephone through to Tongby and let our chaps know," said the coastguard.

In orderly formation the party set off to the place where the pedlar had left his cart. At "Scouts' Pace"—alternately walking and running—the distance was quickly covered. Butterfly and the load were still in sombre isolation. "He made off in that direction," whispered Peter.

"To Black Ghyll Bay then," replied the petty officer. "Artful bounder! He knew when our patrols pass, and chose his time."

With redoubled caution the party set off in single file, the sailor leading the way and Peter following up at the rear of the Scouts. Not a sound betrayed their presence—it was mainly owing to the fact that they all wore well-used foot gear.

Presently Peter found himself on the point of cannoning into the back of the Scout just ahead of him. The party had halted. With out the slightest confusion they concealed themselves behind a row of bushes that grew almost on the edge of the cliff. The petty officer raised one hand and pointed.

Through the darkness Barcroft could just distinguish the outlines of a human form crouching in the gorge barely ten yards on his right front, where the cliff began to fall away and form a ravine known as Black Ghyll.

At intervals the man in hiding raised his head and peered cautiously over the thick bush. Not once did he look behind. His attention was centred solely upon the foreshore or else seaward; he was totally oblivious of the fact that he was being watched intently by eight pairs of eyes.

Out to sea everything seemed swallowed up in pitch-black darkness. Only the measured beating of the groundswell upon the shingly shore gave the watchers any indication, apart from their local knowledge, that the wide North Sea was almost at their feet. The stars, too, had disappeared from view, for the mist had increased and was now threatening to develop into a regular sea-fog.

Suddenly the darkness was pierced by a faint ray of light emanating from a mere pinprick of luminosity. Short flash—obscuration—long flash—obscuration—short flash: that was all, but sufficient to indicate that out in that void of Cimmerian gloom some one was signalling.

The suspect rose and leaned forward. It looked as if he were spread-eagled over the gorse-bush. For quite a minute he remained there, then leaving his place of concealment he made his way towards the beach, crouching as stealthily as a panther behind every obstacle until he made sure of his ground.

Perhaps it was the strain of watching in the darkness; perhaps the thought that the suspect might escape; but whatever the motive the fact remained that one of the Scouts, uttering a loud yell, broke from cover and dashed towards the man, brandishing his staff like a Berserk.

"That's done it!" mentally ejaculated Peter. The premature and unauthorised action left no alternative.

"At him, lads!" shouted the petty officer. The fellow stood his ground, expostulating angrily. But his words fell unheeded. Like a pack of hounds the eager and alert youngsters literally threw themselves upon the suspect, and bore him to the ground.

Over and over they rolled, the gorse crackling under their weight. Only a few gaunt stumps prevented the struggling mob from tumbling over the brink of the fearful abyss. Unable to bear a hand Peter and the petty officer stood well-nigh breathless with suspense, expecting every minute to see the suspect and his assailants topple into space.

The struggle was short-lived. The fellow's efforts at resistance ceased. Bound hand and foot and with the ten-stone patrol leader sitting on his chest he realised that the game was up.

"Get your staves, lads," ordered the patrol-leader. "Form a stretcher. We'll carry him as far as the cart."

"Strikes me I hear engines," declared the coastguardsman. "There, what's that?"

A dull, rasping sound and the splash of disturbed water broke the silence. A moment later the night breeze carried the unmistakable noise of a vessel's engines running at full speed ahead.

The petty officer was quick to act. Raising his hands to his mouth he shouted in stentorian tones:

"Ship ahoy! Go full speed astern instantly. You're heading straight for Black Ghyll."

The clang of the engine-room telegraph bell followed quickly, to the accompaniment of short, crisp orders and the trample of boots upon a metal deck.

It was already too late. With a rending crash the vessel, whatever she might be, ran bows on to the jagged rocks.

"That's done it! Her number's up," exclaimed the petty officer. "Now, lads, four of you come with me. There's work to be done there, I reckon. The others stay with this gentleman and guard the prisoner till we return."

"Look here," said the captive in well-nigh breathless expostulation. "You've made a rotten mistake. Spoilt everything."

Peter felt his heart give a furious beat. Regardless of regulations he bent over the prostrate prisoner and struck a match.

The flickering flame revealed the indignant features of Philip Entwistle.

CHAPTER XXIII
ON THE ROCKS

"So I haven't been able to chuck you fellows yet," remarked Lieutenant-commander Tressidar. "And what is more I see no likelihood at present of so doing. We've just had a wireless to proceed east to a position somewhere off the mouth of the Humber."

"We are not at all fed up with your hospitality, Tress," replied Fuller, "only we ought to have been on board the old 'Hippo' long ago. I think, if there's a chance, we ought to get ashore, report to the Commander-in-Chief and await orders."

The "Antipas" was steaming at a good twenty knots. It was late in the afternoon; the sea calm, the sky slightly overcast. With a steadily-rising glass the weather showed indication of continuing fine, notwithstanding the presence of patches of sea-fog.

Towards sunset the fog increased until it was no longer safe for the destroyer to maintain her speed. Fishing boats, dauntlessly risking the submarine menace, were frequently in these waters. To tear blindfold through the dense mist would be courting disaster.

The slowing down of the engines brought the three airmen on deck.

"Fog!" exclaimed Kirkwood. "Rough luck. I thought that we were entering port when the skipper rang down for easy ahead."

"Pretty thick, too," added Barcroft. "It's as much as I can do to see the bridge. Beastly calm, too; what do you say to returning to our little rubber of dummy?"

"Now I'm here I'll stop," decided Fuller, drawing his coat across his chest. "Hullo! they're taking soundings. That looks as if we were nearing shore."

For nearly an hour the "Antipas" literally "smelt her way." Darkness had fallen, and with it the fog bank increased in density and dimensions. No longer was it possible to discern anything beyond a couple of yards. No discordant hoot blared from the syren, no navigation lights were shown. Beyond slowing down nothing more could be done, owing to war conditions, to safeguard the destroyer from risks of collision.

"Hullo, you fellows!" exclaimed the lieutenant of the destroyer as, clad in oilskins, sou'wester and sea boots, he groped his way for'ard. "Have we made it too comfortable for you down below?"

"Didn't know that it was your 'trick,'" remarked Barcroft.

"Neither is it. That's one of the penalties of serving on a destroyer. You never know when you're off duty. The skipper's just spoken through: we're on the track of a strafed U-boat. Picked her up by microphone."

"Here's to the bridge, then," decided Fuller. "Come on, you would-be card-players. Let's see the fun."

"One of the advantages of going dead slow, I suppose," commented Tressidar as his guests rejoined him. "We've cut across the trail of a submarine, that's certain. Come in, and see how things are progressing."

The lieutenant-commander opened the door of the chart-room. Against one bulkhead stood the receiver of the submarine-signalling apparatus. Standing in front of it was a bluejacket with both ear-pieces clipped to his ears. With his left hand he was alternately actuating the switch that connects both receivers.

"Right dead on, sir," he reported. "Less than a couple of cables' lengths ahead, I'll allow."

Behind him stood the helmsman at the steam-steering gear, his eyes fixed upon the cryptic movements of the operator's hands, as the latter transmitted the course to the quartermaster.

The principle of the microphone signalling apparatus is simple enough. In the vessel's hold and as far beneath the waterline as possible, are two metal tanks each filled with water and containing two sensitive instruments that readily pick up sounds transmitted through the medium afforded by the sea. One tank is placed on the starboard the other on the port side, and both are connected by wires with the receiver in the chart-room.

Supposing the operator hears the thud of a distant propeller, and the sound is more distinct from the port side he knows that the submerged vessel is somewhere in that direction. Conversely, the sound being greater in the right-hand receiver he is able to locate the object emitting the sound as being on the starboard side of the ship. When the volume of sound passing through both receivers is equal the operator knows that the vessel's bows are pointing practically "dead on" to the unseen but audible peril.

"That's all very fine," remarked Kirkwood. "But supposing that man has a cold in one ear. How is he to guard against being misled by the inequalities of hearing? I've heard of a fellow being deaf in one ear and not knowing it for months."

"The inventors have taken that into consideration," replied Tressidar. "That's why both ears are connected with the receiver on one side only of the vessel at a time. As he turns that switch from side to side both ears are listening to the sounds from the port and starboard tanks alternately. What's that?" he added, addressing the operator. "Three cables ahead? This won't do; she's gaining on us."

The skipper quitted the chart-room, followed by the three airmen. Coming from the lighted compartment; they were momentarily dazzled by the transition from artificial illumination to murky, pitch-black night.

"Increase speed to fifteen knots," ordered Tressidar. "Where there's water for that strafed U-boat there's enough for us.... Overhauling her? All right; twelve knots, then."

"Those fellows have plenty of nerve," remarked Barcroft, "or else they've no nerves at all. Suppose fog doesn't make the slightest difference to them when they are submerged, but to us it appears otherwise. What is that U-boat doing, I should like to know, plugging along at twelve knots and in the direction of the British coast?"

"Keeping a pressing appointment, perhaps," said the A.P. with a laugh.

"Many a true word spoken in jest, old bird," rejoined the flight-sub. "It is——"

"A little less talking there, if you please," interrupted Tressidar curtly.

The three airmen took the hint. It was only on very rare occasions that the genial lieutenant-commander "choked any one off." It was an indication of the mental strain upon the skipper of the "Antipas."

"By Jove! if she does come up," thought Barcroft. "It will be Third Single to Perdition for a set of skulking pirates. The fog is lifting, too. I can distinguish the wave-crests nearly a cable's length ahead. We'll be into another patch in another minute, though, worse luck."

Suddenly the watchers on the destroyer's bridge caught sight of a short series of flashes slightly on the port bow, and perhaps at a distance of a mile.

In a trice Tressidar brought his binoculars to bear upon the glimmer of light, thanking Heaven as he did so that a rift in the fog enabled him to spot the presence of the hunted Hun. The powerful night-glasses revealed the outlines of a conning-tower and twin periscopes just emerging from the waves. Then as quickly as it appeared the light vanished. It was enough. The lieutenant-commander could still discern the patch of phosphorescence that encircled the partly submerged U-boat.

"Starboard ten!" ordered Tressidar, at the same time telegraphing for full speed ahead both engines.

Before the destroyer could work up to her maximum speed her knife-like bows rasped and bit deeply into the hull of the doomed unterseeboot. An almost imperceptible jar as the quivering vessel glided over her prey, a smother of agitated water on either hand, and the deed was done. Another of the modern pirate craft had been dispatched to its last home.

"Voices ahead, sir," shouted the look-out man. "Land ahead! By smoke! We've done it."

The engine-room telegraph bell clanged shrilly. As the propeller blades bit the water with reversed action the "Antipas" began to lose way. It was too late.

With a shock that threw almost every officer and man to the deck the destroyer charged bows on to a ledge of rocks. Her forefoot lifted almost clear of the water, while to the accompaniment of the hiss of escaping vapour from a fractured main steam-pipe, the "Antipas" buckled amidships.

"Clear lower deck! All hands fall in facing outboard!" ordered the skipper.

From the mess-deck the "watch below," already roused by the impact of the destroyer with the ill-starred U-boat, came tumbling out, forming up in orderly silence to await further commands. Out of the steam-laden stokehold and engine-room staggered black-faced, partly-clad men, many suffering from the effects of terrible scalds, while others, too badly injured to help themselves, were assisted by their heroic comrades. Risking a hideous death in the partly-flooded engine-room the devoted "ratings" performed acts of valour that, although unseen and unheard of, represent the acme of courage. Fresh from the overheated stokehold and engine-room the survivors of the "Black Squad" found themselves faced with the immediate prospect of involuntary immersion in the chill waters of the North Sea.

"Ahoy!" shouted a seaman at the skipper's instigation. "Where are we?"

"'Ard aground," replied a voice through the darkness.

In spite of their hazardous position several of the crew laughed, and tried to switch on a husky cough to hide their levity from their officers. The unknown's reply was certainly brief and to the point, but hardly the sort of answer that Tressidar required.

"Silence there!" he ordered.

Then a boyish voice penetrated the night air.

"You're on Black Ghyll reef," it announced. "Do you require any assistance?"

"Not at present," replied the lieutenant-commander. "You might stand by, though, in case we do."

The after part of the "Antipas" was now a couple of feet beneath the water, and had settled on the sandy bottom of the bay. With the falling tide—it was just after high-water springs when the destroyer grounded—there was no immediate necessity to abandon ship. Nevertheless it was imperative that the injured men should be taken ashore, and assistance obtained as quickly as possible if there should be any possible chance of salving the wreck.

"Clear away the whaler!" was the next order.

The boat was manned and rowed cautiously towards the shore. Although the sea was calm the men were in total ignorance of the nature of the coast. Lacking local knowledge they were not even at all certain whether a landing might be effected. On either side rose the jagged points of vicious-looking rocks, while looming against the misty starlight could be discerned a range of frowning cliffs with no apparent break in the line of continuity.

"Thank God that there ain't a stiffish onshore breeze," muttered the coxswain of the whaler. "'Tain't 'arf a rotten crib."

"Boat ahoy!" came the same boyish hail from the invisible strand. "Starboard a bit.... You're close on the Double Fang. I'll tell you when to turn.... Now, straight in. It's all sand here."

The whaler's forefoot grounded on the soft shore. The coxswain, producing a small handlantern from the stern sheets flashed it upon the group of figures gathered at the water's edge four Boy Scouts.

"Crikey!" ejaculated the coxswain admiringly. "You're game'uns. Wot are you doing here at this time o' night?"

"We're coast-watching," replied the patrol leader. "We had just collared a spy when your vessel ran ashore. There's a chief petty officer of coastguard up the top of the cliff."

The lad did not think it necessary to explain that the petty officer had rather wisely declined to risk his neck by clambering down the precipitous face of the rugged wall of rock. At his age he lacked the steady head and sureness of foot that were essential for such feats of agility.

"Landing's easy enough when you knows 'ow," remarked the coxswain. "I've been sent ashore to find out. Look 'ere, we've a dozen or more badly injured hands aboard, an' we wants to get 'em off. Any chance of carrying 'em up those cliffs?"

The lad shook his head.

"Not up the cliffs," he explained. "There's a path up the valley. It leads to Scarby."

"Any doctors there?"

"None nearer than Tongby. We'll send a couple of Scouts there, if you like."

"P'raps you'd better," agreed the man. "It's a tidy 'andful for our Pills— our doctor, that is. All right, chummy, you might stand by and give us a hail when we come ashore again. 'Tis a rum crib, swelp me, if it ain't—but it might be worse."

The whaler backed from the shore, to return presently with a heavy load of wounded men and other members of the destroyer's crew told off to carry the injured to the nearest house.

Guided by the patrol leader the grim procession set out on its journey of pain. The fearfully scalded men, temporarily bandaged by the R.N.R. Surgeon Probationer borne on the destroyer's books as doctor, groaned and uttered involuntary cries of agony as, in spite of the care of the bearers, they were jolted along the narrow, uneven path.

Presently the scout came to a sudden halt. "There's a man lying at the foot of the Cliffs," he exclaimed. "Why, it's Pattercough, the man we were looking for when we captured the second spy."

A seaman bent over the body.

"Dead as a bloomin' doornail," he announced. "He's broke 'is bloomin' neck an' saved the 'angman a job, I'll allow that is, if he's the spy you says he was. Lead on, matey. The dead must look after themselves while this affair's under way."

At the meeting of the path with the by-road the patrol-leader stopped.

"It's straight on to Scarby," he explained. "Bennet," he added, addressing his companion. "You go with these sailors and show them the coastguard station. Then come back; bring the other fellows along with you if they've returned. I'll go to the beach again in case there are more to be shown the path up the valley."

Meanwhile Lieutenant-commander Ronald Tressidar was "standing by" his wrecked vessel. He had done everything he could in the interests of the crew. Until day broke it was impossible to form an accurate idea of the extent of the disaster. It was galling to lose his command; there would be a court of inquiry. Of the issue of that Tressidar had no misgivings. The "Antipas" had run ashore in the course of an action with an enemy submarine. The mishap was to be deplored, but it was unavoidable. The destruction of the hostile submarine had been accomplished. That was the object of the destroyer's *raison d'etre*.

"Can we be of any use?" asked Fuller.

"Not in the slightest, thanks," replied the youthful skipper. "The best you fellows can do is to go ashore. Goodness only knows if there's a railway anywhere in the neighbourhood. At any rate, you can make your way back to Rosyth, and better luck next time. If by any possible chance I can keep you clear of the court of inquiry I will do so. I know perfectly well that you want to be hard at it again, and the 'Hippodrome' seems likely to be particularly busy very shortly, according to all accounts."

"Good luck, old man!" said Fuller earnestly, The three airmen shook hands with the skipper, and dropping into the whaler were rowed shorewards.

"Hard lines on old Tress," declared Fuller. "He'll come out with flying colours, of course; but just fancy the poor fellow cooling his heels ashore waiting for another command when out there— —"

And with a comprehensive sweep of his hand he indicated the seemingly limitless expanse of the North Sea—the arena where the question of naval supremacy will be settled, let us hope once and for all time in favour of the glorious White Ensign.

CHAPTER XXIV
ENTWISTLE'S DECISION

"So this is the coastguard station?" asked Billy Barcroft of his youthful guide. "Any chance of getting a conveyance to the nearest station Tongby, I believe?"

"I am afraid not, sir."

"Even this donkey might be pressed into service," continued the flight-sub, indicating Butterfly, who, having been placed "under arrest," was browsing on the green surrounding the flagstaff. "Although I've had enough of donkeys to last me for some considerable time."

Little knowing that the animal under discussion was the self-same one that had given him the slip at Barborough, Billy, accompanied by his two comrades, entered the detached building known as the look-out house. The ground floor was utilised as a kind of store, where arms and nautical gear were kept. Above was a large room furnished like an office, in which was a telephone as well as a large telescope mounted on a tripod so as to command a clear view of the sea. Being night the windows were closely shuttered, while double doors prevented any stray beams from escaping into the night.

"Up aloft, sir," said the scout. "I'll telephone through and see if a trap or a car can be sent from Tongby. This is our mess room," he explained. "There's a good fire going. Hullo! There's some one here already. I think it's the gentleman who told us about the spy."

Seated on either side of the roaring fire were Peter Barcroft and Philip Entwistle. The former's face was turned away from the door, and at first Billy failed to recognise his parent. Nor did he the vet., for Entwistle's face was elaborately and liberally embellished with sticking-plaster, as the result of First Aid on the part of the Scouts following their determined onslaught on the brink of the cliff.

Entwistle had taken his gruelling in rightdown good part. He was still under nominal arrest, for having been made a prisoner he could only be released at the order of a superior officer. Already a report had been telephoned through and a reply was momentarily expected.

"I am not going to explain the whole business to you, Barcroft," said the vet, when Peter expressed his regret at the attack upon his neighbour, and still more so his astonishment at finding him under most peculiar circumstances on the cliff at Scarby. "Some day, perhaps. I had information—no matter how—that some one was in traitorous communication with enemy submarines. To bring home proofs of the principal's guilt it was necessary to tackle his subordinate. Unfortunately my plans were upset by the somewhat injudicious intervention of these youngsters—commendable as regards pluck and all that, but nevertheless it spoilt my investigations."

"I didn't know that you were in the detective line," remarked Peter.

Entwistle shrugged his shoulders.

"Perhaps I had better not commit myself by answering your question," he replied with a laugh that ended in a wince. It was no easy matter to smile with one's face smothered with sticking-plaster. "I hope you understand my reluctance to say anything more on the matter."

Peter nodded.

"All the same I shall look forward to the time when you are able to emerge from your shell," he said.

"By the bye," remarked the vet, "you haven't told me what brought you to this part of the world. It's taking a one-sided advantage when I ask if *you* are doing a bit of detective work."

"I was," admitted Mr. Barcroft.

Entwistle raised his eyebrows in mild surprise.

"Tracing the persons who stole my donkey—Butterfly," continued Peter. "I had the tip that the animal had been taken to Bigthorpe. Went there to follow up the clue, and strangely enough almost the first man I met was Norton."

"What was he doing at Bigthorpe?"

"I hardly know. Said something about a nervous breakdown. He seemed a bit upset, I thought."

"H'm!" Entwistle, gazed into the fire, deep in thought. "Is he returning to Tarleigh?"

"He's there already, I presume," replied Peter. "However, that has nothing to do with the case I am relating (Entwistle thought otherwise, but refrained from audible comment). At Bigthorpe I found that Butterfly had been sold to a man at Scarby, so on I came. Quite by accident I met the fellow on the road, kept out of sight and watched him go towards the cliffs. Went and had a look at his cart, discovered it laden with petrol-cans, so I made off immediately to inform the coastguard. The rest you know."

"As to that— —" began the vet.

The door being opened interrupted his remarks. Turning his head to see who the newcomers might be, he startled his companion by saying—"Bless my soul, it's young Barcroft."

"Hullo, pater!" said Billy in astonishment. "You here? This is a regular surprise." Peter got up from his chair.

"Pleased to see you, boy," he exclaimed. "As for the surprise, it's nothing. To-day has been a day of surprises. What brings you ashore?"

"We were in the destroyer that ran aground," explained the flight-sub. "But let me introduce you to Fuller—you've often heard me speak of him— and Bobby Kirkwood, who, as you know, was, and I hope will continue to be, my observer."

"I thought you were in the 'Hippodrome,'" remarked Barcroft Senior, after mutual introductions and when the three airmen had drawn their chairs close to the comforting fire.

"Officially we are now—at the present moment," said Fuller. "Unofficially we are toasting our toes on dry land. Before long we hope to be up in the air; I think I am correctly interpreting the wishes of my two energetic chums?"

Conversation was proceeding briskly when one of the Scouts, called to the telephone, reported that a car was on its way to Scarby to convey the airmen to Tongby, and that there was a train leaving the little place at eight in the morning for Bigthorpe, whence by the main line to the north they could reach Edinburgh by about noon.

"And this breaks up the party," quoth Billy as the motor drew up outside the station. "Well, good-bye, pater. Sorry time has been so short."

"Not so fast with your good-byes, my son," protested Peter. "We— Entwistle and I—are going into Tongby by this car. It may be a tight squeeze, but we'll risk that."

"But how about Butterfly?" asked Billy.

His father waved his hand deprecatingly.

"I've done with the brute," he replied. "She absolutely refused to greet me. I'm going to make a present of her to these youngsters as a kind of reminder of this night's work. If they don't want her, I suppose there are plenty of people in this village glad to keep her. Now, Entwistle, best leg forward. It's a long, long way to Tarleigh. By Jove! you'll have to explain those scratches when you return to your virtuous home."

Philip Entwistle merely responded with "Yes" with a preoccupied air. His work in connection with the affair had only just begun. Although a veterinary surgeon he was also an accredited member of the Secret Service, and upon the *soi-disant* Andrew Norton's arrival at Tarleigh as a new resident he had been informed of the suspicious nature of the newcomer. It was by design that he had misdirected Barcroft in the matter of the wrong train on the eve of the Barborough Zeppelin raid; but that was owing to the fact that he had mistaken the occupier of Ladybird Fold for the suspect, von Eitelwurmer.

Now arose the difficulty. Could he warn Barcroft of the dangerous character of the spy, without prejudice to his plans? At present it was undesirable, even on the damning evidence he had found at the spy's house, to cause von Eitelwurmer to be arrested. Better to let the fellow prosecute his activities a little longer, complete the chain of evidence and rope in his accomplices, if any, than to make the spy a prisoner without being able to make a clean sweep of all his works. Premature action would mar the elaborate mass of evidence that Entwistle was on the road to collect— evidence that would be far-reaching as far as the network of German espionage in England was concerned.

So for the present he decided to keep his own counsel regarding Andrew Norton. Not even a hint would he throw out concerning the tenant of The Croft. If he did so, Barcroft could not help showing antipathy to his friend Norton, and the latter, scenting danger, would be doubly wary.

Yet, knowing that there was a price on Peter Barcroft's head, although he did not as yet connect Norton's presence at Tarleigh with the Kaiser's blood-moneyed decree, Entwistle realised that he would have to keep a watchful eye upon his newly-found friend in order to guard him from the possibility of impending peril.

CHAPTER XXV
THE BOMBING EXPEDITION

OFF Zeebrugge once more. In the pale grey dawn of a November morning yet another strafing operation was about to take place. The Huns, who had converted the peaceful little Belgian fishing port into a hornets' nest, were to be allowed no rest.

Approaching the coast, the undulating dunes of which were just visible against the pale light of the eastern sky, were eight monitors, their powerful guns cocked up at a grotesque angle in readiness to open fire at a six-mile range. At a considerable distance astern were the seaplane-carriers "Hippodrome," "Arena" and "Cursus," while in a far-flung line ahead, astern and abeam, were the swarm of destroyers and patrol boats whose mission it was to promptly "scotch" any U-boat that, more daring than the rest of the cowardly crew, might attempt to let loose a torpedo at the converted liners. Already the Hun had learnt the lesson that it was almost a matter of impossibility to sink a monitor by torpedo, even though the weapons were "set" to run only a few feet beneath the surface. Coupled with the knowledge of the fact that it was "unhealthy" to be anywhere in the vicinity of craft flying the White Ensign, when there were others proudly displaying the Red Ensign and which were practically incapable of defence, the U-boats took good care to give the bombarding flotilla a wide berth.

Already the "Arena" and "Cursus" had dispatched their complement of seaplanes for the purpose of registering the result of the monitors' fire, but up to the present the airmen on board the "Hippodrome" had received no orders to board their respective "buses" and hie them to the scene of action.

"They've opened the ball," exclaimed Kirkwood, as the monitor on the left of the line let fly with her 14-inch gun.

"An obvious performance," remarked Fuller. "Unless one were both blind and deaf. More to the point: why are we being held in reserve, I wonder?"

"Dunno," added another flying-officer. "In the case of you three fellows there might be a plausible explanation. You've been so jolly keen on getting away from the ship that the skipper won't give you another chance. By Jove! That was a good one!"

Somewhere in the vicinity of Zeebrugge a dense cloud of black smoke had been hurled hundreds of feet into the air. One of the British shells had found a particularly satisfying target, for either a petrol depôt or an ammunition "dump" had been sent sky-high, with, possibly, a few hundred Huns to boot.

Yet no sound of the explosion could be heard, for the monitors' guns outvoiced that. The coast-defence craft were letting fly as quickly as the hydraulic loaders performed their task, and the gigantic yet docile weapons could be trained upon the practically invisible objective.

It was by no means a one-sided action. From cunningly concealed shore batteries, that seemed to multiply with hydra-headed persistence, German shells hurtled through the air, for the most part ricochetting harmlessly. A few, however, "got home." One monitor, listing badly to starboard, was already crawling slowly out of range. Another had been set on fire, but, the conflagration being quickly subdued, she "carried on" with calm and awful deliberation.

It had been one of the tenets of war that armoured ships were more than a match for shore batteries. The mobility of the former and the knowledge of the fixed position of the latter accounted for the theory—a theory that had been justified by the bombardment of Alexandria. But in the greatest war that the world has yet seen this idea received a rude shock. The skill with which huge guns can be loaded, ranged and trained upon a moving target rather more than equalised matters. Thus the old forts on the Dardanelles were quickly reduced to a heap of ruins by the guns of the "Queen Elizabeth," but this did not prevent the Turks bringing heavier ordnance to bear upon the Allied squadrons as they attempted in vain to force the historic Straits.

But there has been yet another swing of the pendulum. In an engagement betwixt ships and forts there was a deciding factor—the command of the air. Provided airmen from the attacking squadron could assist by observing the hits of the naval guns and by dropping quantities of powerful explosives on the hostile batteries the advantage would rest with those who held command of the sea. Nor was mere observing and bomb-dropping on defended positions sufficient. It was necessary to harass the enemy's lines of communication and prevent reserves of men and ammunition being rushed up to the coast.

"Ten to one we're down for a 'stunt,'" hazarded Barcroft. "That's why we are cooling our heels here. Ah! I thought so," he added, as the airmen were summoned to receive instructions preparatory to a flight.

A quarter of an hour later Billy Barcroft felt like dancing a hornpipe on the quarter-deck. He had been given a task after his own heart—to bomb the German hangars at Lierre, a town about six or seven miles south-east of the fortress of Antwerp and a distance of eighty miles, as the crow flies, from the position taken up by the seaplane carriers. To Fuller was deputed the business of wrecking the important railway station of Aerschot, while the other pilots were likewise given definite instructions to drop their cargoes of explosives on specified places of military importance. The airmen were enjoined to avoid as far as possible encounters with hostile machines on the outward journey, the importance of reaching their respective objectives being paramount to the excitement of aerial duels with Hun flying men.

"We'll be within sight of one another most of the time, Barcroft, old man," said Fuller, as he signed to his observer to take his place in the machine. "Now, Gregory, all ready?"

Fuller's companion, a sparely-built sub-lieutenant, whose long, hooked nose and obliquely placed eyes gave him the appearance of a bird, nodded assent.

"Well, good luck!" shouted Barcroft.

The words were drowned by the roar of the engine, but the lieutenant instinctively realised their meaning. With a cheery wave of his gauntletted hand he started on his long flight.

Thirty-seconds later Barcroft got away, with Kirkwood as his observer. There had been a slight rivalry between Billy and Fuller as to who should take the A.P., for the lieutenant had regarded the latter as his own right-hand man since the night of the encounter with the Zeppelins, while Barcroft claimed priority. The matter had been decided by the spin of a coin, with the result that the A.P. was now on his way to Lierre with Barcroft.

High above the bombarding monitors flew the powerfully engined seaplane, now nearly half a mile in the wake of Fuller's "bus." At regular intervals astern came the rest of the aerial raiders, all rocking slightly in the disturbed air caused by the concussion of the heavy guns.

Ten minutes were sufficient to bring Barcroft's machine over the Belgian coast. Acting upon previous instructions he maintained an altitude of eleven thousand feet, at which height it was practically invisible from the shore, across which clouds of smoke and dust were slowly drifting as the British shells burst with devastating effect upon the Huns' positions.

No Archibalds greeted the raiders; neither Fokkers nor Aviatiks appeared to bar their way. For the present the flight was nothing more than an exhilarating joy-ride.

Once Kirkwood turned his head to watch the following seaplanes. Only one was in sight. The rest had already turned off for their respective objectives, and even that one was beginning to plane down towards a broad canal on which were dozens of loaded barges, their cargoes consisting of heavy gun ammunition destined for the batteries of Zeebrugge and Ostend.

For the present the A.P.'s task was practically a sinecure. There was no necessity to use the wireless instrument: two hundred feet of trailing aerial wire is apt to be in the way during bomb-dropping operations; besides, the raiding seaplane, not having to register for the guns of the fleet, could refrain from reporting progress until her return to her parent ship. So having made sure as far as possible that the bomb dropping gear was in working order this time, and having fitted a tray of ammunition to the Lewis gun in order to be ready for use in case of emergencies, Kirkwood leant over the side of the fuselage and contemplated the country beneath; the features of which as seen from the air he knew better by this time than any of his native land.

From Ghent Barcroft followed the course of the River Scheldt until the town of Antwerp appeared in sight. At this point Fuller was observed to be turning away to the right. Both seaplanes were approaching their respective objectives.

"Bestir yourself, you lazy bounder!" shouted Billy through the voice tube. "There's something ahead. Looks like a balloon. Get your glasses and see what it is."

"It is a balloon," declared Kirkwood after a brief inspection. "A captive one."

"And right over the Lierre hangars," thought the pilot. "What for? There's nothing to observe from a belligerent point of view, unless the bounders are expecting us. It may be that the balloon is in use for instructional purposes. If so, I'll give the young pups cold feet, by Jove!"

"They've spotted us," announced the A.P. "They've begun to haul the thing down."

"Then they are too late," added Barcroft grimly. "Gun all right? Stand by to give 'em a tray."

Tilting the ailerons the pilot swooped down towards the unwieldy, tethered gas-bag. As he did so mushrooms of white smoke burst into view all around the descending seaplane. The German anti-aircraft guns were firing upon the British raiders.

Barcroft held steadily on his course. He was quite used to shrapnel by this time. He knew, too, that soon the Hun gunners would have to cease fire for fear of hitting their own captive balloon.

Already the German officers in the car of the balloon realised that it was impossible for the gas-bag to be hauled down in time. Three of them leapt into space. The fourth remained, grasping the edge of the basket-work and staring terror-stricken at the approaching seaplane.

In spite of the tax upon his mental energies Barcroft watched the descent of the three. For nearly two hundred feet they dropped like stone, then they were hidden from his view by three umbrella-like objects. Before taking their desperate leap the Germans had provided themselves with parachutes.

Apparently there was not one left for the remaining Hun. Suspended betwixt earth and sky he realised the horror of his position, until, seized by a forlorn resolve, he clambered over the side of the car and began to swarm down the wire rope that held it in captivity.

It was hopeless from the first. In spite of the protection afforded by the leather gloves. The metal wire cut into his palms like hot iron. Before the luckless German had lowered himself fifty feet his grip relaxed. Like an arrow he crashed to the ground, a thousand feet below.

"Don't fire!" ordered the flight-sub, realising that if merely perforated by small-calibre bullets the gas-bag would fall harmlessly to earth. "Stand by to drop a plum—now."

The A.P. jerked the releasing lever. As he did so Barcroft set the seaplane to climb steeply. Ten seconds later the bomb hit the balloon fairly in the centre of its convex upper surface. The next instant there was a vivid flash, followed by a crash that was audible above the roar of the seaplane's engine. Sideslipping the machine dropped almost vertically. Not until she had passed through the outlying portion of the dense cloud of smoke from the destroyed balloon did the pilot regain control.

A hurried glance showed that the flaming wreckage of his victim was plunging earthwards, leaving a fiery trail in its wake. It was falling upon the triple line of sheds in which German aeroplanes were stored.

Like a swarm of ants the air mechanics scattered right and left to avoid— in many cases ineffectually—the gigantic falling firebrand. If Barcroft had any qualms concerning the fearful havoc he was about to create upon the throng of human beings he showed none. He remembered those bombs dropped upon the defenceless civil population of Barborough.

"Let 'em have it hot!" he shouted.

At that comparatively low altitude there was little chance of missing the expansive target. The ground was literally starred with diverging jets of flame. The burning sheds collapsed like packs of cards, the debris bursting into a series of fires. In half a minute the hangars ceased to exist save as a funeral pyre to the mechanical birds that would never again soar through the air.

A severed tension wire, one end of which cut Billy smartly on the head despite the protection afforded by his airman's padded helmet, reminded the flight-sub that again the Archibalds were having a chip in. The planes, too, were ripped in several places, while jagged holes through the sides of the fuselage marked the accuracy of the shrapnel. It was, indeed, a marvel that either pilot or observer escaped injury.

Barcroft heaved a sigh of relief as the seaplane drew away from the shell-infested zone. In the heat of the bombing business his blood was tingling through his veins; he was excited almost to the point of recklessness; the risk of being "winged" by a bursting projectile hardly troubled him. But once clear of the scene of action he realised what a tight corner he had been in, and, although all immediate danger was at an end, he let the motors "all out" in desperate haste to gain a safe altitude.

He found himself comparing the recent situation to a cat and dog encounter. So long as the feline faced the dog the latter generally contents itself by barking and making "demonstration in force"; but directly the cat turns tail it tears away at full speed, its sole anxiety being to get away from its assailant for which, up to a certain point, it had shown contemptuous bravery.

The flight-sub's thoughts were suddenly interrupted by Kirkwood shouting through the voice-tube.

"There's Fuller a couple of miles on our left," announced the A.P. "What's more, he's tackling three Hun machines."

CHAPTER XXVI
A FUTILE RESCUE

WITHOUT a second's hesitation Barcroft turned the rudder-bar. Almost on the verge of sideslipping the seaplane swung round and headed straight for the enemy aircraft.

"Something wrong with friend John," muttered the flight-sub, "or he wouldn't turn tail to half a dozen strafed Fritzes."

Everything pointed to Barcroft's surmise being correct. Fuller's seaplane was in flight in a double sense. He had lost the superiority of altitude. His observer was replying to the machine-gun fire converging upon the fugitive craft from three different points. A hundred feet higher and about three hundred yards astern of the British seaplane was a large, double-fuselaged biplane. To the right and left but practically on the same horizontal plane were two Fokkers—a tough set to be up against, but in ordinary circumstances the dauntless flight-lieutenant would not have hesitated to engage.

Presently the British seaplane's Lewis gun barked. It was evident that the machine was running uncontrolled, as she was wobbling considerably. Barcroft was now near enough to see what had happened. There was just time for a brief glance, for his plane was approaching the on-coming Huns at an aggregate speed of nearly 180 miles an hour.

There was no sign of Gregory, but Fuller, abandoning the joy-stick, had climbed into the observer's seat in order to work the automatic gun. This he did so successfully that within five seconds of the weapon opening fire one of the Fokkers crashed earthwards, completely out of action. Then the British gun was silent.

This was all that Barcroft could see as far as Fuller was concerned. He had devoted all his attention to the double-fuselaged craft.

While Kirkwood was letting loose a drum of ammunition from the Lewis gun Barcroft employed his usual tactics. He steered straight for his antagonist. If the gun failed to do its work in time, and if the Hun pilot's nerves did not desert him, the result would be a rending crash in mid-air as the two swift-moving craft collided. The interlocked wreckage, a mass of flame, would drop like a firebrand to earth—a swift yet terrible death for friend and foe alike. But Billy knew how the odds were against such a mutual catastrophe. The Hun, if he managed to avoid the stream of bullets, was not likely to "stand up" to the resistless onrush of the British seaplane.

Suddenly the double-fuselaged biplane nosedived. Only just in time did Barcroft tilt the ailerons, for the seaplane literally scraped the tail of his vertically-descending foe. For nearly a thousand feet the machine "plumbed," then like a silvery dart it flattened out.

"Old trick, Fritz," muttered Barcroft. "Well, you've lost your altitude advantage. I'll renew your acquaintance later."

The flight-sub knew that some minutes must elapse before the double-fuselaged machine could climb to renew the encounter. During that interval he had time to devote his attention to the remaining Fokker that, following Fuller with deadly persistence, was firing the while but receiving no reply from the British craft.

Already Fuller was a couple of miles away. His antagonist was gaining slightly. It seemed remarkable that with such a prodigious outlay of ammunition the Huns had not succeeded in strafing their quarry.

Suddenly Fuller's seaplane dipped. Barcroft gave vent to an involuntary groan, but the next instant he wanted to cheer, for his chum had looped the loop two or three times and was now heading in the opposite direction.

"I see the move," thought Barcroft. "He's luring Fritz towards us."

The two seaplanes passed one another at less than a hundred yards. Fuller raised his arm by way of greeting as they swept by. As he did so shreds of canvas flew from the lower plane, and dipping abruptly the crippled machine dropped, lurching hideously as it did so.

Almost simultaneously the Hun pilot of the Fokker collapsed across the decking of the fuselage. The machine, no longer under control, swayed through a distance of nearly a quarter of a mile, and then, tilting obliquely, began a terrific tail spin that ended in a jumble of wreckage on the unsympathetic soil of Belgium.

"Now for the double bus," muttered Billy. "The Huns will pay dearly for strafing poor old John."

But the remaining aeroplane of the two had had enough, for, seeing the British seaplane swooping down to engage upon round two, she promptly sought safety in flight.

Pursuit, Barcroft knew, was futile. Not only was the fugitive going in an easterly direction, which meant that had Billy held on in chase he would be lured further and further away from his floating base, but the Hun machine was more powerfully engined and possessed an undoubted superiority of speed.

"By Jove!" shouted the A.P. "Fuller's planing down. He's got the old bus under control of sorts."

The flight-sub looked downwards. A small rectangular patch of grey eighteen hundred feet down confirmed the truth of Kirkwood's statement. The injured seaplane was volplaning in wide circles. Her pilot was about to make an involuntary landing. This, in itself, was a highly dangerous performance, as the floats were very unsatisfactory landingskids. It was a hundred chances to one that the seaplane would bump hard and collapse, pinning the pilot under the wreckage. Even if Fuller escaped with his life or without broken limbs, he was confronted with the additional danger of being made a prisoner.

Without a moment's delay Barcroft switched off the ignition and commenced a volplane. At least he would be able to discover whether his chum was able to make a safe landing. Beyond that—

"Good old Fuller!" almost yelled the A.P. "He's spotted a canal. I see his move—artful bounder!"

Running in a direction approximately east and west was a long stretch of artificial water. The straightness of its course showed that it was not a river. It was bordered on either side by a broad tow-path, which in turn was fringed by a line of poplars. With the exception of a string of barges being towed down by a small tug (and they were nearly two miles away) the canal looked deserted.

It was for this expanse of water that Fuller was making. Provided there was sufficient width for the extreme breadth of his wing spread and a margin to boot, there was little doubt of the experienced flight-lieutenant's ability to make a safe descent.

"He's done it!" announced Kirkwood.

"If he has managed it there is no reason why we shouldn't," thought Barcroft grimly. "Stand by, old man; we'll shove down and pick him up."

The canal appeared to expand in size in order to meet the descending seaplane. It required all the skill and nerve at the youthful pilot's command to carry out his desperate plan. An error of a few feet to right or left meant irreparable damage to the frail craft and failure of his devoted efforts on behalf of his stranded friend.

With admirable judgment Billy brought his "bus" down, making a fine "landing" on the surface of the canal at a distance of less than a hundred yards from the crippled aircraft, Then, drifting gently, the seaplane brought up alongside the bank, with one of her floats rubbing against the edge of the tow-path.

"Nip out and hold her on, old man!" exclaimed Billy.

The A.P. obeyed promptly. Fortunately this required little or no effort, for the thick-set though leafless trees broke the force of what wind there was.

Barcroft quickly followed Kirkwood to the bank. Already Fuller had got ashore, and was preparing to destroy his machine when, to his utter astonishment, he had seen another seaplane skim over his head and alight at a short distance off.

Running by the path Billy approached the lieutenant.

"Come along, old man!" he said hurriedly. "There's no time to be lost. We'll give you a lift in our bus back to the old 'Hippo.'"

"Thanks," replied Fuller coolly. "What's the hurry? No Huns in sight. I'll do this job properly."

The odour of petrol vapour wafted to Barcroft's nostrils. Fuller had allowed the spirit to escape from the tank, and was engaged in wrapping a piece of oil-soaked paper round a stone.

"No explosives left, I hope?" asked Billy. "None except the petrol," replied Fuller. "That's explosive enough, I reckon, for this job. No, I dropped all my plums over Aerschot. Gregory's gone (s'pose you can see that for yourself?); shot through the head; he gave a sort of leap—he wasn't strapped in, you'll understand—and flopped right over the fuselage."

"You've been strafed!" exclaimed Barcroft, for Fuller's quick sentences, coupled with the fact that he winced frequently, pointed to that.

"The child is correct," agreed the flight-lieutenant. "Machine-gun bullet clean through the left arm. It stings a bit, but nothing much. No, don't trouble about it now. It'll keep. Now for a blaze."

Striking a match he set light to the oiled paper and tossed the flaming missile into the fuselage of the doomed seaplane. With a rush of air and a lurid flare the petrol vapour caught. In an instant the machine was enveloped in fire.

"Good enough," declared Fuller, with an air of satisfaction. "Hard lines on the old bus, though. She was a beauty. I was just getting used to her, too."

"Come along, old man," urged Barcroft again.

Giving a farewell glance at the burning wreckage, Fuller turned reluctantly away and accompanied his chum to the waiting seaplane.

"We're going to pitch you out of your perch, my festive," announced the flight-sub addressing the observer. "Fuller's tried to stop a bullet. He didn't succeed, and as a result the nickel's left a hole through his arm. Now, all aboard. We're lucky not to have a swarm of Huns about our ears."

Having assisted the wounded flight-lieutenant on to the float and thence into Kirkwood's seat in the fuselage Barcroft swarmed up and took his place at the joy-stick.

Standing on the float and steadying himself by holding on to a strut, the A.P. gave a vigorous push with his foot against the canal bank. As the seaplane drifted towards the centre of the artificial waterway he clambered nimbly to the deck of the fuselage and, lying at full length, steadied himself by grasping the coaming surrounding his surrendered place.

"All right?" asked Barcroft.

The motor fired smoothly. With the engine throttled down the pilot taxied cautiously for a short distance, then increasing speed and tilting the ailerons he started to climb.

At barely twenty feet from the ground a sudden and furious gust of wind caught the seaplane fairly abeam. Quickly Billy actuated the rudder-bar in order to turn the machine sufficiently to counteract the side-drop.

It was too late. Swept bodily sideways the seaplane failed to clear the line of poplars. The left-hand planes struck a tree-trunk and crumpled like brown paper. The next instant the whole fabric crashed to the ground across the tow-path.

CHAPTER XXVII
FUGITIVES

BOBBY KIRKWOOD was the first of the trio to recover his scattered senses. The impact had hurled him violently forward, and cannoning off Barcroft's back he had slid more or less gently to the ground. The shock had forced Billy against the for'ard side of the coaming, well-nigh winding him, while at the same time his head came into contact with the framework, thus causing him to see a most gorgeous galaxy of stars.

Well it was that the observer's body glanced off that of the pilot; otherwise the A.P. would have been instantly killed by the swiftly-revolving propeller. As it was he escaped by a hairbreadth.

Fuller was not so fortunate. The sudden change of momentum had the result of crushing his already wounded arm, besides giving him a nasty blow on the forehead. He, too, began to wonder dimly whether he was witnessing a superb display of Brock's fireworks.

As Kirkwood regained his feet the wreckage subsided still more. The propeller blades striking the ground were shattered to fragments, while the motor, released of its "load," began to race with terrific speed.

It was this nerve-racking sound that recalled Barcroft to a sense of action. Switching off the ignition he slid from the chassis and surveyed the scene of desolation.

"Come along, Fuller. Let's give you a hand!" he exclaimed.

Awkwardly the flight-lieutenant descended from his precarious perch. The two stood in silent contemplation for some seconds. Verily they realised that they were very much "in the cart." Stranded in a country overrun by hostile troops, far from the coast—always the preliminary goal of a seaman who is making a bid for freedom—their chance of seeing the inside of a German prison loomed large upon their mental horizon.

"Let's get rid of the old bus while she's warm," suggested Barcroft. "There's no possible chance of getting her repaired sufficiently for even a short flight, and it won't do to let the Huns patch her up."

"Shoulders to the wheel, lads," exclaimed Fuller. "One of mine's a bit groggy, but I feel like shifting a steam-roller with the other."

By their united efforts the wrecked seaplane was toppled over into the canal. The sudden contact of the cold water with the hot cylinders would, they knew, fracture the castings and make the motor useless until complicated and costly repairs had been executed—even if the Germans succeeded in fishing the debris out of the mud at the bottom of the canal.

"Now we'll make tracks," decided Fuller. "Wonder there aren't soldiers on the spot already."

"Yes, we'll make tracks," agreed Barcroft, "but not the ones you are keen on leaving behind."

He pointed to the muddy tow-path and to the comparatively dry ground on the other side of the row of poplars.

"We'll walk backwards as far as the field," he continued. "The Boches are bound to examine the footprints. If they see that they lead in the direction of the canal it may baffle 'em a bit. We must look sharp. I see the water falling an inch or so."

"But the canal isn't tidal," remarked Kirkwood.

"I agree," assented Billy. "The slight fall tells me that the nearest lock has been opened. That means a barge is on its way, and, much as I regret missing the sight of a Hun cargo boat bumping on the wreckage of the old bus, prudence demands that we sheer off."

Having walked backwards until they reached hard ground the trio set off cautiously. The country consisted of tilled fields—the work of impressed Belgians, forced by their taskmasters to cultivate the ground to provide foodstuffs for the Huns. The absence of hedges gave the land an unfamiliar appearance as far as the three British officers were concerned. What was of more pressing significance there was a lack of efficient cover, the only means of securing shelter being by keeping close to the trees that bounded the fields.

"There's a spinny of sorts in there," said Kirkwood, pointing to a circular cluster of bushes. "I vote we make for that and repair damages."

"And find ourselves surrounded by dozens of Boches," added Fuller. "Naturally, once they found the wreckage of our machine they would search the nearest cover. We must make for those woods What say you, old bird?"

"Yes, and remain till nightfall," added Barcroft.

The wood was nearly a mile away, and presented an expanse of leafless trees extending nearly twice that distance. The depth of the wood the fugitives had no means of discovering.

For the last four hundred yards the three officers crawled and crouched, for the ground was as flat and unbroken as a table-top. Away on the right could be discerned a red-tiled farmhouse, close to it a roofless barn, with the two charred gables standing up clearly against the sky. Further away was a village of considerable size, but in all directions there were no signs of human beings or of cattle.

"Thank goodness we are here at last," exclaimed Fuller, throwing himself upon the ground. "I don't want you fellows to think that I'm piling it on, but my rotten ankle's played old Harry with me. Fractured it on a ringbolt on the 'Cursus' at Harwich," he explained. "Had six weeks in hospital, and thought it got fixed up all right, but it isn't."

"And your wound?" asked the A.P.

"Pooh! Nothing," replied Fuller unconcernedly. "That's a simple matter. If this ankle crocks properly, I'll make you fellows carry on without me. I can hang out a couple of days until you're clear and then give myself up."

"I'm jolly well sure you don't," said Barcroft firmly. "We three sink or swim together. Think you'll be able to swarm up that tree if we give you a hand?"

The flight-lieutenant eyed the gnarled trunk somewhat dubiously.

"Might," he replied. "I'll try, anyway. What's the idea?"

"To lie close until it gets dark."

"But why that tree? It's on the edge of the wood. Why not go further in, where it's ever so much thicker?"

"Because if the Huns track us this far they'll naturally conclude that we've bolted for cover. They'll doubtless beat the interior of the wood and not pay much attention to the part nearest the canal. Besides, from this particular tree we can command a wide outlook without running much risk of detection."

By the aid of their belts Barcroft and Kirkwood succeeded in assisting the wounded officer to gain the lowermost branch. Thence it was a comparatively simple matter to climb another thirty feet. Here two huge limbs gave a tolerably secure perch, wide enough to hide the fugitives from the sight of any persons passing underneath, and yet able to afford an outlook over a wide expanse of open country.

"Now let's look at that injured arm," said Barcroft, producing his "first aid" outfit. "Slip his coat off, Bobby; we don't want to cut that away. H'm! clean hole, by Jove! Iodine and gauze, old man. That's capital. I've morphia tablets here; if you feel in much pain I'll give you half a one and no more. Can't afford to have your brain dulled by morphia at this stage of the proceedings, John.',

"That's easier," said Fuller with a sigh of relief. "Now if you'll be so good as to unlace my boot I'll massage this low-down ankle."

"You'll keep still," ordered Barcroft firmly, "We'll do the rubbing business—if only to keep our blood circulating."

"Did you save your map?" inquired Fuller.

"I burnt mine."

"Yes, I have mine," replied the flight-sub. "I make it about sixty miles from the Dutch frontier—not much use making a shot for the coast, I take it?"

"Phew! Sixty miles—I did that distance once on a walking tour. For pleasure, mark you," said Fuller. "Plenty to eat, a decent show to put up at every night, and quite fine weather and I had galled heels by the end of the second day."

"If we could sneak a captive balloon like you did at Sylt," remarked the A.P. "That would be top-hole."

"A bit of sheer good luck," said Fuller reminiscently. "That sort of dose isn't often repeated. Tressidar and I broke into a house and collared suits of mufti. That won't do here, though. We were on Danish soil then; now we are in occupied Belgium. Caught and we are shot as spies, while the unfortunate civilians to whom the clothes belong would be strung up for assisting us to escape, whether they did it knowingly or otherwise. Time for more amateur burglar work when we're on Dutch soil. That's my opinion. You see, if we cross the frontier in uniform we'll be interned. I remember——"

"Look!" ejaculated the A.P., pointing in the direction of the farmhouse.

Making their way across the fields were about a hundred people, men and women, herded together in rough military formation and escorted by grey-coated German infantry. The civilians were on their way to forced labour in the fields. Woe betide the luckless Belgian, male or female, who showed the faintest resentment, or lagged behind. Blows and kicks were administered with impartial severity by the brutal guards, while some did not hesitate to prod the helpless human cattle with the butt-ends of their rifles.

"And yet there are worms in England who cry out about the dilution of labour and the encroachment of the rights of the working man," remarked Barcroft. "This is the sort of rights they'd get if the Huns once occupied even a portion of the Homeland."

"Poor bounders!" exclaimed the A.P. as he fondled the holster of his revolver. "I'd like to put a shot through that red-faced swine's head."

"You'd only make it worse for us and for them," said Fuller.

"True," assented Kirkwood, "but a fellow cannot disguise his feelings in such circumstances. One thing seems certain: the Boches haven't got wind of our presence."

"Don't know so much about that," said Billy. "Unless I'm much mistaken there's a patrol coming this way—and dogs, too, by Jove!"

In less than ten minutes (it had taken the trio an hour to cover the same distance) the patrol gained the field in which the Belgians were literally slaving. Apparently the crowd of workers disturbed the trail, for the bloodhounds, three massive-limbed, heavy-jowled creatures, no longer kept their noses close to the ground and followed the fugitives' track without the slightest deviation. Instead they wandered round in circles, growling rather than baying, and showing every indication of having lost the scent.

Followed a heated controversy between the Huns with the dogs and the Germans guarding the field labourers, until the latter, ordering their charges to assemble, marched them into the field next adjoining and nearer to the canal. Four Belgians, however, remained. These, after what was evidently a homily as to their behaviour, followed the patrol with the bloodhounds.

The scent once lost took some time to pick up again, but eventually one of the animals stopped at the foot of the tree in which the fugitives were hiding and set up a succession of low, deep cries. The other dogs, apparently on a different trail, disappeared in the wood, their keepers having all their work cut out to hold them in leash.

"One at least of the English swine is up this tree, Max," said a corporal, addressing one of the two privates with him. "That is certain. The others have gone elsewhere. I wonder that they had the sense to separate."

"We'll make sure of this one," said Max grimly.

"Ach! That is so," agreed the corporal. "Here, Karl, you speak this outlandish language. Tell this fellow to climb and see if the Englishman is there."

Turning to the Belgian who had been compelled to remain with them, Karl spoke to him in Flemish. Being ignorant of the Walloon language Barcroft was unable to understand his reply.

"The fool says he is hungry and has not enough strength to climb," said Karl, translating for the primary benefit of the corporal and for the secondary information of Billy Barcroft.

"Tell him," replied the Hun, "that he must go—and be quick about it. If he succeeds in finding the Englishman, then I will inform the commandant and see that the fellow gets a double ration to-night. That ought to satisfy his hunger."

Lying at full length upon the sturdy branches the three airmen could distinctly hear the rasping of the Belgian's boots against the bark and the short sharp gasps that betokened a man obviously out of condition.

The A.P. glanced at Barcroft and pointed to his revolver. The look indicated clearly enough what he meant. There were but three Germans. There were also three determined Britons all armed with revolvers. It would be an easy matter to settle the hash of the Huns and trust to flight before the rest of the patrol, alarmed by the shots, could arrive upon the scene.

But the flight-sub shook his head. The risk was too great. Reprisals would automatically follow upon the luckless peasants, who were bound to be regarded as accomplices in the attack upon the three soldiers.

Presently a pair of hands gripped the rough bark of the bough on which Barcroft was lying—long, lean, gnarled fingers almost claw-like in appearance. The next instant the Belgian's head and shoulders appeared above the rounded edge of the bough.

For a brief second Billy's eyes met those of the climber. The fugitives were discovered.

CHAPTER XXVIII
TRACKED

AT the sight of the lean, cadaverous features of the Belgian Barcroft had to exercise a tremendous lot of restraint to control his desire to utter some sort of exclamation. He had no wish to harm the fellow, who, as he knew, was acting under compulsion, with overt bribery thrown in. In fact he felt sorry for the man, whose pathetic eyes and drawn features portrayed both hunger and misery.

Yet in an instant the climber turned his face aside and resolutely hauled himself upon the branch on which Billy was lying. He was now in full view of the other officers. Fortunately neither of them spoke nor moved, yet the mental tension was acute.

Standing upright upon the bough and carefully preserving his balance the Belgian outstretched his arm to grasp the branch above.

"The bounder doesn't want to take unnecessary chances," thought Barcroft. "He wouldn't shout while he was only holding on by his fingers. Now he's able to get a firm grip in case he thinks we'll heave him out of it."

But no. The flight-sub was totally wrong in his surmise. The man, deliberately ignoring the presence of the three fugitives, climbed still higher, until he gained the topmost branch capable of supporting his weight.

Then, having leisurely scanned the surrounding tree-tops, he shouted something to the Germans standing at the foot of the British officers' hiding-place.

For a moment Barcroft and his companions were again plunged into the throes of suspense. "The pig says that there are no signs of the Englishmen," interpreted Karl.

"Donnerwetter!" grunted the corporal. "So much for the bloodhound, and Herr Major is ever boasting of what the brute can do. He's wrong for once at least, only I dare not tell him so. Tell the Belgian to come down. I'll soon send him up another tree a little further on."

"That's right," agreed Max. "Make the fellow work till he drops. If he breaks his neck there's one of the rabble the less."

At the order the climber descended, as before paying no heed to the three officers. Upon regaining the ground he was marched off to make another ascent on a useless search. An hour later, having, as they thought, thoroughly searched the wood, the patrol withdrew, cursing and grumbling at their ill-luck, since, it appeared, a reward of two hundred and fifty marks for the arrest of the fugitives had been offered.

"A proper sport, that Belgian," said Fuller in a whisper, realising the wisdom of speaking in a low tone lest the Huns had left men to guard the woods. "He could have given us away as easy as winking."

"Perhaps he'll inform the Boches now he's out of sight," hazarded the cautious A.P.

"Great Scott! I hope not," ejaculated Fuller. "In fact I'm willing to lay long odds that he won't. I'd like to meet that chap on the quiet again. I'd make it worth his while."

"So would I," added Barcroft. "Well, this affair has done us a good turn. The Huns have evidently satisfied themselves that we are not anywhere in this wood. The coast will be clear for to-night. How's that arm, old bird?"

"Feeling a bit stiff," replied Fuller. "The air's so confoundedly cold."

"It is a bit fresh," agreed Kirkwood. "And probably it will freeze hard to-night. And your ankle?"

"Can't feel any sensation in it," replied the flight-lieutenant. "The damage, if any, will assert itself when I place foot to ground. What an ass I was not to have brought my Thermos. Full of good old hot tea, too. I left it on the bank, after the smash."

"You deserve a vote of censure for importing food stuffs into German-occupied territory, old man," said Barcroft. "Can't you imagine a thirsty Hun mopping that stuff?"

"You speak for yourself, my festive," retorted the flight-lieutenant. "What did you do with *your* flasks?"

"They went down with the wreckage," replied Billy.

"Yours, perhaps," said Kirkwood. "My Thermos got smashed when we crashed. I heard the glass go, and I remember the hot liquid escaping and running over my gloves."

"Then you are all right for a feast," retorted Fuller. "Goatskin soaked in tea, eh? Sort of cannibalistic feast."

"Don't insinuate that I'm a giddy goat," protested the A.P. "It is like a case of—oh, dash it all!"

Kirkwood's exclamation was occasioned by the binoculars slipping from his benumbed fingers and falling to the ground. Rolling a few feet they lay in clear view silent evidence to the hiding place of their owner.

"Then you are a goat—that proves it," said Fuller. "Hullo! What's the move?"

Kirkwood slipping out of his leather coat, was already about to descend to retrieve his lost property. So far the coast seemed clear, for the Belgian labourers and their guards had moved to a field beyond range of vision. Since it was safe to conjecture that they would return to the farm buildings for the night the danger lay in the fact that they would almost assuredly spot the conspicuous binoculars as they repassed.

The A.P. dropped after swarming down about twenty feet of trunk and alighted softly. His first care was to obliterate his footprints in the bare earth, for the ground surrounding the tree trunk was absolutely devoid of grass, and although sufficiently hard to withstand the impression of a person walking it was not proof against the impact of a man wearing a pair of heavy boots and dropping from a height of seven or eight feet.

Then, crouching, he made his way towards his cherished binoculars. Just as he picked them up and placed them in his pocket, for he had left the sling case with his comrades, there was a rustling in the undergrowth. The next instant a huge dog, growling savagely, leapt upon him.

The animal was of the lurcher breed—a type encouraged in the German army for various duties, including field ambulance work, guarding and tracking prisoners and drawing machine-guns. Although smaller than the bloodhound it possessed greater swiftness, while its strength and ferocity were only slightly inferior.

Luckily Kirkwood did not lose his presence of mind. Used to dogs, the experience he had had with playful canines would be turned to good account.

Clenching his leather-gloved hand the A.P. let out with his left. His fist, taking the lurcher fairly on the point of the nose, sent the animal reeling. The respite was but momentary. Like a dart the dog flew straight for the young officer's throat.

Kirkwood met the animal as it leapt in midair. His right hand, with its protection of the undressed leather gripped the lurcher round the muzzle, his fingers and thumb meeting inside the brute's wide-open jaws. Instantly the A.P.'s left hand grasped the dog's lower jaw.

So far so good. The animal, unable to bite, attempted to shake himself clear. Foiled in this direction he planted his hind legs firmly in the ground and, giving his body a series of jerks, sought to pull the A.P. off his balance.

"Shoot the brute!" exclaimed Barcroft from above. "Risk it! It can't be helped. Clap the muzzle close to the brute's hide."

But Bobby thought otherwise. Even if he could afford the risk of letting go the dog's jaws with one hand and draw his revolver the muffled report would still be sufficiently audible to alarm the Huns.

For perhaps half a minute he stood his ground, contenting himself by prising the lurcher's jaws apart. Then, slowly at first, he began to bend the animal's head backwards. It was a horrible yet necessary task—one that taxed the A.P.'s strength and endurance to the uttermost. Already he could feel the dog's teeth penetrating the gloves, and those saliva-streaming fangs meant trouble once they pierced the flesh.

Yet the man was winning through. Back and back he levered the animal's head. The brute's breath was coming in short, irregular pants; its blood-flecked eyes were almost bursting from their sockets. Still it struggled furiously, striving in vain to break away from the A.P.'s vice-like grip.

"By Jove! He'll never do it," thought Barcroft. "The brute's tiring him out."

At the risk of barked shins and elbows the flight-sub descended from his perch. Gaining the ground he drew his revolver, wrapped his scarf several times round the weapon to muffle the sound of the explosion, and cautiously approached the combatants.

Extreme care was necessary, for the lurcher, driven to desperation, was turning his antagonist round and round. Kirkwood, his whole energies devoted to twisting the animal's neck, was unable to counteract the dog's movements, nor did the animal remain sufficiently still to enable Barcroft to plant the muzzle of his weapon firmly against its ribs.

The end came with unexpected suddenness.

With a distinctly audible crash the lurcher's vertebra snapped. Its body seemed instantly to grow limp. The sudden cessation of resistance caused Kirkwood to fall forward across the still quivering body of his enemy.

Barcroft lifted his chum and set him on his feet. The A.P., now the duel with death was done, was as pale as a sheet and trembling in every limb.

"I'll be all right in a minute," he gasped. "Feel as ill as a seasick cat."

"Sit down," ordered Billy, and grasping his comrade by the nape of the neck he bent his head until it rested on his knees.

"Keep like that a while," he continued. "I'll get rid of incriminating evidence. My word, what a lump!" he added, as he lifted the dead brute by its hind legs. "Half a hundredweight, I should imagine."

Keeping the carcass clear of the ground the flight-sub carried it quite fifty yards through the wood before depositing it under a bush.

This necessary task performed, he retraced his steps.

"Chirpy again?" he inquired.

"Quite," replied Kirkwood.

"You look jolly warm," continued Barcroft.

"I feel it."

"Then get a move on and swarm up here," interrupted Fuller's voice. "I'm as cold as charity and could do with a human warmingpan."

"All clear?" inquired Barcroft.

"By Jove, no!" was Fuller's hurried rejoinder. "Look sharp, you fellows. There are half a dozen of 'em coming this way."

Making sure that they had left behind them no evidence of their presence the two airmen re-ascended to their lofty perch.

"You're steaming like an overworked horse, old man," said Billy addressing the A.P. "I'll throw your coat over you. You can't sit up or the Fritzes will spot us."

Trudging across the tilled land were eight or nine greatcoated Huns, armed with rifles. Two of their number were drawing a light cart.

"What's that for, I wonder?" whispered Kirkwood, for the Germans were still a considerable distance off, yet making almost in a straight line for the tree in which the three chums were hidden.

"Can't say," replied Fuller. "I never saw Huns with a contraption like that before. Rations, possibly: they may mean to camp out here just to keep us company."

The fugitives were not left long in doubt, for on arriving at a spot twenty yards from the edge of the wood the party halted and proceeded to don flexible metallic masks with hideous-looking snouts. This done, the corporal in charge inspected each man's face-protection with deliberate thoroughness, while from a distance two Hun officers in the uniform of the Engineers watched the proceedings.

"By smoke!" muttered Barcroft under his breath. "They're going to have a shot at gassing us."

At a brisk order the lid of the cart was thrown back revealing a couple of cylinders to which were attached lengths of armoured metallic hosepipe terminating in elongated nozzles. First the cylinders were placed upon the ground and air pumped into them until the required pressure was obtained. Then each apparatus was strapped to a man's back, a soldier being in attendance to hold the nozzle.

It was fairly safe for the three British officers to watch the proceedings since the height of the branch enabled them to look down upon the heads of the gassing party, while the latter could not look up owing to the straps that secured the lower portion of their masks to their shoulders.

"Reminds me of goblins at a panto," thought Bobby. "Wonder when they're going to start?"

As a matter of precaution he tied his handkerchief over his nose and mouth, an example that his companions hastened to copy. They realised that it was but a sorry protection—useless against the full strength of the deadly chlorine, but sufficient, perhaps, to ward off the effects of a "tail-end" of the poison-cloud.

Weirdly fascinated the fugitives watched the proceedings. It seemed strange to witness the diabolical preparations for their intended execution. Dimly Barcroft wondered whether he would be conscious when he fell from the bough, or whether the gas would overcome him instantly.

"The first whiff and I'll shoot," he thought grimly. "I'd like to shatter the nozzles of those pretty masks and let the brutes have a good sniff at their vile mixture."

A faint hiss betokened the fact that the taps controlling the discharge tubes had been turned on. Clouds of black vapour, eddying and seething, issued from the nozzles and rose sullenly in the cold, damp air.

CHAPTER XXIX
GASSED

SOMETHING fluttered past the flight-sub's ear. It was a dead leaf. Whisked by a sudden gust it disappeared. Simultaneously the wind moaned dismally betwixt the gaunt branches.

Hitherto the air had been heavy and still. Now, almost miraculously, a stiff breeze had sprung up, blowing in the direction of the infernal gas cylinders, just as they liberated their poisonous contents.

The rolling columns of vapour, forced back by the wind, literally enveloped the hideously masked operators. More, the deadly cloud, keeping close to the ground, travelled at prodigious speed towards the two Hun officers, who hitherto had been thoroughly enjoying the proceedings.

Quickly their brutal hilarity changed to an attitude of terror, as the death-dealing gas, spreading from the right and left of them, bore down at a rate exceeding that of a trotting horse. For a brief moment Barcroft had a vision of two grey-coated forms, two pairs of heels in the air and two pairs of outstretched arms. Then the cloud hid them from sight.

Already the operators, finding that the gas had been misdirected, had shut off the controlling valves. But the mischief was already done. When the cloud had drifted away before the now steady breeze the German officers could be discerned lying on the ground and beating a frantic tattoo with their elbows and heels as the poisonous vapour tore their lungs.

Aghast the corporal watched his superiors' death agonies. While his men hastened to render aid—a useless task—the luckless non com., tearing away his mask and liberating the poisonous vapour, held his face close to the hissing nozzle. Then he, too, dropped, writhing on the ground in mortal pain.

Finding that the gas-masks impeded their action the men who gathered round the dying officers discarded their protection, since the fumes of the first discharge had passed far beyond the scene. But they had not reckoned on a repetition of the dose. Suddenly overwhelmed by the fumes that issued uncontrolled from one of the cylinders, five of the men were stricken down.

The remaining few, who had not deprived themselves of their masks, made no attempt to check the outpouring cloud. They promptly fled.

"By Jove, if the wind lulls we are done for!" thought Barcroft. "A fellow wouldn't stand a ghost of a chance after a sniff of that stuff. Wonder how long the gas lasts?"

A back eddy sent a faint tinge of chlorine over the prostrate trio. It was as much as Billy could do to restrain himself from tearing his handkerchief from his mouth and gasping for breath. Fuller coughed heavily, while the A.P. rose to a kneeling position. Had not Barcroft grasped him by the arm he would have toppled off the bough. Then came another rush of pure air and the danger was past.

It was nearly twenty minutes before the apparatus exhausted itself. For nearly half a mile the track of the gas could be followed. The rich dark earth was turned a sickly yellow. Trees on the edge of the adjoining field were literally bleached by the corrosive vapour, while its effect upon the bodies of the victims of their own infernal contrivance was to make it difficult to distinguish between the colour of their uniform and that of their hideously drawn features.

"I vote we shift," suggested Barcroft. "The Boches evidently have a suspicion that we are somewhere in this wood. It's positively not healthy to remain."

"I think otherwise, with due deference to you," objected Fuller. "Granted the Huns imagine we are here. Those bloodhounds told them that; but after this delightful fiasco of the gas-business they'll take it for certain that if we are here we've been done in. So it would be well to sit tight till dark—much as I want to be on the move."

"What is the effect of chlorine gas upon food?" inquired the A.P.

"Rotten, I should imagine. Why?" asked Billy in surprise.

"Because there's food and drink down there," continued Kirkwood, pointing to the body of the corporal. "These fellows, for some reason, are in heavy marching order. There's almost certain to be grub in his pack and I can see his water bottle. We can't afford to be too squeamish, you know."

"Don't fancy German tack steeped in poison," remarked Fuller. "Although I feel as if I could eat almost anything. As for water—well, there's plenty of that about."

"And that's what makes me think that the fellow has something better than water in his canteen. At any rate, here goes."

Giving a glance round to see that no one was in sight the A.P. again descended to earth. Gingerly unbuckling the dead soldier's knapsack he produced half a loaf of black bread, a tin of meat and a hermetically-sealed box that afterwards proved to contain biscuits. One sniff at the bread was enough. Kirkwood promptly replaced it and carefully rebuckled the straps of the pack. The man's water-bottle he risked taking. Unscrewing the cork he found that the bottle contained neat Schnapps.

"One teaspoonful only for you, Fuller," he announced as he rejoined his comrades with the spoils. "Raw spirit will play the deuce with that wound of yours."

"You are quite right," agreed the flight-lieutenant as Barcroft proceeded to prise open the meat tin. Its contents consisted of tightly packed sausages. "For the same reason I suppose I must abstain from rich food. Give me a biscuit, you despoiler of the dead."

Late in the afternoon another party of Germans arrived upon the scene, this time merely to collect the victims of the gas and to remove the instruments of retribution.

"Double patrols at all cross-roads to-night, curse it!" said one of the soldiers. "Always more work. These Englishmen must be stiff by this time. Why send us out to arrest corpses?"

"We don't know that the gas has settled them," replied his companion. "Although it did the trick very neatly for Johannes Muller. I'm sorry for him. As for the ober-leutnant— —"

He shrugged his shoulders expressively. Evidently the officer was a typical Prussian.

"These English airmen played the deuce at Aerschot and Lierre," continued the first speaker. "It will go badly with them if they're caught, but, as I said, it's my opinion that they are done for already. Double patrols on a night like this. It's as bad as the trenches at Ypres."

"Fortunately I am warned for the Golden Lion cross-roads," said his companion. "As soon as the leutnant has made the rounds our party will make tracks for the cabaret. I am an old campaigner, Fritz."

"Ach! Do not, then, get caught," cautioned the other as he slammed the lid of the box on the cart. "It will be safe enough between midnight and two o'clock. I've a mind to join you, only it's a goodish step from Quatre Vents."

"Where's the map?" inquired Fuller, after the fatigue party had disappeared. "The 'Golden Lion' he said? That's it—*le Lion Doré*—it's marked here. Luck, boys! It's on the way to the frontier. Roll on, eleven o'clock. Only six hours more. Why didn't we bring a gramophone, or even a pack of cards?"

Slowly the leaden-footed hours sped. Darkness fell upon the scene. To add to the cold and discomfort; a chilly rain followed the "piping down" of the wind. The gnarled bough, rendered slippery with the moisture, was hardly safe. Its condition presaged danger when the time came for the three fugitives to attempt to descend the tree trunk. What was more there was every indication of the wet turning into ice.

Even the airmen's thick leather coats and fleece-lined gloves afforded but scant protection against the rigours of the penetrating air. Again and again Billy consulted the luminous hand of his watch. Would the hour of eleven never come?

"Why wait any longer?" asked the A.P., his teeth chattering with the cold. "We can make our way cautiously through the wood. We'll be a mile nearer to the Golden Lion crossroads when we get to the other side. We'll be too benumbed if we stop here."

"All right," agreed Barcroft. "Belts together, lads. We'll lower you as far as we can, John. Mind that ankle of yours when you drop."

It was an eerie business lowering Fuller through the darkness, but without mishap he alighted on the soft ground. Then having thrown down the water bottle and the rest of the provisions his two comrades rejoined him.

"All right?" whispered Barcroft.

"Right as ninepence," replied the flight-lieutenant. "Lead on, Macduff."

Guided by a luminous spirit-compass Billy plunged into the wood, his companions following in single file. Already the rain had been sufficiently heavy to moisten the ground in spite of the protection afforded by the leafless branches. Here and there a dry twig cracked under their feet; again and again they had to make detours to avoid thick-set undergrowth; once their progress was impeded by a knee-deep but sluggish brook, but without mishap the fugitives gained the remote side of the wood.

Beyond all was dark as pitch. The sky being overcast even the starlight was denied them. Presently a lantern gleamed in the distance, its yellow glimmer lighting up the high-pitched roof and quaint chimneys of a tall building that had evidently escaped the ruin of war.

Barcroft nudged the A.P.

"The 'Golden Lion'," he announced. "And another hour and a half to wait."

CHAPTER XXX
THE BARN BY THE RIVER

THE distant light from the lantern glittered on the bayonets of the sentries, who, sheltering as best they might from the rain, paced stolidly to and fro at the bleak cross-roads. Presently the gleam increased in intensity, throwing distorted shadows upon the gaunt poplars of the road-side.

"The lieutenant going the rounds," whispered Fuller. "Fancy the fool taking a lantern with him. Wonder if he's afraid of the dark?"

The quivering bayonets stiffened into immobility as the Hun officer approached the now alert sentries. The fugitives could just distinguish the guttural 'Wer da?' of the challenge, then an unintelligible exchange of words.

The German officer and his escort moved on. The sentries, sloping arms, resumed their monotonous beat until the round had disappeared from sight and hearing.

Seemingly interminable minutes passed, until just as midnight was approaching there came a low whistle through the darkness.

"*Hier!*" replied one of the men.

"All safe," rejoined the new-comer. "Yes, both of you. What a night! It's not fit for a dog to be abroad."

"Now," whispered Barcroft at the expiration of another long ten minutes. "Ankle all right, old man?"

"Quite," replied Fuller mendaciously. It was far from right, but the flight-lieutenant, game to the core, had no intention of letting his chums know that every time he set foot to the ground excruciating pains racked him.

Across the clayey soil, now almost knee-deep in mud, the daring trio literally floundered, their immediate objective being the endmost of a line of tall trees at a distance of fifty yards from the cross-roads.

"Steady!" cautioned Billy as the *pavé*, glistening even in the gloom, became visible. "I'll push on and see that the coast is clear. Back in a brace of shakes."

The trees cast sombre shadows as the flight sub drew near; rain, closely approaching sleet, fell in a steady downpour; the wind had resumed its doleful whine. Altogether the climatic conditions were horrible.

"This is absolutely the limit," thought Billy, until his characteristic optimism reasserted itself. "Perhaps it's as well, though. The Huns don't like sticking it and have departed. A fine night and our risks would be greatly increased."

He pulled up with startling suddenness. Less than ten paces ahead of him was a German sentry. Sheltering under the lee of the outer most tree the fellow was actually looking straight in the flight-sub's direction.

For several seconds Barcroft stood stock still, debating whether to throw himself upon the man or seek safety in flight. The sentry, his coat-collar turned up and his hands resting upon the muzzle of his rifle, appeared as immobile as if fashioned of stone. He was an oldish man. The flight-sub was certain of that fact; more, he wore glasses.

"A Landsturmer, and as blind as a bat," thought the young officer. "There were three sentries, then; two have gone to the estaminet, the old boy is told to remain at his post. Now what's to be done? Something, or Fuller and Kirkwood will be forging ahead to find me and then there'll be damage done."

Very cautiously Barcroft began to back away from the unsuspecting Hun. The man coughed and hunched his shoulders still more. At the sound Billy again stood rigid, half expecting the sentry to slope arms and resume his beat. Nothing happening, the flight-sub withdrew as silently and stealthily as the slippery state of the *pavé* permitted.

"Well?" whispered the A.P.

"Hist!" was Barcroft's only reply, then grasping his companions by their arms he led them back until they were well out of the sentry's hearing— even supposing that he possessed the normal use of his ears.

"A Boche over there," reported Barcroft. "Nearly rammed him broadside on. Blind as a bat; a regular septuagenarian. We'll make a slight detour and have another shot at crossing the road. It's open country beyond."

This time the highway presented no difficulty, and with renewed vigour the trio struggled through the tenacious slime beyond.

It was Barcroft's plan to keep to the fields as much as possible and follow the road on a parallel course. It was infinitely harder going, but there was less risk of blundering upon a German outpost, while at intervals military motor-cars tore at break-neck speed over the slippery *pavé*, their iron-shod wheels slithering dangerously on the slimy stones.

In almost total silence the dreary trek was maintained throughout the night, with the exception of two brief halts. Gamely Fuller "stuck it," although his ankle was getting worse under the strain. His left arm, too, was throbbing in spite of careful bandaging, yet no word of complaint came from his lips.

At half past six in the morning Barcroft called a halt.

"By dead reckoning I estimate we have covered twenty-five miles," he announced. "That's not so dusty. It will be dawn in another hour. We'll have to find a place and lie doggo until to-night. How's the victualling department, purser?"

"I can spare a couple of biscuits apiece," declared the A.P. "And a small tot of Schnapps. You'll have to wait till lunch time for the sausage tack. I'm counting on a three days' basis, you know."

"Very good," replied Barcroft approvingly. "There is a hovel or barn ahead. We'll make for that."

The outbuilding consisted of stone walls and a tiled roof, the latter in a state of dilapidation. The massive oaken door had been partly wrenched from its hinges. Within, the floor was of trodden earth mixed with lime. The place was absolutely bare.

"Not even a bundle of straw," declared the A.P. "The roof leaks like a sieve. Still, it is better than nothing at all."

"The only place to hide in is under the rafters," said the flight-sub. "Those two planks lying over the beams will serve that purpose should necessity occur. I would suggest that we keep watch by turns—two-hour tricks. That will give each man four consecutive hours' rest. I'll take first trick; you, Bobby, will relieve me and John will follow on. Now to bed, you roysterers."

Fuller and the A.P. needed no second bidding. Rolling themselves in their leather coats that fortunately acted as waterproofs, and with their heads pillowed on their padded flying helmets, they were soon sound asleep.

Taking up his post by the open door—he made no attempt to close it lest the fact would be remarked by people living in the district—Barcroft commenced his dreary vigil. Although bodily and mentally tired he knew that his comrades were more in need of rest than he. It was merely a case of "sticking it"; happy in the knowledge that the guerdon, in the shape of precious liberty, was twenty-five miles nearer than it had been seven hours previously.

Gradually, as the sullen dawn overcame the blackness of the night, the dreary landscape unfolded itself to the watcher's eyes—an expanse of flat country broken here and there with isolated buildings. Within fifty yards of the barn where the fugitives sheltered was a fairly broad river, that described almost a complete semicircle around the building.

"It's running north," soliloquised Billy. "Wonder if it's the Aa? Hanged if I can fix our position with certainty! We've crossed five or six railway lines, and half a dozen small streams. Hang it all! We can't be more than five or six miles from the frontier. By Jove, we are close to the road, though! Wonder if that bridge is guarded?"

After a short interval a convoy of motor waggons thundered past. The A.P., roused out of his sleep, sat up.

"What's that—an air raid?" he asked drowsily.

"No, only traffic," replied Billy. "No cause for alarm. You've another forty minutes yet."

A little later on a barge, quite eighty feet in length, manned by a couple of Belgians and towed by a miserably gaunt horse, descended the river. As it rounded the bend the cumbersome craft ran aground. Its stern, being still afloat, was swung round by the force of the wind and jammed against the opposite bank.

At the impact, slight though it was, the hatch of the after cabin was thrown back and German soldiers scrambled on deck. One of them was smoking a long pipe with a bent stem. He evidently regarded the situation with philosophical stolidity, but not so his companion. The latter, cursing and reviling the luckless Belgians, danced like a madman on the sodden deck, till, losing his balance, he subsided heavily against the massive tiller.

"Bring the horse back, you swine!" he shouted to the man on the bank. "There'll be trouble in store for you if the barge doesn't reach Wuestwezel by noon. Himmel! What will Herr Kapitan say?"

Peering through a crack in the door Barcroft watched the proceedings. The German had mentioned Wuestwezel. Consulting the map the flight-sub found that it was a small Belgian village on the frontier, where in pre-war days a customs station was situated.

For the best part of an hour the men strove unavailingly to extricate the barge from the tenacious mud. Even the two Huns condescended to assist in the operation but without the desired result. So interested was Barcroft in their frantic efforts that he quite overlooked the fact that it was time for Kirkwood to relieve him.

"You'll have to go to Hulstweelde and get additional help, you lazy dogs!" bellowed the infuriated Fritz. Then he said something to his companion, but speaking in a lower tone the words were unintelligible to the young British officer. Apparently there was an argument in progress as to which of the two Germans should accompany the bargees, lest the latter took it into their heads to decamp. Finally all four trudged off, leaving the horse to nibble at the scanty pasture on the bank.

"You rotter!" exclaimed Kirkwood. "It's gone nine. Why didn't you turn me out? And what are you so interested in? Come, now, you were very keen on ordering me to turn in. Try this luxurious *salle-à-coucher*."

"Before I do so," replied Barcroft pointing to the abandoned barge, "I'm going to do a bit of burgling if there's anything in the food line. Keep a sharp look-out, old man—towards that bridge especially. I won't be long."

It was a comparatively simple matter to board the deeply-laden craft. Almost the whole of the space amidships was covered by huge tarpaulins, leaving a narrow gangway on either side. Making his way aft Barcroft boldly descended the short ladder leading into the cabin—a somewhat spacious compartment with the small "cuddies" on barges working British canals.

"Black bread and cheese," said the flight-lieutenant to himself. "Well, that's better than nothing. Bacon, too: useless when one cannot light a fire."

He had no qualms about despoiling the Philistines. Before the food would be missed the barge would doubtless have resumed its voyage. When the theft was discovered the Germans would to a certainty blame the men who came to their assistance.

"Wonder what the cargo is?" continued Billy as he regained the deck.

Unfastening one corner of the tarpaulin he made the discovery that the contents of the hold consisted of bales of old clothes packed tightly and labelled in large lettering with typical German thoroughness. They were commandeered Belgian civilian articles of clothing, those of cotton being kept apart from those of wool. Their destination was Aachen (Aix-la-

Chapelle) via Wuestwezel, Turnout and Tongres, and at Wuestwezel they were to be transferred to the railway.

"I think I see the move," thought Barcroft. "The stuff is to be converted into cloth for the Huns. The cotton gear, perhaps, will be utilised in the manufacture of explosives, since they cannot get the raw material. By Jove! The very thing. I'll collar a bale of this gear. We'll have to be in mufti of sorts when we cross the frontier, otherwise it means internment."

A low whistle from the barn warned the flight-sub to a sense of danger. It was too late. Riding at a steady trot along the river bank was a German officer.

CHAPTER XXXI
THE FRONTIER

RESISTING his first impulse to rejoin his companions Barcroft crouched upon the unsavoury bundles and drew the corner of the painted canvas cover over his head. In breathless suspense he waited.

The clatter of the horse's hoofs ceased. He heard the rider dismount as his boots struck the ground.

"You there, Corporal Pfeil?" he shouted. "Donnerwetter! what do you mean by getting your charge in this fix?"

Receiving no reply the German began cursing volubly, at the same time expressing his belief that Pfeil and Co. were dead drunk in the barge cabin and that those rascally Belgians had given them the slip.

The fellow came on board. It required considerable effort on his part, for by the time he gained the deck he was puffing and blowing. As he walked aft his spurs jangled on the metal deck. So close did he pass the hiding Barcroft that the latter could have grasped his ankles.

"Schweinhund!" exclaimed the major, for such was his rank. "I'll give Pfeil something to remember this business. Confound this rain! I'll wait for him in the cabin."

He went below. Presently Barcroft could hear the rasping of a match, and the tantalising odours of tobacco from the after-cabin.

"Now I'm done," soliloquised the flight-sub. "The penalty for inquisitiveness, I suppose. Properly dished unless— —"

Seized by a sudden inspiration Billy softly threw back the corner of the tarpaulin, crept aft and closed the sliding hatch of the cabin. Before the astonished major could completely realise what was happening Barcroft had shut the massive metal hasp and had secured it by wedging a belaying pin through the staple.

"Shout as hard as you like, my festive!" chuckled the flight-sub; then he, too, realised that he had "put his foot into it." Not only that—he had jeopardised the chances of his companions.

Throwing a sack of clothing to the bank Billy leapt ashore, picked up the weighty bundle and made for the barn.

He found Fuller awake, for Kirkwood had informed him of the danger that threatened the explorer.

"We were just coming to your rescue," announced the A.P., "only we saw that you had boxed the Boche up. What's this bundle for, old bird?"

"For to-night's fancy dress ball," replied Barcroft. "A suit of mufti for each of us. We appear in the characters of the Continental knockabouts."

"What do you mean?" asked Fuller.

"Simply that we must make tracks at once, before Corporal Pfeil and Company return. Obviously we cannot hope to wander unmolested over the country if we stick to our flying kit, so with my characteristic regard for your welfare I have procured a stock of second-hand clothes for your inspection and choice. We'll push on for a couple of miles or so and then hide until it's dark. Then, with luck, over the frontier we jog, without running the risk of being interned by the Dutch authorities."

The contents of the bag were emptied upon the floor—a weird collection of musty and for the most part dirty and ragged clothes.

"Must we, or musty?" inquired Kirkwood sniffing disdainfully

"Both," replied Barcroft decidedly. "Look alive. Pity to have to sacrifice our coats, though. Mine cost me eighty-five shillings only a month ago. Keep your revolvers. They'll stow in the coat-pockets."

The change of raiment was speedily effected. The discarded gear, folded in as tight compass as possible, was stowed away on the beams of the barn.

"Who knows," remarked the A.P., "but that we may have a chance of recovering our kit, when the Boches have been driven out of Belgium? My word, Billy, you look absolutely IT! Tired Tim or Weary Willy must be your character."

"You speak for yourself, old sport," retorted Barcroft laughing. "You're positively not respectable. We tolerate your presence only on sufferance. Matter of fact, Tired Tim does suit me," he added, stifling a yawn. "I'm as dog-tired as a fellow can possibly be. And what might you be supposed to represent, John—a Belgian hare?"

"That's about it," replied Fuller languidly. "The main thing is to keep warm, and trust to luck to get a hot bath later. Some fit, eh, what?"

The flight-lieutenant had appropriated a long cloth coat liberally trimmed with fur. In its prime the coat might have done credit to a wealthy bourgeois of Brussels, but now it would ill-become a city scavenger.

The rest of the clothes were returned to the sack, with the addition of a couple of heavy stones. Barcroft and the A.P. carried the "incriminating evidence" to the river and hurled it into the water.

"Don't suppose our boots will excite suspicion if we fall in with any one," remarked Kirkwood. "It is impossible to say whether they are black or brown."

"Or sabots," added Billy. "Without exaggeration we are carrying half an inch of mud about on them. Now, easy ahead."

Keeping clear of the highway, and following the river at a respectful distance the fugitives covered a distance of about three miles in less than a couple of hours. The rain was falling heavily again, blotting out everything beyond a distance of fifty yards, but by this time the dauntless trio regarded the discomfort with equanimity and as a blessing in disguise.

"By Jove!" exclaimed Puller, suddenly coming to a halt. "There's the frontier."

Before they were aware of the fact they had arrived within a few feet of the seemingly interminable barbed wire fence that separated occupied Belgium from coveted Holland. As far as could be seen the barrier was unguarded.

"How about it?" inquired Barcroft. "Shall we make a dash and risk it?"

"Steady," cautioned the flight-lieutenant. "Suppose, as is more than likely, there's a high tension wire running along that contraption? We don't want to be pipped on the post, you know."

"I'll test it," declared Billy promptly.

"How?" asked his companions in one breath

"By this," replied the sub indicating the wristlet compass. "You hang on here. I won't be long."

"Be careful, then," said the A.P.

"Trust me for that," answered Barcroft cheerfully. "Lie low and keep a sharp look out."

On either side of the fence was a belt of reeds and coarse grass. In ordinary circumstances its height would be five or six feet, but the wind and rain had beaten down the reeds considerably. In places the tangle of grass was almost flat, and, combined with the slippery soil, formed a trap for the unwary.

"H'm! a fair amount of traffic on either side of the fence," commented Barcroft as he arrived upon the scene of his investigations. "They've had sentries patrolling up and down, but evidently they don't like the weather."

Kneeling in the slime the flight-sub unbuckled the strap that secured the little spirit compass to his wrist, then cautiously he held the delicate instrument towards the lowermost wire.

The needle was unaffected, even though he brought the compass close enough to risk a short circuit should the wire be highly charged with electricity. Three parallel wires he tested with similar results. At the fourth, which was about three feet from the ground, the needle oscillated. Whether it was owing to the deviating effect of an electric current or that he had unintentionally jogged the compass Barcroft could not decide. Withdrawing the instrument he waited for the sensitive index to come to rest.

"Dash it all!" he ejaculated as he resumed his investigations. "That wire is charged. It will mean a fine old job getting through this fence. Might squeeze through under the lowermost one if it could be prised up. But supposing the electrified wire isn't always the fourth from the ground: what then? I'll apply another test further along."

So intent was the flight-sub in his work that he failed to hear the faint sound of footsteps stealthily approaching through the squelching mud. Entirely at a disadvantage since he was crouching on his knees, Barcroft was most disgustedly surprised to hear a guttural exclamation, the form of which left no doubt as to the nationality of the speaker.

Turning his head Billy found himself at the mercy of a German sentry, whose levelled bayonet was within a foot of his shoulderblades.

CHAPTER XXXII
AN AVERTED CATASTROPHE

"MORNING, Norton; you are an early visitor," exclaimed Peter Barcroft. "Five minutes later and you would have found me out—to use a contradictory phrase. I'm just off for a morning with the rabbits. Care to come along?"

"Delighted," replied the spy. "I suppose you won't mind my calling at The Croft to get a gun?"

A couple of weeks had passed since Siegfried von Eitelwurmer's return to Tarleigh. During that time Peter had seen or heard nothing of Philip Entwistle. The *soi-disant* Andrew Norton had resumed his former habit of dropping in at Ladybird Fold at all hours, somewhat to the detriment of "The Great Reckoning—and After," which was now approaching completion.

Von Eitelwurmer was trying to muster up courage to earn single-handed the reward offered by his Imperial Master for the obliterance of the man whose writings had so greatly offended the Potsdam Potentate who was seeking in vain for a place in the Sun. The spy had a wholesome dread of British justice should he bungle in the attempt and find himself under arrest. He had been told by the authorities at Berlin that he must not expect further co-operation by means of a Zeppelin. Evidently the rough handling the German aerial squadron had met with on the return journey had upset the hitherto implicit faith of the Huns in this branch of frightfulness. Since, then, von Eitelwurmer had no opportunity of getting Peter Barcroft conveyed to Germany, he set about a means to "remove" him. After all, he decided, half the reward was better than nothing.

In his many conversations with Peter the spy never mentioned the subject of their meeting at Bigthorpe; and Barcroft, putting down his reticence to a fear of being rallied on his mental lapse, studiously avoided any reference to the event. Nor did von Eitelwurmer say a word on the subject of the raid. In fact, he had never discussed the war with the tenant of Ladybird Fold, and had shown such a casual disinterestedness whenever Peter had touched upon the matter that the omission to say a word about the Zeppelin's visit to Barborough occasioned no surprise.

"Haven't you a double-barrel?" inquired Peter as the spy brought out a twelve-bore single-barrelled sporting gun with a breech action resembling that of a Martini rifle. "If I had known I could have lent you one—a hard-hitting choke bore."

"Thanks all the same," replied von Eitelwurmer. "I'm used to this. I've got in two shots at a running rabbit before to-day. Where are you making for?"

"Over the moors towards Windyhill," replied Barcroft, signing to the two dogs to come to heel. "We'll cut through the Dingle Dell. It's a bit rough going, but we'll save a mile or so."

The Dingle Dell was a narrow valley between two rugged cliffs of Millstone Grit. Through the defile rushed a foaming mountain stream fed by the recent rains and now possessing a tremendous volume of water. Centuries of erosion had worn the rocks that confine the torrent to its course to a remarkable smoothness, while the water as it leapt from one level to another had undermined the banks almost throughout the entire length of the Dingle Dell.

Tarleigh Moors had been experiencing a variety of weather during the last fortnight. Following the heavy rain came a hard frost that in turn gave place to the first of the winter snow. Although most of the white mantle had disappeared, patches of snow still remained in the sheltered sides of the valleys, while in the Dingle Dell the trees still retained their seared and yellow leaves.

Crossing a dilapidated wooden bridge the two men ascended a steep bank, on the top of which ran a narrow path, slippery with the exposed roots of the abundant trees. On the left the ground dropped steeply to the foaming stream; on the right was a "cut" or artificial waterway that supplied power to the neighbouring bleach-works, the smell of which, hanging about in the dank atmosphere, was the acknowledged drawback to the sylvan beauties of the Dingle Dell.

"I haven't been this way before," remarked von Eitelwurmer untruthfully. He knew the district far better than his companion, and perhaps his knowledge was equal to that of the majority of the inhabitants of Tarleigh. It was his business to acquaint himself with the locality of every place in which his secret service work had led him. "Shouldn't care to walk along this path on a dark night, especially after one of your 'night-caps,' Barcroft."

"Yes, it is a sort of 'twixt the devil and the deep sea business," rejoined Peter. "Steady!" he added as the spy stumbled over a protruding root. "Gun's not loaded, I hope?"

"Rather not," replied von Eitelwurmer, pulling down the breech-block lever and holding up the weapon for his companion's inspection. "I'm used to a gun, remember."

"You may be," retorted Barcroft grimly, "but these roots are not.... dash it all!"

He sat down heavily, a patch of slippery ground having been responsible for the mild catastrophe. His cap, falling from his head, rolled down the bank and finally stopped on the top of a rounded boulder on either side of which the water swirled furiously.

"The result of moralising," declared Peter. "And I've lost my cap. Bang goes five and sixpence if I don't recover it."

Resting his gun against a tree, Barcroft descended with considerable agility till he gained the brink of the torrent. The two dogs, unused to the sight of their master on his hands and knees, capered behind him. To his disgust he found that the lost head-gear was just beyond the reach of his outstretched hand.

He was not going to be done, he reflected stubbornly. By grasping the stem of a hazel that grew close to the stream he could lean out further without losing his balance.

The stem seemed stout and supple enough, but unfortunately its looks belied its actual strength. It parted, and the next instant Peter was struggling in the foaming torrent.

Flung against the hollowed water-course with a thud that almost deprived him of the little stock of breath left after his sudden immersion in the icy water, Barcroft was unable to make an effort to save himself from being swept over a miniature waterfall. Full six feet he fell; then, almost blinded by the spray that enveloped his head, he found himself struggling in a small but powerful eddy, while the rocks that almost surrounded the pool were too high and too slippery to afford a hand-grip.

Upon seeing their master topple into the stream Ponto and Nan leapt in after him, although Peter was then ignorant of the fact. Swimming ineffectually against the strength of the current both dogs were swept away, without being able to be of the slightest assistance, through a portion of the water course which, though only a couple of feet across at the top, had been worn away to four times that distance underneath.

Meanwhile Siegfried von Eitelwurmer was stolidly contemplating the catastrophe. He saw the two animals being swept away, and marked the semi-subterranean channel. A man carried under those overhanging rocks stood little chance of escape. Even if Barcroft were able to resist the remorseless pressure of water that threatened to sweep him through the contracted gully the numbing effect of the water would quickly tell. Yet the luckless man maintained silence; not a cry for assistance came from his lips.

From the path only the tip of Peter's head was visible. The spy still stood immovable. He had no wish for his unfortunate companion to witness his apathy. He chuckled with fiendish glee. Fate was playing into his hands.

Suddenly a maddening thought flashed across his mind. Barcroft drowned—inquest—verdict: "Accidental Death." Would the German Government pay the blood-money in these circumstances? He doubted it. Being a Hun he had no faith in a Hun's interpretation of the accident.

It was not a sense of duty, the call for heroic action, that spurred von Eitelwurmer to the rescue. With admirably acted zeal he descended the declivity, and followed the bank until he reached the pool in which Peter was still maintaining a precarious foothold.

Grasping the benumbed man's wrists he exerted his full strength in an attempt to extricate him. The effort was in vain: Barcroft, encumbered with his saturated clothing and now too exhausted to help himself, was too heavy to be hauled into safety.

"Run to the works and get assistance," exclaimed Peter, fancying that his supposed friend was in danger of slipping off the rocks into the swirling cauldron. "I can hold on some time yet."

Thoroughness was one of the spy's characteristics. Having undertaken to rescue his companion he was not going to be thwarted if it could be helped. Glancing around he spotted a stout branch of a tree lying on the ground. Its length was more than sufficient to bridge the distance between the projecting sides of the stream.

"Hold on for ten seconds, Barcroft," he exclaimed, and releasing his hold he made his way to the severed branch and secured it.

"Hang on!" he said, at the same time lifting Peter sufficiently to enable him to grip the span of wood. Then, pulling off his woollen scarf, he leant over the edge and passed it round Barcroft's waist, slackening the "bight" until it sank low enough to go round his companion's knees.

"Now," he continued, "together!"

With a steady heave von Eitelwurmer raised Peter's legs until his feet were fairly over the edge of the bank, while his head and body supported by the suspended branch were still hanging over the stream. So far so good. The German's next step was to shift the scarf until it formed a loop round Barcroft's shoulders. Another strong pull and the rescued man was lying safe but exhausted on the bank, while the two very wet dogs were frantically licking his face. The animals, after being carried down stream, had succeeded in finding a foothold, whence they had leapt clear of the dangerous stream.

"You've saved my life, Norton," said Peter, stating a perfectly obvious fact.

"It is nothing," protested von Eitelwurmer.

"Perhaps, but it is precious to me," rejoined Barcroft, unable, even in his exhausted condition, to resist the temptation of "pulling up" his companion for a badly-expressed declaration.

"What I did, I meant, of course," added the spy. "How about your cap?"

"I'll have another shot for it," said Peter with sudden determination. "If you'll hold my hand I'll reach it easily enough."

"No, you don't," decided the German firmly. "I don't want the trouble of fishing you out again. Come along."

Having assisted Barcroft to the path, von Eitelwurmer again descended, cut a short stick and deftly hooked the cause of the accident.

"Here you are, Barcroft," he exclaimed, handing the cap to its rightful owner. "Quite easy, you see. I suppose rabbit-shooting is off at present?"

"Until to-morrow," replied the undaunted sportsman. "At ten, sharp. You must have an opportunity of making up for what you missed to-day, Norton; 'pon my word you must."

CHAPTER XXXIII
VON EITELWURMER'S OPPORTUNITY

AT eight the following morning Siegfried von Eitelwurmer was considerably surprised when the tenant of Ladybird Fold appeared at The Croft, booted and gaitered and carrying his gun.

"You are two hours too early, Barcroft," he exclaimed. "What is wrong? Couldn't you sleep after your involuntary bath?"

He spoke jocularly, yet in his mind there was a haunting suspicion of doubt. Not that there was any reason for it as far as Peter Barcroft was concerned, although—did he but know it—Philip Entwistle was "speeding things up" in his work of investigating the case of Andrew Norton otherwise von Eitelwurmer.

"I slept soundly," replied the unruffled Peter. "Notwithstanding hot-water bottles and mustard poultices, cough-mixtures and various bronchial remedies. It's one of the penalties of being married; but, 'twixt you and me, I like being made a fuss of in that direction. Now, I wonder how you would fare, Norton, if you were taken ill, living practically by yourself?"

"Make the best of it, I suppose," replied the spy hurriedly. He was an arrant coward where illness was concerned. "But why this early call? Thought you didn't rise much before nine?"

"I had a note from the parson this morning," exclaimed Barcroft. "I happened to mention that I was going shooting and told him that I would hand over the bag to the village soup kitchen. Personally I loathe rabbits as food. However, the vicar informed me that the soupkitchen opened at eleven-thirty, and asked if it would be convenient for me to send the rabbits down by ten o'clock. Don't suppose we'll get back in time, but we'll try."

"First get your rabbits," said von Eitelwurmer banteringly.

"Trust me," declared Barcroft with conviction. "But are you busy? I'm afraid I've interrupted you."

"Only catalogues of early spring seeds," replied the spy. "They can wait till to-night. I'll be ready in a couple of minutes."

So saying the *soi-disant* Norton threw the books on the floor with feigned unconcern, recorked a small bottle of lemon juice and pushed it out of sight behind a pile of sporting papers. Then, getting his sporting gun from the rack and stuffing a handful of cartridges into his pocket, he signified his readiness to start.

"I wonder," mused the spy as the two men walked briskly down the lane—"I wonder what Barcroft meant yesterday: 'You must have an opportunity of making up for what you missed to-day.' Very strange that he should say that. Yet can he know anything? I have been careful enough, in all conscience."

His fingers came in contact with the loose cartridges. Grimly he reflected that they were of English manufacture. Previous acquaintance with sporting cartridges coming from the Fatherland had made him chary of using ammunition of German origin. There must be, he reflected, no misfires. An initial failure would upset his nerve. He could not muster up courage to make a second attempt on the same day.

"You're rather quiet to-day, Norton," remarked his companion, as the two passed the scene of yesterday's adventure. "Not feeling quite up to the mark, eh? Or have I turned you out of house and home too soon after breakfast?"

"I wasn't aware that I was," replied von Eitelwurmer. "In fact I feel remarkably fit. Those dogs of yours trained to the gun?"

"Quite, by this time," said Barcroft. "And as for turning a rabbit out of cover they're great. You wait till we set to work."

"Powerful-looking animals," continued the spy. "I suppose they would pull a man down?"

"They might," answered Peter cautiously. "But since an occasion for testing their capabilities in that direction has not yet occurred—and I hope it will not—I haven't any definite data upon which to base my assumption. They were a bit of a handful as puppies," he continued warming to his subject, for the two sheep-dogs were practically part and parcel of Barcroft's existence. "The predatory instinct was very strongly developed. They would go to my neighbours' houses early in the morning and systematically and deliberately steal the milk. I've known them to take a jug as well and bring it back unbroken and deposit it as a kind of trophy on my lawn."

"You might have cut down your milk-bills," remarked his companion. "For a Biblical precedent you have the case of the prophet who was fed by ravens. I presume they stole from his neighbours. Were their efforts confined purely to the milk-business?"

"Hardly," replied Peter. "In one instance they brought home a boot."

"Only one?"

"Only one," declared Barcroft solemnly.

"It was in an almost new condition. I made inquiries all over Alderdene but without success. No one had lost a boot. Quite a month later I discovered that a parson living at Barcroft, a village three miles away, had missed one of his boots, and sure enough the one Ponto and Nan brought in was the missing article. Apparently they had walked into the parson's scullery, and finding nothing in the edible line, had picked up the boot as a souvenir of the visit."

"They showed a total lack of common sense," said von Eitelwurmer. "Now, if they had carried off the pair——"

"I should have had to return two boots instead of one," added his companion. "But here we are. We'll work up against the wind and keep the dogs to heel."

The sportsmen had gained the gently-sloping rise of Windyhill. It was the only side on which the ascent could be described as easy. The ground was grass-grown and interspersed with clusters of bushes, although the cover was by no means extensive. At the foot of the rise flowed a small brook, which was crossed by a single plank. Beyond a hedge somewhat of a rarity in the North—through which was a gap with a stile. From this point to the summit of the hill, a distance of nearly a mile, the only obstructions consisted of two rough stone walls running athwart the slope.

"We'll load after we're over the stile," said the cautious Peter. "Be careful, there's quite a lot of snow under this hedge."

Von Eitelwurmer's answer was to slip and measure his length in the soft snow.

"Donner—dash it all!" he exclaimed, hastily checking the natural yet hitherto carefully avoided habit of forcibly expressing himself in the language that came easiest to the tip of his tongue-that of the Fatherland. "You're right, Barcroft. It is confoundedly slippery."

Picking up his gun that had fallen from his grasp the spy followed Barcroft over the stile. Here the two men loaded and Peter called the dogs to heel.

"Plenty of evidence that the bunnies are about," he remarked. "We'll keep twenty yards apart. I don't suppose we'll catch sight of a rabbit until we get to the bushes."

Stealthily and in silence the sportsmen approached the nearmost patch of cover. Suddenly, a startled rabbit broke away and ran down wind. Up went Peter's gun, and the next instant bunny was kicking on the ground.

"Why didn't you fire?" inquired Barcroft, as the two converged upon the spoil. "The animal was across your path."

"Why didn't I?" repeated von Eitelwurmer. "I did. That was my shot. You didn't fire."

"But I did," declared Peter.

Both men ejected a still-smoking cartridge from their respective guns. They had fired simultaneously and the report had prevented each sportsman from hearing the other's shot.

"Honours even," cried the spy. "It was certainly remarkable."

"Very," agreed Barcroft as he reloaded.

The first enclosure produced no further trophy. Scaling the low wall the two men gained the second stretch of grazing land. Here the cover was slightly greater in extent.

"That's a favourite warren," said Barcroft, pointing to an irregular line of bushes. "You take the left side and I'll work round to the right. Ten to one you'll get a rattling good shot there. I'll keep the dogs with me."

The sportsmen separated. Von Eitelwurmer, treading softly and crouching under the bushes, allowed three rabbits to bolt almost under his nose. It was not through preoccupation of mind but by deliberate intent.

Once he stumbled over an exposed rock, and dropped his gun.

"That's the second time. This snow is dangerous," he muttered with a curse. "Is it an omen? And on the last occasion I nearly gave myself away."

He stopped to wipe some melting snow from the stock of his gun, wiping the walnut wood carefully in order to ensure a good grip; then still crouching, he continued his way.

Two shots rang out in quick succession on his right, then, after an instant, he saw Barcroft emerge from behind a bush and make for the next patch of cover.

"Twenty yards—absolutely safe, shots will hardly have time to spread," soliloquised the spy, giving a quick glance over his shoulder to see that there was no possibility of being overlooked from behind.

Then, setting his jaw firmly, he deliberately raised his gun to his shoulder, took careful aim at the back of the unsuspecting Peter and pressed the trigger.

CHAPTER XXXIV
KIRKWOOD'S WINDFALL

"So you've turned up again like three bad halfpennies," remarked the Senior Officer of the base to which the "Hippodrome" was attached, as the three airmen reported themselves. "Did you have much difficulty in getting across the frontier?"

"Very little, sir," replied Fuller, who by virtue of his higher rank acted as spokesman for the trio. "Nothing to brag about. Had a little bother with a sentry guarding the electrically-charged wire on the Dutch frontier; but, while he was preparing to tackle Barcroft with the point of his bayonet, Kirkwood and I contrived to deal with him very effectually. The Hun, you see, sir, had provided himself with a combined hook and wire cutting arrangement with an insulated handle, and it came in jolly useful. That's about all, sir, and we are ready to rejoin our ship at the earliest opportunity."

"I am afraid that's out of the question for a week or ten days," replied the Rear Admiral. "The 'Hippodrome' is away on special service, and I won't run the risk of sending you away on a destroyer, bearing in mind your previous trip for the same reason. The best thing you can do is to go on leave. You look as if a rest and a good feeding up will do you good. Should anything arise requiring your recall you will be sent for by wire, so hold yourselves in readiness for such a possibility."

The Senior Officer shook hands with the three subordinates and the interview was at an end.

"S'long, you fellows," exclaimed Fuller, when they were once more outside the Rear Admiral's office. "I'm catching the twelve-fifteen to Town. See you later."

"What are your plans, old man?" asked Billy, addressing the A.P.

"My plans? I haven't any," replied Kirkwood, who, having lost his parents early in life, had no home but that represented by His Majesty's ships. "I could go to my uncle's place, but I'm not very keen, and I fancy the sentiment is reciprocated by him, although I am his heir. He's a lawyer, you know, and about as musty as parchment."

"Then run up with me to Tarleigh," said Billy cordially.

The A. P, was not one of those fellows who affect a ridiculous hesitation when given an invitation.

"Thanks, awfully, old man," he replied. "I'm on absolutely. Is there time to look in at the Naval Club? I expect letters awaiting me."

"Right-o!" assented Billy. "By the powers, 'tis good to find oneself in England after our little jaunt. Makes a fellow completely bucked, especially after a jolly good bath, fresh clothes and all that. Ugh! Those togs we took from that barge!"

"Coming in?" inquired Kirkwood, as the pair arrived at the entrance of the Naval Club.

"No, not now," replied the flight-sub. "I'll go to the post office and send a wire to let my people know we are on the way. I'll pick you up at the station."

Barcroft had sent a telegram to his parents from the Hook of Holland announcing his safety. He had also gone to the post office immediately upon his arrival in England, but the place did not open till nine. It was now nearly noon.

He had not gone more than a hundred yards when Kirkwood overtook him, flushed with excitement.

"Here's a business!" he exclaimed. "Don't know whether to be sorry or glad. I've just had a letter informing me that my uncle, Antonius Grabb, has shuffled off this mortal coil. This is from his partner, who, apparently, is executor to the will. He wants me to call at his office as soon as possible. Billy, my festive, I'm afraid I'm a rich man. The thought of it appals me. I've handled thousands of Government cash in my time, but never had as much as a hundred to my credit before."

"Congrats, you lucky bounder!" said Billy heartily.

"And so I have to run up to Town," continued the A.P., "there to face an interview of momentous import. Frankly I funk it. How about it? Will you come with me? We can put up at the Whatsname Hotel—you know where I mean—and take the first train in the morning to Tarleigh."

"All right," assented Barcroft, after a brief consideration of the proposal. "We'll have to look sharp if we're to catch that twelve-fifteen. Here's luck—a taxi."

"Well, that is playing a low-down game," remarked Fuller as they rejoined him on the platform. "You two unsociables, declining my invitation to run up to Town, have evidently hatched a plot to have a stunt on your own account. But I've spotted your little game, you sly dogs. Now own up—what's the move?"

"We did change our minds," confessed the A.P. "Force of circumstances, you know. Fuller, I'm a millionaire of sorts—in pence, I fancy. At any rate, my uncle Antonius has died, and we're off to see his executor. Come to his office with us? The more the merrier, you know, and I'll stand dinner at the Carlton, if it hasn't been 'taken over.'"

Arriving at Ely Place the three officers were ushered into the presence of Mr. Fasly Gott, junior partner of the firm of Grabb and Gott.

The lawyer regarded his callers with well concealed interest.

"Mr. Robert Kirkwood, I presume," he exclaimed addressing Fuller.

"Almost wish I were," muttered the lieutenant to himself as he indicated the rightful bearer of the name.

"Ah, yes, of course," murmured Mr. Gott, re-adjusting his pince-nez. "I can see a strong resemblance to your late relative, my esteemed partner."

"That's not a compliment," thought the A.P. "In fact, it is a downright perversion." The lawyer cleared his throat. Obviously he did not like the presence of three officers in naval uniform. His reason was soon apparent.

"Your uncle's will," he continued, "is, to say the least, somewhat out of the ordinary. First let me impress upon you that its contents were absolutely unknown to me, his executor, until after his decease. He leaves the whole of his real and personal estate, representing a sum of at least seventy thousand pounds, to his nephew, Robert Angus Kirkwood——"

"Lucky dog!" interposed the irrepressible Fuller.

Mr. Gott gave a deprecatory cough. Levity was a rare emotion in that gloomy office, the motto of which in the vast majority of cases ought to be—'Abandon Hope, all ye who Enter Here.'

"Subject to one condition," he continued. "My late partner, as you might know, was a man of pacific temperament. Here I must hasten to explain that the will is dated 1913, that is, a twelvemonth previous to the outbreak of this deplorable war, and there is no codicil. The condition is as follows:—That the said Robert Angus Kirkwood resigns his commission in his Majesty's Navy, otherwise the bulk of the estate goes to the Society for the Encouragement of the Discovery of Antediluvian Remains."

"In that case," rejoined Kirkwood calmly, "I think you had better communicate with the secretary of the Society for the Encouragement of the

Discovery of Antediluvian Remains and inform him that my uncle's legacy is at his disposal. I am rather surprised that you should have written asking me to call. The proposition is an insult to His Majesty's Service."

"You show the proper spirit, Mr. Kirkwood," said the lawyer, with genuine admiration for the young officer's *esprit de corps*. "It is a peculiar will, and, if you desire to dispute its terms, you may be successful at the Courts; I should be happy to undertake the case. However, there is one clause. The bulk of the estate goes to this eccentric Society. The residue, consisting of deeds of real estates to the value of seven thousand pounds, goes to you unconditionally."

The interview lasted about twenty minutes, at the end of which the three officers prepared to leave.

"By the bye," remarked the A.P., "I suppose you can let me have a copy of the list of securities?"

"Yes, a copy," replied Mr. Gott. "The deeds will be handed over when probate of the Will has been declared. You will understand that the duties will be considerable?"

"Lucky to have to pay 'em," commented Kirkwood. "Thank you, Mr. Gott. Good afternoon."

It was not until the following morning when Barcroft and the A.P. were speeding north by the 5.15 express on their way to Tarleigh that the flight-sub mentioned a matter that was on his mind—a delicate request the reason for which Billy could not very well explain.

"By the bye, old man," he began "what do you propose doing with those deeds when they are handed over to you?"

"Hanged if I know," replied Kirkwood. "Haven't troubled much about them. Simply carry on and make good use of the interest, I suppose. Seems a fairly safe investment, but personally I'd rather sell out and shove the money into the War Loan."

"Are you willing to hand one of the deeds over to me?" asked Billy.

The A.P. looked at his companion in surprise. "Certainly," he replied. "Didn't know—hang it!—I'd no idea you were in need——"

"No, not that," interposed Barcroft. "A cash transaction, most decidedly. There's one—originally belonging to a Mrs. Deringhame—I'm rather keen on having. Can't very well explain why, unless you insist upon an explanation, only I thought——"

"Don't worry, old bird," said Kirkwood. "It's yours on your terms. I see by the list that old rascal Gott gave me that this particular document is included. That's settled, then."

"Thanks awfully," said Billy gratefully. "Some day I'll be able to tell you why I wanted it. When do you think the business in connection with your late uncle's will will be settled?"

"About a week, I should say," replied the A.P. "At any rate, if it isn't I think I can reasonably apply for an extension of leave."

It was after nine when the two officers arrived at Barborough. Here they found that the next train on to Tarleigh would not leave for another hour and a half.

"There's no particular hurry," remarked Billy. "But, all the same, I don't see why we should cool our heels in this draughty show. I vote we walk."

He could not help wondering why his father had not been waiting for him on the platform. Perhaps he was even now on his way with the car—that wretched magneto ought to be repaired by this time.

"I'm on," assented the A.P. "How about our gear? We can't lug it those five or six miles."

"Hanged if I haven't overlooked that problem," said Barcroft. "Let's take a taxi."

The taxi deposited the two chums at the door of Ladybird Fold at precisely the same moment that a telegraph boy was delivering a couple of telegrams.

"You did look awfully surprised to see us, mother," remarked Billy after the preliminary exchange of greetings. "This is my great pal, Kirkwood—Billy Kirkwood. You've heard me mention him many a time."

"Of course we are delighted to see you, Mr. Kirkwood," said Mrs. Barcroft. "It is, as Billy says, a surprise."

"But didn't you get my wire?" asked the flight-sub.

"I suppose it is one of these," remarked his mother, opening one of the envelopes.

She read the contents, a puzzled expression on her face. Then, without a word she handed it to her son.

"Silly asses!" exclaimed Billy, for the wire was from the Admiralty expressing regret that Flight-sub-lieutenant William Barcroft was reported missing. "However, it doesn't much matter now. Would have been awkward if we weren't here to show that it's a mistake. Look here—handed in three days ago. Delayed in transmission. Didn't you get my wire from Holland?"

Mrs. Barcroft shook her head.

"I gave that rascally hotel porter a couple of gulder to take the telegraph form to the post-office," declared the flight-sub. "Ten to one he stuck to the tip and the money for the wire as well. Where's the governor?"

"He went out early this morning with Mr. Norton," replied Mrs. Barcroft.

"The fellow who got adrift on the night of the Zep, raid? He turned up all right after all, then. Where have they gone?"

"Towards Windyhill. They went rabbit-shooting."

"Windyhill? Where's that, mater?" asked Billy. "We may as well stroll over that way, Bobby. No, thanks, mater, we don't require any lunch at present. Had second breakfast on the train. You can hang out till one o'clock, my festive?"

"Rather," declared the A.P. "Let's go and meet Mr. Barcroft and help carry back the spoils."

Receiving directions from Mrs. Barcroft the two chums set off on their quest. Half way down the lane leading to the Dingle Dell they suddenly encountered Philip Entwistle.

"Mornin'," said Billy with a laugh. "How are you? Recovered from that donkey-trip of ours yet?"

"Quite—absolutely," replied Entwistle. "So you are on leave again? I'm glad—very glad. There's a little matter upon which I should like to speak."

He paused and glanced inquiringly at Billy's, companion. The A.P. discreetly began to walk on.

"I say, Kirkwood," called out the flight-sub. "Let me introduce you."

"So you are the man who was flying with our friend here when the German airman who bombed Alderdene was strafed," said Entwistle, after the introduction was made.

"I believe I had a hand in it," admitted Kirkwood.

"That was when the document setting a price on your father's head was discovered, Barcroft," continued the vet.

"I say—how did you know that?" asked Billy. "Funny how things like that leak out."

"It's part of my business," replied Entwistle gravely. "That is the matter on which I wish to speak to you, and since Mr. Kirkwood is 'in the know' up to a certain point I do not see any reason why he should not be admitted into our conference. First of all, let me say that for the present I must get you to promise not to say a word to your father, or in fact to any one concerning what I am about to divulge." The two officers gave the required promise.

"It concerns Andrew Norton," continued Entwistle. "He is a secret agent of the German Government. On the night of the Barborough raid he had planned to have your parent made prisoner by the crew of the Zeppelin. Unfortunately for him his plans went adrift, and, as a result, he himself was kidnapped and taken to Germany."

"How on earth do you know this?" asked Billy incredulously.

"From definite and unimpeachable information," replied Entwistle. "I am—this is of course strictly confidential—also a Secret Service man, belonging to an opposition show. In due course—we have been giving him a good amount of rope—friend Norton will be arrested."

"But why cannot the governor be informed?" was Billy's next question.

Philip Entwistle smiled.

"Your father is—well, too imaginative, and, perhaps, a little too impulsive. I don't think he would believe me at first, if I were to broach the subject. He would, I feel inclined to think, even start bantering friend Norton."

"Yes, perhaps he might," admitted young Barcroft.

"And so I am just off to the house to see your father," continued Entwistle. "There are one or two questions I want to ask him, indirectly put but directly bearing upon the Norton case."

"'Fraid you won't find him there," remarked Billy. "He's gone rabbit-shooting with the man under discussion."

"With Andrew Norton?" asked Entwistle anxiously, then—gripping the flight-sub's arm—"Where, man, where? We must find him at once."

The three set out at a rapid pace through the Dingle Dell. The Secret Service man's hand went to his hip pocket, his fingers coming in contact with the butt of a small but powerful automatic pistol. For more than two years the weapon had been Entwistle's constant companion, yet no one, not even his personal friends, were aware of the fact.

"Thought Barcroft would speed things up a bit," he soliloquised. "Going rabbitting with that beauty has done it. Wonder if we are too late?"

Somewhat breathless in spite of their fine physical condition the trio arrived at the foot of Windyhill. As they crossed the stile two shots rang out in quick succession.

"They're up there," announced Billy, pointing to the second field. "I saw some one moving to the right of that clump of bushes."

Over the stone wall the men scrambled. As they did so a single report, more of a crash than the sharp, short detonation of a charge of smokeless powder, came from behind the gorse, followed by a scream of agony that trailed off into a long-drawn groan.

"Good heavens!" exclaimed Billy, spurting ahead of his companions.

Rounding the patch of cover he came upon the scene of the tragedy. Lying at full length upon the grass was a man; over him, with his back turned towards the new arrivals, was another—Peter Barcroft.

CHAPTER XXXV
ONE CARTRIDGE LEFT

"AN accident," declared Peter confusedly. The appalling event had completely unnerved him. He hardly seemed to realise that his son had turned up at a most opportune moment. "An accident. His gun burst, goodness only knows why. By Jove, he'll bleed to death if we don't look sharp!"

Von Eitelwurmer's injuries were ghastly at first sight. His left hand and wrist were simply a mass of scorched and lacerated flesh, his right hand was badly cut, while his face, ashy grey with a dreadful pallor, was pitted with embers from the smokeless powder. By his side were the remains of his gun, the barrel completely fractured for a distance of more than six inches.

For a brief space the spy opened his eyes. He saw the two officers in naval uniform.

"*Gott in himmel!*" he gasped, and straightway fainted.

Entwistle glanced knowingly at the two chums and nodded significantly. Peter, in his agitation, had not grasped the significance of the exclamation uttered in the injured man's native tongue.

"There's a gate yonder," remarked Entwistle, while he and young Barcroft were engaged in checking the flow of arterial blood. "You two might fetch it. It will be just the thing to carry him to the village."

Pulling himself together Peter hurried towards the gate, followed by Kirkwood, but not before the latter had been again warned by Entwistle to keep a discreet silence on the subject of the injured man's identity.

"We'll take him to his house," declared Entwistle. "I don't think the injuries are dangerous, although they are bad enough. The correct course would be to run him into Barborough and put him in the infirmary, but I have good reasons for the steps I propose taking. Excellent, Barcroft," he exclaimed when the gate was forthcoming. "Now, together, lift."

"What happened, pater?" asked Billy during the journey down the hillside.

"Hanged if I know exactly," replied Barcroft Senior. "I was ahead of him when it happened. Heard a fearful bang, turned round and found Norton on the ground."

"Frozen snow in the barrel, most likely," remarked Entwistle. "I've known guns to burst before to-day through that reason."

"He did slip when we crossed the stile," admitted Peter, "and plenty of snow had drifted down there. But that theory won't hold. He fired his gun after that."

"He may have fallen down again, or unknowingly poked the muzzle into another lot of snow," suggested Entwistle. "There was a good depth under the lee of those bushes, you'll remember, and I noticed by the footprints that he had walked through the drift."

"It's awfully unfortunate," declared Peter.

"Awfully—for the spy," thought Entwistle, "otherwise you might be taking his place on this improvised stretcher."

The wounded man was taken to The Croft and put to bed. Two doctors, summoned by telephone, were quickly in attendance.

"He'll pull through," was the verdict, "unless complications ensue. Shock to the system is more to be guarded against than the actual injuries. Some one will have to be constantly with him, particularly to see that an even temperature of the room is maintained."

"I'll stay," volunteered Entwistle.

"We'll take turns," suggested Peter. "I'll relieve you at two o'clock. Lunch will be ready for you then. If we cannot get a trained nurse (there is a dearth of them in Barborough, I understand) I'll be with him to-night. Come on, boys; we'll get back to Ladybird Fold."

During the meal Barcroft Senior spoke hardly a word. His appetite was poor. He was not used to scenes of physical violence. Even the unexpected arrival of Billy and the A.P. did little to help him to regain his normal spirits.

Lunch over, Peter left the two chums to their own devices and wended his way to The Croft.

He encountered Entwistle on the landing.

"Well?" he asked.

"He's just recovered consciousness," reported Philip. "A little light-headed, perhaps, and temperature up a bit. I'll come again at four. If you don't mind I'll arrange to stop here to-night."

"You're awfully good," said Peter, who had perhaps unconsciously taken upon himself the duties of deputy master of The Croft. "Well, lunch is awaiting you. Make yourself at home at my place. If there's anything you require don't hesitate to ask for it."

Entwistle had undertaken his self-imposed duties as sick-bed attendant with conscientious zeal; but he had also found time to make a complete investigation of the spy's papers, securing several that promised to become incriminating documents when subjected to professional scrutiny. At any rate, if he could be undisturbed he anticipated an interesting afternoon's search.

"I'll tell Barcroft all about it when I have completed the chain of evidence," he reflected. "He'll have a nasty shock, poor fellow, when he learns that his so-called pal tried to murder him. The whole thing's as plain as daylight to me; von Eitelwurmer meant to shoot him in the back, only the bursting of his gun saved Barcroft."

Left in charge of his treacherous friend, Barcroft found the patient had fallen asleep. Since nothing more was to be done Barcroft Senior took up a book, at the same time sighing for a pipe, a luxury that out of praiseworthy consideration for the injured man he had temporarily abandoned.

"By Jove!" said Peter to himself about an hour later. "That fire's getting low."

As silently as possible he heaped more coal upon the smouldering embers. Tending fires was not in his line. Often at home he would allow the study fire to die out simply through neglect to make use of the poker.

Somewhat anxiously he watched the gradually dimming glow. He was half-minded to ring for Mrs. Crumpet, until reflecting that the housekeeper at The Croft was evidently a person who made more noise in proportion to the work done than was desirable in the circumstances, he decided to tackle the recalcitrant fire himself.

Vainly he looked for a pair of bellows. Foiled in that direction he suddenly remembered having seen a smouldering fire roused into activity by means of a newspaper held over the grate.

"This might do," he soliloquised, picking up a couple of sheets of printed paper, since no newspaper could be found. "A catalogue of sorts: wonder if Norton wants it particularly?"

Slowly, very slowly, the dying fire began to revive, until under the forced draught a respectable flame rewarded Peter's efforts. Patiently holding the printed sheets across the grate until his arm ached, he whiled away the time by reading the technical description of Someone's patent combined washtub-and-dryer.

Suddenly his interest was aroused.

"Bless my soul!" he ejaculated. "That's funny. It wasn't there half a minute ago."

Under the heat of the now glowing fire letters hitherto invisible took semblance upon the warm paper. To his utter surprise the name "Barcroft" appeared in view.

Hardly able to credit his senses Peter read the damning evidence of the supposed Andrew Norton's treachery. It was written in German, for, owing to Entwistle having on a previous visit taken possession of the cypher (a circumstance that had caused the spy hours of uneasiness until he had been lulled into a sense of false security), he had been obliged to resort to ordinary writing pending the arrival of another code-book.

"Your request for immediate action noted," read Peter. "Expect Barcroft's removal to-day. Notifying impending accident to substantiate claim. Also hope to secure his manuscript to-night. Will destroy it if unable to retain without exciting suspicion."

There were also statistical particulars of the output of one of the Barborough munition factories, including the number of new gigantic shells, but Peter had not time to read that far.

A reverberating report filled the room. A bullet, whizzing close to the head of the startled man, shattered into a thousand pieces a mirror on the wall.

The spy, awaking from his sleep, had seen Barcroft poring over his secret—the same paper that he had been compelled to take hurriedly to his room that very morning when Peter disturbed him at his work.

Von Eitelwurmer realised that the game was up. Visions of a firing party in the moat of The Tower gripped his mind. Anything but that: he would make Barcroft pay for his discovery, and afterwards send a shot through his own head.

Under his pillow the spy habitually kept a Service revolver. This he fumbled for with his partly crippled right hand, and taking aim fired at Peter's head.

In his weak state von Eitelwurmer had not taken into sufficient consideration the "kick" of the powerful weapon. At the first shot the revolver jerked itself from his feeble grasp and clattered upon the floor.

"Thank you," said Peter firmly, as he stooped to pick up the weapon. He was surprised at his own almost unnatural calmness. "Might I ask the reason for this—er—outrage?"

"You have discovered everything," muttered the spy. "That was sufficient reason."

"Accidentally," added Barcroft. "Even then why should you seek my life and, what is almost as important to me, to destroy my labour—my writings? Look here, Norton, the position is this. You are a spy, caught redhanded, and the penalty is, as you know, death."

"And I meant to settle you before that," hissed the recreant.

"But Providence decided otherwise," continued Peter. "I thought you a totally different kind of person. You partook of my hospitality, yet descend to attempted assassination. Yet I do not forget that yesterday you saved my life. I wonder why? However, we are now quits, but I feel inclined to do you a favour. In ordinary circumstances you would be nursed back to health merely for the purpose of undergoing trial and suffering execution. There is yet another way."

"How?" asked the spy eagerly.

"By this," answered Peter holding up the revolver. "I will extract all but one cartridge and return you the weapon. If you are still intent upon my life the instrument is in your hands—only, remember, you cannot fire a second shot. Here you are. I give you five minutes to decide."

Slowly Barcroft crossed the room and descended the stairs. Only then did his calmness give way—and it required plenty of courage to deliberately turn away from a loaded weapon in the hands of a vindictive spy.

Entering the dining-room Peter sank into a chair and rested his head on his hands. Only the loud ticking of the grandfather clock disturbed the silence until the door was pushed open and Philip Entwistle entered.

"Hullo!" he exclaimed. "What's wrong now? Has Norton——?"

"I have made a very remarkable discovery," said Peter. "Andrew Norton is a German spy."

"Indeed?" was Entwistle's rejoinder.

"Accidentally I found some incriminating writing. He saw what I had done and let rip at me with a revolver. Needless to say he missed."

"That's the third lucky escape you've had from his murderous intentions," remarked Entwistle quietly. "I can tell you now. He tried either to murder or kidnap you by means of the Zeppelin that came to Barborough.

That the authorities gathered from one of the crew when the airship was wrecked in the North Sea a few days ago and the men rescued by a British patrol boat. Secondly, he did his level best to shoot you in the back this morning— —"

"Is that so?" asked Barcroft. "I can just understand a man doing such a thing through violent personal motives, but for a mere international reason— —"

"My dear fellow, there was the sum of ten thousand marks waiting to be earned."

"Yes," admitted Peter. "I know that. But only yesterday he fished me out of the Dingle Dell stream when I was almost on the point of being drowned. For why?"

"Ask me another," replied Entwistle. "At any rate, you will have cause to realise the actual existence of the Unseen Hand. But what happened just now, after he fired and missed?"

Peter Barcroft glanced at the clock. It wanted thirty seconds to complete the stipulated five minutes.

"I talked to him pretty straight," he said. "Shamed him a bit, I think. Anyway, I took four unused cartridges out of the revolver. Being a six-chambered weapon one cartridge remained."

"Well?"

"I handed the pistol back to him; told him if he were still of the same mind he had yet another chance to settle with me. He didn't—"

"Great Scott!" exclaimed Entwistle striding towards the stairs. "You left him with a loaded revolver?"

Peter laid a detaining hand on the Secret Service man's shoulder.

"I gave him five minutes," he said. "And the time's up."

A pistol shot rang out from the upstairs room.

Siegfried von Eitelwurmer, otherwise Andrew Norton, had paid the penalty.

CHAPTER XXXVI
THE ELUSIVE OBJECTIVE

"By Jove! old man," exclaimed Kirkwood, "we're up against a big thing to-morrow."

Billy Barcroft merely nodded. It was "a big thing," this impending movement. Something that was well worth the risk, but at the same time the chances of the participators in the business returning were very remote.

The two chums were pacing the port side of the quarter-deck of the "Hippodrome"—a long and comparatively narrow space betwixt the rise of the deck-houses and the stern, and separated from the corresponding part on the starboard side by the inclined launching platform.

The seaplane-carrier was lying in a certain East Coast harbour, with steam raised ready to proceed at a moment's notice, and although her destination was supposed to be a strict secret, the nature of the forthcoming operations was known to all on board.

It was nothing less than a raid on Cuxhaven, where a considerable portion of the German High Seas Fleet was known to be "resting" after a speculative but cautious cruise off the west coast of Jutland, the object being twofold—to exercise the crews and to impress upon the incredulous Danes the fact that the fleet of the Black Cross Ensign were willing and anxious to meet the British navy.

With their U-boats well out to sea, their ocean-going torpedo-boats forming a far-flung screen, and Zeppelins hovering overhead, the Hun "capital ships" had steamed in and out, keeping within their protective mine-fields: Having accomplished this imposing evolution the battleships of the fleet returned, part going to Cuxhaven, the rest to Wilhelmshaven, while the bulk of the torpedo flotillas anchored off the east side of Heligoland.

Once more the German Press had burst forth into a panegyric on the invincible and undaunted prowess of the fleet of the Fatherland, taking good care to impress upon the people that, although every opportunity had been offered to the British to engage in battle, the challenge had been declined.

The projected raid upon Cuxhaven was a reply to the Huns' empty boast. The seaplane carriers "Hippodrome," "Arena," "Cursus" and "Stadium," escorted by light cruisers and destroyers, were to proceed to a rendezvous twenty miles west of Heligoland. Sixty miles away the British battle cruisers were to "standby," ready, at a wireless call for assistance, to tear off at full speed to the succour of the small craft should the latter, regarded as an easy prey, be attacked by the big-gun ships of the German navy.

At the first blush of dawn twenty seaplanes were to start from their parent ships on their perilous flight over the Heligoland Bight and drop their powerful bombs upon the naval port of Cuxhaven—a feat that, knowing the formidable anti-aircraft defences, promised to be a forlorn hope; yet there was the keenest competition amongst the airmen of the fleet to participate in the "grand stunt."

The A.P. had carried out his promise to Barcroft. He had sold Billy the deeds of Mrs. Deringhame's house at Alderdene, and the flight-sub had sent them anonymously to Betty's mother.

It was a tremendous financial sacrifice on Billy's part. It had practically wiped up the bulk of his capital, but Barcroft cared not one jot for that. What troubled him was the fact that he could not ask Betty to marry him on his meagre pay. He had very little doubt but that the girl would do so, for during his last leave he had been much in her company.

"It wouldn't be fair to Betty," he soliloquised. "I must rake in some more cash, but goodness only knows how long it will take. One thing, we are both young, or I'm hanged if I would have the nerve to ask her to wait! Well, if this raid comes off successfully it will mean promotion. That's one blessing. If it doesn't—well, Billy Barcroft won't be in a position to worry about anything, I guess."

The flight-sub had completed his preparations. Two letters, one to his parents and one to Betty Deringhame, had been written, sealed and handed to the fleet-paymaster to be forwarded in the event of the writer's death. This unpleasant but necessary business performed, Barcroft dismissed the matter from his mind and concentrated his thoughts and energies on the work in hand.

"All correct, Jones?" he asked, addressing the air-mechanic who was putting the finishing touches to the seaplane that was to carry Barcroft and Kirkwood on their adventurous flight.

"All correct, sir," was the reply. "I've advanced the spark a trifle, sir she ought to simply buzz; but perhaps you'll see that everything's to your satisfaction."

Carefully Billy tested his controls, examined unions, contact breaker, and automatic lubricators. Success depended upon motor efficiency almost as much as upon the skill and courage of the pilot. The slightest hitch might spell disaster.

"There's the permission to part company," announced Kirkwood as a signal, made in response to a display of bunting from the yard-arms of the respective seaplane-carriers, was hoisted from the naval signal station. "Wonder if I'll see Old England again," he added in an undertone.

Already the cruisers were steaming out of harbour; not in the pomp of pre-war days with guards drawn up on the quarter-deck and bands playing as each vessel passed the flagship. Silent and grim, huge emblems of seapower, they glided past the harbour batteries and, increasing speed to twenty-two knots, were soon out of sight.

With destroyers preceding and following, the four seaplane-carriers were next to leave. On gaining the open sea they formed line abreast, surrounded by their vigilant escort; the light cruisers, reducing speed to that of the convoy, taking up station two miles astern.

In this formation the flotilla reeled off knot after knot without incident, until late in the evening, when two of the destroyers on the "Hippodrome's" starboard beam began a rapid fire that lasted nearly five minutes, breaking station and circling in a fashion that recalled the preliminary manoeuvres of a pair of cautious boxers.

"U-boat, somewhere over there," commented Fuller, who with Barcroft and the A.P. was on deck in preference to the somewhat boisterous ward-room. "I don't think they've got her. Wonder if she's dived and avoided the cordon. If so we'll have to look out."

"Hope she won't bag us at this stage of the proceedings," said Kirkwood. "At any rate, our quick-fires are manned, and it will be dark in another half-hour."

The two destroyers had resumed station, having signalled to the effect that no definite result was observed but it was believed that the U-boat's periscopes had been smashed by gun-fire.

"The trouble will come later, I think," said Barcroft when the message was communicated to the "Hippodrome's" officers. "If she isn't winged she'll rise to the surface after we're out of sight and wireless the news to the Heligoland signal station. The mere mention of seaplane carriers will put the Huns on the *qui vive*. However, that can't be helped; I'm turning in, you fellows, and I advise you to do the same."

Well before dawn the airmen detailed for the raid were roused from their sleep, or rather their efforts to slumber, since few were sufficiently proof against the excitement of the forthcoming expedition to enjoy a good night's rest.

Breakfast over, the members of the forlorn hope donned their leather coats and flying helmets, and assembled aft for final instructions from the wing commander.

"There is to be no easing down to keep pace with the slowest machine," were his instructions. "Each man is to go for his objective at top speed. You have noted the positions of the various batteries, I trust? It would be well to leave the Glienicke Redoubt well on your left. It's the only one, I believe, that mounts the latest Krupp's antis. On no account must the bombing seaplane attempt to encounter hostile aircraft on the outward flight: leave that task to the escorting planes. If, however, you fall in with any Zeppelins, attack immediately. One more point: should the situation necessitate the withdrawal of the seaplane-carriers and their escorts you know your instructions? Good. Well, gentlemen, that is all I have to say, beyond wishing you the best of luck and a safe return."

Barcroft's machine was the last to leave the "Hippodrome's" launching platform, and the last but one of the raiding craft. It was still dark. The misty outlines of the nearmost biplanes could be just discerned as they rose swiftly and steadily above the invisible destroyers. The crews of the latter gave the airmen three rousing cheers as they swept overhead, but the tribute was wasted. The farewell greetings were drowned by the roar of the engines.

As dawn began to break Billy made a rather disconcerting discovery. His seaplane was now the last of the procession. It had been over hauled by the one from the "Cursus," and what was more she was slowly yet surely dropping astern.

It did not appear to be the fault of the engine. The timing and firing seemed perfect. The motor was running like a clock, yet the rest of the raiding aircraft, most of which he knew were usually slightly inferior in speed, were distinctly gaining.

With the growing dawn the four escorting battle seaplanes could be distinguished, two on either side of the long-drawn line of bomb dropping air-craft. It was the duty of the former to engage any hostile aeroplane that attempted to bar the progress of the latter. Armoured and carrying two light quick-firers they were more than a match for the German airmen, and the latter were fully aware of the fact.

"Hang it all!" muttered the flight-sub as he actuated the rudder-bar and tilted the ailerons in order to check a cross-drift and to increase the altitude. "It's getting jolly misty. Hope it doesn't mean fog."

The rearmost of the rest of the air-squadron was now almost invisible, the others entirely so. As a matter of precaution Barcroft took a hurried compass bearing, fervently hoping that the mist would clear by the time he reached his desired objective.

"We're odd man out, old bird!" he shouted through the voice-tube. "Keep your eyes skinned. I don't want to get out of touch with McKenzie if it can be avoided."

"It can't," replied his observer. "He's just been swallowed up by the mist."

"I'll climb higher still," decided Billy. "There must be a limit to this rotten patch of vapour."

For another ten minutes Barcroft held on his course. He could not be far from land, he decided. Already the leading raiders must have achieved their object, if it were possible to see their target, and were on their return journey. The chances of a collision in mid-air with one of the British seaplanes suggested itself. The idea was not an inviting one—the impact of two frail and swiftly moving objects at an aggregate rate of nearly two hundred miles an hour, and the sickening crash to earth. There would be some satisfaction in knowing that an enemy aircraft was destroyed in this fashion, but the possibility—remote, no doubt—of sending one's fellow airmen and oneself to instant destruction was a proposition for which the misty air was responsible.

"I'm going to shut off the juice," announced Billy to his observer. "Keep your ears open, my festive."

With the switching off of the ignition the seaplane commenced a long glide. The almost total silence, save for the swish of the air against the planes and struts, was broken by a succession of loud rumbles. Some of the British raiders were at work.

"In which direction?" shouted Barcroft.

"Ahead on your left, I think," replied Kirkwood.

"Seems to me that the smash came from the right," declared the pilot. "Can you see any flashes?"

"Not a sign," replied the observer. "The sounds seem as if they are coming from the right now abaft the beam, if anything."

"It's a proper mix up," thought Barcroft. "Fog plays the very deuce with sound. If the other fellows are able to drop their bombs it proves that the mist is confined to the upper air. Dash it all! Are we never going to get clear of this muck?"

He jerked his goggles upwards until they rested on his cap. For all practical purposes they were useless, although guaranteed to be immune from the effect of moisture. The front of his coat was glistening with particles of ice. Everything he touched was slippery with rime. Jets of vapour, caused by the cold moisture coming in contact with the warm cylinders, drifted into his face and buffeted his bloodshot eyes.

"It's almost as bad as the night when Fuller and I strafed that Zep.," thought Kirkwood, who, although in a more sheltered position than his companion, came in for a generous share of the atmospheric discomforts.

A sudden jerk, so severe that it was a wonder the huge wing-spread did not collapse under the rapid change of pressure as Barcroft tilted the ailerons, told the observer that something had been sighted. Almost simultaneously the motor was restarted and the seaplane rising and banking steeply almost grazed the topmasts of a number of ships.

Kirkwood grasped the lever of the bomb-dropping gear and hung on till the order to let rip. But Barcroft gave no indication for the work of destruction.

"Sailing craft," he said to himself. "I could see their topsail yards. They are not what we want. Evidently we are over the commercial part of the harbour, if this is Cuxhaven. I'll buzz round and see if we have any luck."

Round and round in erratic curves, ascending and descending, the seaplane sped, yet without sighting any more shipping. Twice she came within sight of the ground, descending to within fifty feet in order to do so, but only an expanse of tilled fields rewarded the pilot's efforts. Then, climbing to a safe altitude he again volplaned in the hope of being guided by the sound of the bombardment. Again his endeavours met with no success. All was quiet, beyond the discordant clanging of a distant bell. The raiders had come and gone. Whether the fog had cut short their operations, or whether the air had been sufficiently clear to enable them to locate their objective, he knew not. The fact remained that Billy and the A.P. were lost in the fog and unable to carry out their allotted part of the strafing affair. They might be ten, twenty, or even thirty miles over German territory, so vague had been their course. Unless they speedily made tracks for the rendezvous they stood a good chance of running short of petrol should the fog extend sufficiently seaward to prevent them sighting the waiting seaplane carriers.

"What's the move, old man?" shouted the A. P,

"Off back," was the reply. "Nothin' doin' this trip."

"Hard lines," rejoined Kirkwood. "It's getting worse, if anything."

Which was a fact, for the frozen particles of moisture were increasing in size, and, driven into the airmen's faces by the rush of the seaplane through the air, were lacerating their skin until their features were hidden by congealed blood. Goggles being worse than useless, the two officers were compelled to close their eyelids to within a fraction of an inch and suffer acute torments from the biting air.

Very cautiously Barcroft planed down until the altitude gauge indicated a hundred feet, Seeing and hearing nothing he descended still further, restarting the engine as a matter of precaution.

Presently a rift in the wall of vapour enabled both pilot and observer to discern a flat, greyish expanse of sand through which several small channels wound sinuously.

"Good!" muttered Billy. "Now we know, more or less. We're over the sandbanks off the mouth of the Elbe unless it's the Weser. Anyway, nor' west is the course until we get away from this fog."

Ten minutes later the bank of vapour showed signs of diminishing in density; then, with a suddenness that left the two airmen blinking in the watery sunshine, the seaplane dashed into the clear daylight.

The sight that met their eyes was particularly cheerful. Ahead, at a distance of about four miles, lay the island fortress of Heligoland. But for one reason Barcroft would have made unhesitatingly for this strongly fortified rock of sandstone, drop his cargo of explosives and trust to luck to get clear. There was a more tempting inducement, for almost directly underneath the British seaplane was a large German warship.

CHAPTER XXXVII
"THE GREAT STRAFE"

THE sight was an unfamiliar one. Many a' time had Barcroft seen a British battleship from above, but never before one of the firstclass units of the Kaiser's navy. This one was a two-masted, three-funnelled vessel, the peculiar shape of the "smoke stacks" proclaiming her to be one of the "Deutschland" Class—built thirteen years previously, and carrying as her principal armament four 11-inch guns. She was not under her own steam. Tugs were lashed alongside, a third towing ahead. She had a decided list to starboard and appeared to be slightly down by the head.

"She's been hammered a bit," thought Billy. "We'll do our level best to shake her up a lot more. Pity she's not one of the 'Hindenburg' type, but half a loaf is better than no bread, so here goes."

As a matter of fact the battleship had been knocked about a week previously, owing to having bumped against one of the drifting German mines. Brought with difficulty into the outer roadstead, she was being repaired as secretly as possible in order to return to Kiel for completion of refit. The disaster having been concealed, at least officially, from the German populace, it had been considered necessary to keep the injured vessel off Heligoland rather than take her through the Imperial Canal in her nondescript state.

The British naval air raid upon Cuxhaven had completely upset this arrangement. News of the impending attack had been wirelessed, as Barcroft had surmised, from the U-boat that had been driven off by the seaplanes' escort, and, not knowing what the raiders' objective actually was, the Germans had hastily sent the crippled battleship from the roadstead in the hope that she might lie safely in the Kiel Canal before the aerial bombardment took place.

All three tugs were blowing off steam vigorously. The hiss of the escaping vapour had prevented the Huns from hearing the noisy British seaplane's approach, and now at an altitude of five thousand feet Barcroft had the huge target at his mercy. It was, however, necessary to descend considerably. There must be no risk of missing the slowly-moving battleship.

Descending in short right-handed spirals the pilot brought his craft within five hundred feet of his enemy. A bugle-blast, followed by the appearance of swarms of sailors as they rushed to man the light quick-firers, announced that the impending danger had been sighted. At all events, it was not to be a one-sided engagement, for almost simultaneously two anti-aircraft guns, mounted on the battleship's for'ard turret, came into action.

Both shells passed so close to the seaplane that the pilot distinctly felt the "windage" of the projectiles, The frail aircraft reeled in the blast of the displaced air, but fortunately the time-fuses of the shells were not set accurately. The missiles burst over eight hundred feet above their target.

Deftly Kirkwood released a couple of bombs. Both found their objective, one striking the fo'c'sle between the steam capstan and the for'ard turret, the other slightly in the wake of the bridge and chart-house, completely wrecking both. In a few seconds the whole of the fore-part of the battleship was hidden by a dense cloud of smoke.

"Not so dusty," thought Billy as he manoeuvred to enable the observer to drop another couple of "plums." As he did so a shell burst almost underneath the seaplane, ripping a dozen holes in the wings and severing a strut like a match-stick.

Out of the enveloping mushroom-shaped cloud of white smoke the seaplane staggered. For the moment Billy fancied that she was out of control and on the point of making a fatal nose-spin.

"Let's hope, then, that she'll drop fairly on top of that strafed hooker," was the thought that flashed across his mind.

But no; grandly the gallant little seaplane recovered herself. A touch of the pilot's feet upon the rudder-bar showed that she was capable of being steered, while apparently the controls were still in order.

Billy gave a quick glance over his shoulder. To his relief he found Kirkwood cool and imperturbable at his post, awaiting the opportune moment to release another pair of powerful bombs.

One burst aft, utterly knocking out the crew of the anti-aircraft gun that had so nearly strafed their attackers; the other, missing the warship's deck, landed fairly and squarely upon the tug lashed to the starboard side.

The little vessel, totally ripped up amidships, sank amid the roar of escaping steam, but still secured by fore and aft "springs"—wire hawsers stout enough to withstand the strain—she acted as a tremendous drag upon the huge bulk of the battleship.

In vain the latter attempted to check her tendency to swing to starboard by liberal use of the helm. The other tugs, still straining at their task, only made matters worse, until finally the towing craft, unable to check the side strain on her hawser, slewed completely round, and in this position was rammed by the steel prow of the battleship.

By this time Billy had manoeuvred for a third attack. So great was the confusion on the German's decks—most of the men who had survived the explosion bolting from their dubious cover that the seaplane was no longer subjected to a peppering from the Archibalds.

For years naval architects had been increasing the strength of a battleship's side-armour, while the thickness of the "protected" deck, considered only liable to glancing hits, was kept at about three inches of steel. The present war quickly found the defects of insufficient deck armour. Enormous shells, fired at a range of eighteen thousand yards, fell almost vertically upon the decks of battleships during the Jutland fight, while the menace from bombs dropped from hostile aircraft was only beginning to be realised.

Slowing down Barcroft again approached his quarry. This time Kirkwood released three of the high-explosive missiles. Two, fairly close together, by the after 11-inch gun turret, completed the business.

With a rush and a roar, indescribably appalling in its titanic power, the battleship's after magazine exploded. The seaplane, whirled like a feather in a hurricane, was enveloped in a cloud of black smoke tinged with flames and mingled with flying fragments from the disintegrated ship. In utter darkness Billy found himself on the underside of the overturned machine. Only the resisting strength of his broad securing strap saved him from being hurled downward like a stone.

Almost rendered senseless by the asphyxiating fumes, thrown about as far as the "give" of the strap permitted, his head shaken like a pea in a box, Barcroft was only dimly conscious that the job had been done almost too well. In spite of the danger of his hazardous position he was filled with a sense of elation. The seaplane had scored heavily, and for the present nothing else mattered. Deafened by the thunderous explosion, unable to see a hand's length in front of his face, he was at a loss to ascertain whether the motor was still running or whether the seaplane was engaging in a final tail-spin.

Mechanically he grasped the joy-stick. The seaplane was then looping the loop for the third consecutive time. Something—what it was he was unable to ascertain—hit the fuselage with a resounding crash. The lightly-built fabric trembled under the impact. It seemed as if the body of the machine had been ripped asunder.

At nearly a hundred miles an hour the seaplane cleared the edge of the drifting smoke. She was then "on an even keel," but about to nose-dive towards the surface of the sea, barely a couple of hundred feet below.

The sudden transition to the light of day recalled Billy to a sense of his responsibilities. The engine was working, although he heard only a very subdued buzz. Something had to be done to avoid the impending violent impact with the waves.

Billy did it—how, he could never remember, but, as in a dream, he regained control of the badly-shaken craft and began to climb resolutely from the scene of his exploit.

A hasty glance at the planes revealed the unpleasant fact that huge rents were visible in the fabric. It seemed marvellous how the greatly-reduced wing-surface could impart sufficient lifting power to the machine; yet, with a disconcerting wobble she held her own against the attraction of gravity.

He turned his head, half expecting to find that Kirkwood was no longer his companion, but to his unbounded satisfaction he saw the A.P. still in his seat. Not only that, but Bobby was grinning with intense glee at the successful issue of the encounter between the giant and the pigmy. His face was as black as a sweep's and streaked with blood, his flying helmet had vanished, leaving his scorched hair rippling in the furious breeze.

Picking up the voice-tube the irrepressible observer shouted something to his companion. Only a strange rumble reached Barcroft's ear. He had been rendered absolutely deaf by the concussion.

Pulling his diary from his pocket Kirkwood scribbled a few words and handed his paper to the pilot.

"How's that?" read Billy. "Fritz got it in the neck that time. That's a great strafe." Billy held the voice-tube to his mouth in order to reply, but no sound came from his lips. Like a blow from a sledge-hammer the awful truth came home to him. He was deaf and speechless.

CHAPTER XXXVIII
SNATCHED FROM HER PURSUERS

KIRKWOOD was quick to grasp the nature of the calamity that had overtaken his chum. Although considerably shaken by the concussion the observer was still in possession of his senses, except that his hearing was slightly impaired.

Again a slip of paper passed between the two chums. On it Kirkwood had written:—"Enemy torpedo craft leaving Heligoland. Are you fit to carry on? Want any help?"

Barcroft, reading the slip, nodded. The mere suggestion of relinquishing his command "bucked him up" considerably. A glance showed that Kirkwood's announcement was correct. From the anchorage on the northeast side of the island a regular swarm of hornets was emerging some of the boats steaming towards the scene of the disaster to the battleship, others heading in the direction taken by the seaplane responsible for the great catastrophe.

The new danger could be treated lightly provided the seaplane was able to carry on and fall in with her parent ship. The torpedo-boats were not within range of their guns, while the speed of the seaplane was more than double that of the swiftest of her pursuers, even in her damaged condition. Should the chase be maintained for any length of time there was a chance of the British destroyers cutting off some, if not all, of the hostile craft.

"Wireless the 'Hippo,'" wrote Barcroft, receiving the laconic reply "Can't." The delicate apparatus had been put out of action when the seaplane staggered under the force of the explosion.

"Then that's done it," thought Billy, pulling off his gloves and running his finger over a slight, almost imperceptible, dent in the petrol tank. The engine was missing badly, and although able to note the fact by observation the pilot guessed rightly that the precious fluid was leaking. Holding his fingers to his nostrils he could faintly smell the volatile fluid. The petrol was leaking, and evaporating as fast as it came in contact with the air.

The application of a piece of soap to the minute fracture temporarily remedied matters, but the mischief was already done. The petrol was almost exhausted.

By this time the German torpedo-boats were almost out of sight, mere dots upon the horizon, their position indicated by long trailing clouds of black smoke. Some uncanny knowledge must have urged the commanders of the various boats to hang on to what appeared to be a fruitless chase. To them the seaplane would be almost invisible unless they kept her under observation by means of their binoculars. In that case they must have noticed the little aircraft gradually dropping towards the surface of the sea.

Anxiously Barcroft scanned the expanse of water in front—a clear field of sea bounded by an unbroken horizon. The seaplane carriers and their strong escort had steamed homewards, taking it for granted that one at least of the raiders on Cuxhaven had been brought down by the heavy hostile fire.

The attempt had been only moderately successful. The fog that had baffled Barcroft had enveloped the rest of the British seaplanes before they had time to get properly to work. Altogether a dozen bombs had been dropped upon the naval port, before the thick bank of haze enveloped them and hid their desired object from their view.

Greeted by a tremendous fire from the German Archibalds, the raiders returned in safety; for the Huns, baffled by the thick weather, could only fire at random. With a few minor damages the airmen regained their respective parent ships, and then it was discovered that Barcroft and Kirkwood had not returned. None of the other flying men had sighted their machine after the first few minutes of the outward flight. It was therefore concluded that the two men were lost, and notwithstanding Fuller's request to make a search, the "Hippodrome" and her consorts steamed westward.

Although Barcroft felt acute disappointment at finding that the vessels had left the rendezvous, he realised that no blame could be attached to the officers responsible for the order to return. Had he flown straight back he might have been in time, but it was the bombing of the battleship that had delayed him.

"It's jolly well worth it," he soliloquised. "But we look like being in the cart again. I begin to think that Kirkwood is a bit of a Jonah, although hitherto he's managed to turn up safely. Hope his luck—and mine—will still hold good."

A motionless blade of the propeller, coming across his field of vision, betokened the unpleasant fact that the motor had refused duty. Almost imperturbably Billy held on to the joy-stick, guiding the seaplane on her long seaward glide.

The A.P., thinking that something had befallen his chum, leant over the curved deck of the chassis and touched his shoulder.

Barcroft smiled in reply and pointed to the empty petrol-tank—a smile that restored his companion's confidence. Nevertheless the vol plane was a dangerous one. The reduction of the wing-spread, bad enough when the machine was driving furiously through the air, caused the seaplane to slip badly while solely under the attraction of gravity. Should a "slip" occur just before the floats took the water the chance of a fatal capsize were almost a dead certainty.

Realising such a possibility the A.P., who had already unbuckled his waist-strap, kept on the alert, ready at the first sign of a disaster to hack through his companion's belt with a keen knife. Even then he wondered what was the use? With no help in sight their fruitless struggle for life would only be unnecessarily prolonged. Then came the opposing thought: while there's life there's hope, and never say die till you're dead.

Again the volplaning craft side-slipped. Barcroft was only just in time to regain control, and making a faultless "landing," brought his command to an aerial rest upon the surface. It could not be termed other than an aerial rest, for the simple reason that the waterborne fabric was rolling and pitching in the short steep seas that are to be met with off the flat Frisian shore.

"For one thing the day is long," thought Billy as he stood upright upon the deck of the swaying chassis and, supporting himself by one of the struts, looked fixedly in the direction of the pursuing torpedo-boats. They were no longer visible, the difference in altitude having put them below the horizon, but the ominous clouds of smoke told the flight-sub that the Huns were still persisting in their search. It was just possible, however, that they might pass some miles to windward and not sight the inconspicuous disabled seaplane in that waste of waters.

Even supposing such to be the case, what fate was in store for the crew of this helpless machine? This part of the North Sea on which they had alighted was a sort of nautical No Man's Land. Fishing vessels gave it a wide berth, fearing the deadly and unseen menace of the mines. Merchantmen no longer followed the once busy maritime highway that led to the erstwhile prosperous port of Hamburg. Save for rare excursions on the part of the German torpedo flotillas and the occasional "sweeps" of Beatty's light cruisers and destroyers nothing afloat was likely to pass that way. Should the seaplane remain seaborne sufficiently long she might drift ashore, but from the direction of the wind it was pretty obvious that she would do so somewhere on the German Frisian group outside the southern portion of the chain of islands belonging to neutral Holland.

The A.P. nudged his companion and tendered his cigarette case. Kirkwood was already smoking a pipe on the principle that he never knew when he might have a chance of another. Billy took the proffered cigarette and lit it. The tobacco seemed tasteless. With his lack of speech the flavour of the fragrant weed was denied him.

Nearer and nearer came the smudges of smoke. The Huns were hard on the track of the crippled seaplane. Already Barcroft could distinguish the grey funnels just visible above the sky-line.

"We must destroy our maps and documents," he wrote. "When I give the word smash the floats. Don't forget your air-collar."

Fumbling in the locker the observer produced a pneumatic life-saving arrangement, which, when inflated, was capable of supporting its wearer for an indefinite time.

Suddenly in the midst of the task of inflating the collar Kirkwood removed the tube from his lips. The air rushed out, and the rubber fabric collapsed like a punctured pneumatic tyre, while the A.P. stared with wide-open eyes at something not more than a hundred yards distant above the surface of the water.

"A periscope, by Jove!" he exclaimed, making a grab at his maps and papers. They, at all events, had to be destroyed.

Although his companion heard not a sound his attention was attracted by Kirkwood's manner. He, too, saw the spar-like object forging slowly ahead—so slowly that the cleavage of the water was insufficient to throw up the usual tell-tale feather of spray.

Deliberately, almost human-like, the eye of the periscope turned slowly in a complete circle. The submarine, satisfied that there was no immediate danger to be anticipated, shook herself clear of the water, disclosing her conning-tower and a portion of the hull of one of the British G Class.

Hardly able to credit their good fortune the flight-sub and his companion thrust their maps into their pockets and began to wave for assistance a quite unnecessary act since the lieutenant-commander of G 21 had already concluded rightly that the airmen were his compatriots in distress.

Five or six of her crew appearing on the long, narrow deck, the ungainly hull of the submarine, skilfully manoeuvred, approached sufficiently close to enable Kirkwood to catch a coil of rope, and the seaplane was hauled alongside.

"Jump, sir!" shouted a petty officer.

Although unable to hear the words Barcroft understood the gesture. He waited until his observer had leapt, then seizing a small axe from the body of the fuselage, he shattered each of the frail floats, and as his command sank beneath his feet he scrambled up the bulging side of the rescuing submarine.

"Barcroft's deaf and dumb," Kirkwood explained to a sympathetic lieutenant. "You'd better look sharp. There are a dozen strafed torpedo-boats after us."

"P'raps it's as well if we do," commented the officer. "I'll trouble you for your yarn when we are snugly down below."

In less than a minute the crew and the rescued airmen were hermetically sealed in the hull of G 21, and descending to a depth of fifteen fathoms the submarine rested upon the bed of the North Sea until the German torpedo-craft, foiled in their endeavour to locate their quarry, steamed back to the security of the inner roadstead of Heligoland.

CHAPTER XXXIX
AND LAST

A WEEK later found Flight-sub-lieutenant Barcroft a patient in a large Naval Hospital somewhere on the East Coast. His case was an interesting one as far as the medical officers were concerned, but far from it from a strictly personal point of view. The medicos, expressing their belief in their ability to restore the young officer's powers of speech and hearing, were unremitting in their attentions, so far without success.

Billy, after the first fit of despondency had passed, was still far from sanguine as to the result of the numerous operations and experiments performed by the hospital staff. Unable to communicate with any one except by means of paper and pencil, he had already come to the conclusion that his flying days were over. He might hope for a partial restoration of his lost senses, but nothing more. There was one thought to console him. He had not been rendered blind by the terrific glare as his gigantic victim was blown sky high. The blessing of sight was still his.

It irritated him beyond measure to see other patients conversing, to watch their lips move, their expressive gestures of understanding, and yet to live in an atmosphere of profound silence. It was humiliating to have to approach a fellow-creature and laboriously commit to paper a request for a most trivial thing; exasperating to follow the comparatively tedious pencil as the person addressed in this manner wrote his reply.

Still living in hopes Barcroft had studiously concealed the news of his affliction from his parents and from Betty. His letters to them were as light and cheerful as of yore, yet he felt that they were a sham. Sooner or later, unless medical science was able to conquer the baffling case, he would be compelled to have to admit that he was—a useless encumbrance: those were his thoughts.

Almost every one of his brother airmen had visited him since his arrival at the hospital, for the "Hippodrome," having returned to her base, was lying in harbour almost within sight of the huge building. Some tried, rather dismally, to be funny, hoping to cheer their luckless comrade; others were so sympathetic that they depressed Billy almost to a state of desperation. It was difficult to appear at ease in the presence of a deaf and dumb man—and Barcroft knew it.

One afternoon John Fuller came to see him. It was the second visit that day. The lieutenant was practical even when in the presence of his afflicted shipmate, for instead of sitting down and laboriously writing out the preliminaries to a long-drawn-out conversation he drew a paper from his pocket and handed it to his chum. And this is what Barcroft read:—

"Congrats, old man. Just heard from 'topsides,' absolutely official: the battleship you strafed was the 'Schlesien,' complement 660. Our skipper has put in a claim on your behalf at £ 5 a head. Unless the judge decides that the prize money is to be divided between the 'Hippo's' ships-company, which is unlikely, Kirkwood and you split £ 3,300 between you. You are also promoted to Flight-lieutenant and have been awarded the V.C. and Kirkwood the D.S.O. You'll see that in to-morrow's *Gazette*."

For a full half-minute Barcroft looked with strained inquiry at his chum. His head seemed whirling round and round, then like a roar from a cannon something seemed to beat upon his ear-drums.

"It's too good to be true," he said.

"Absolute fact," replied Fuller. "Bless my soul, Billy, you can speak!"

"And hear, too," almost shouted the delighted newly-fledged lieutenant. "Come along, John; I'm off to the telegraph office. Keep on speaking, old bird. It's a delight. I hardly expected to hear you again."

The hospital post-office was at the far end of the building. Entering the somewhat crowded room, Billy, with a trembling hand, filled in a form and gave it to a girl clerk.

The girl took the form, counted the words and scribbled something on a piece of paper and offered it to the flight-lieutenant.

"Thank you," said Billy smiling. "But it isn't necessary now, thank Heaven. I can both speak and hear."

"I am glad, Mr. Barcroft," replied the girl, who knew all about the circumstances under which he had received his injuries. "Reply paid? That will be eighteen-pence. You may get a reply in an hour."

The telegram that Billy had dispatched was to Miss Betty Deringhame. It was:

"Am applying for leave. Will you fulfil your promise?"

After a seemingly interminable wait Billy's reply was received.

His message consisted of nine words; hers of one only: "Yes."

It was all that Flight-lieutenant Barcroft, V.C., desired. His cup of happiness was filled to overflowing.